HARVEY DRINKWATER

&

THE CULT OF SAVINGS

Charles A Cornell

Charles Cornell Creative Partners LLC

FORT MYERS, FLORIDA

Charles Cornell Creative Partners LLC
10020 Coconut Road STE 138 #655
Bonita Springs, FL 34135
www.BigCorpSurvivor.com

Publisher's Note: This is a work of fiction. Names, characters, places, and incidents are a product of the author's imagination. Locales and public names are sometimes used for atmospheric purposes. Any resemblance to actual people, living or dead, or to businesses, companies, events, institutions, or locales is completely coincidental.

Book Layout ©2013 BookDesignTemplates.com
Book Cover Design by Andrew Lounds
Book Cover Graphics licensed from Shutterstock.com

Harvey Drinkwater & The Cult Of Savings/Charles A Cornell. -- 1st ed.
ISBN 978-0-9990889-2-0

*Harvey Drinkwater & The Cult Of Savings
is dedicated to every person who helped me
survive thirty-nine years at my BigCorp.
Your guidance, wisdom and kindness
made it possible. Thank you.*

—Charles A Cornell

*The best way to understand the absurdity of reality
is to write about the reality of absurdity.*

—Charles A Cornell

CONTENTS

INTRODUCTION

When common sense leaves the building, things can get a little bizarre. If it wasn't so serious, you might think it was comical. It wouldn't be out of the realm of possibility, you sigh, that a complete idiot could run your BigCorp and do a better job.

Which got me thinking, what would happen if a complete idiot actually did run a BigCorp? Could it really get any worse? Writing through the eyes of an idiot was an immense amount of fun for me. In truth, I am Harvey (or I was before I retired). I think there's a bit of Harvey in everyone. And I would guess there's a bit of Harvey in you too. You've put up with BigCorp's lunacy for a long time, haven't you? Thought so. Sometimes the only true way to survive in a BigCorp is to look at the events around you as if you're seeing them through the eyes of a complete idiot. That way, everything will make sense.

— Charles

CHAPTER ONE

What does Fate have in store for me today? Harvey thought.

Harvey Drinkwater gazed up through the glass roof over the train station's escalator as it whisked him and hundreds of other minions from the darkness of the station platforms into the perpetually gray skies that hung over Ocean City, Oregon.

Not much, he concluded.

Today was like every other day.

He'd gotten up at the same time he always did. Made toast the same way he always made it. The train was late as it always was. And the people were as rude as they always were.

Mr. Fortinelli, the newspaper seller greeted Harvey with, "Itza greata day in Ocean City!" as if it always was and always would be as he handed Harvey a copy of *The Daily Oregonite*.

Harvey's eyes looked up from the headlines on the newspaper towards the horizon. *What on earth were they building?* he thought. There were cranes all over the place. Huge cranes. The biggest he'd ever seen. All over the waterfront. And big wrecking balls, pulverizing what was left of Sam's Sardine Processing Plant.

"What's going on, Mr. Fortinelli?" Harvey asked, bleating like a sheep.

"You buy a paper from me-a every day, you fool. Do you notta read it?" said Fortinelli, exasperated. "Itza…Globallica, dummy."

"Globallica?"

"Santa Maria! For Godda's sake-a, Harvey, read da Business Sectzzione," he demanded.

Harvey was not deliberately ignorant. He just never read the Business Section, that's all. He found it depressing. All those stories of layoffs and plant closings and recessions. Poor people losing their jobs and their life savings. He usually took it home for his Chihuahua, Lopez to poop on.

Harvey preferred the comics. But today, as Fate would have it, he took Mr. Fortinelli's advice and opened the Business pages with an unusual gusto. He read the headlines out loud, softly at first, then in a squeaky, excitable voice that trumpeted his astonishment: 'Construction on Globallica's New World Headquarters in Ocean City Continues. When it's completed, the 147-storey Globallica Tower will be the tallest building, not just on the West Coast, but in the entire United States of America.'

"Oh my gosh," Harvey said to no one in particular. "The tallest building in America? *Here?* In Ocean City, Oregon?"

Harvey bundled the paper under his arm and stared at the huge construction site and its massive dust cloud rising in the distance.

"Wow! Wait 'til I tell Mr. Dortmann," Harvey exclaimed as he leapt ankle deep into the puddle that was always there. He ran across the street to his job at Dortmann's Zipper Emporium, a red-bricked building desperately clinging to life since the 1880s. The letters carved in stone over the door—letters that said *The Great Western Fish Company*—were a lie. Because Mr. Dortmann couldn't afford a new sign.

Harvey strode into the tiny office at the back of the shop, exuding a renewed sense of purpose and a heightened inquisitiveness bristling from more excitement than he'd ever felt before.

"Hilda," he said to the rotund woman overflowing her desk chair. "Have you seen what they're building?"

"You mean the Globallica Tower?"

"You know about it?"

Hilda Ausfahrt, an unfortunately plump lady in her mid-forties, with an unfortunately well-pronounced mustache, looked up from doing her nails. Her reading glasses slid down to the end of her bulbous nose. "Harvey, only an idiot doesn't know about the biggest news to hit Ocean City in over a hundred years."

"Well," Harvey said, his enthusiasm lowered somewhat. His face twisted into an all-knowing nonchalance. "I mean, well…um, have you seen…how far they've progressed? Um…over the weekend?"

Hilda gazed at her cuticles. "Harvey, they've been prepping that site by the waterfront since Christmas. And today is the fourteenth of April. So what's so special about it today?"

Harvey fumbled through the newspaper, deciding it might be wise to actually read the article instead of just the headline.

"Well—" he said, twitching his nose like a ferret.

"*Well?*"

Harvey started to sweat. "Well…um—"

Hilda, tired of waiting for nothing in particular like she always did, brushed the file over her nails. "Well, Harvey? Well *what?*"

Harvey shifted from side to side. His wet sneakers squelched. "I don't have time for idle chitchat, Hilda. I have important work to get done before lunch. I'm going to eat by the waterfront today and see the fireworks."

"Harvey, they don't shoot off fireworks during the day."

He shot a volley across Hilda's bow, "Well, they could if they wanted to."

"Globallica's chairman kicks off Ocean City Founders Week tonight, Harvey. Not at lunchtime. *Tonight.* When it's dark."

"Yes. Of course. Tonight. I knew that." Harvey shuffled through the pages of the newspaper. "At 8:00 PM. At the Old Bandshell."

Despite a constant state of obliviousness to his surroundings, Hilda Ausfahrt still loved Harvey Drinkwater. Well, maybe not 'loved'. But she liked him a lot. Well, 'like' is a strong word. *Pitied?* He might be the saddest excuse for a purchasing agent that anyone could ever expect to find but somehow Harvey Drinkwater always pulled it together. Long enough to convince Mr. Dortmann, a distant relative of

Harvey's on his great-aunt's side, that he wasn't a total moron. Mr. Dortmann that is. For employing Harvey.

Tonight at 8:00 PM? Harvey thought. *Drat. I can't go out tonight.* He had to take Lopez to obedience class. Which was not what Lopez thought at all. Lopez was taking Harvey to obedience class. If only Harvey would wear the leash, maybe they could make some progress. And free up their evenings to see fireworks.

Harvey slumped dejectedly into the oak chair behind his desk, miffed that Fate would be so cruel to exclude him from Ocean City's festivities. The same Fate that he didn't believe in. Except when it was about to appear on his doorstep.

Harvey's phone rang. Harvey set aside his hatred of Fate. His job demanded it. He answered politely, but his usual professionalism was dampened by a sulk. "Dortmann's Zipper Emporium. Harvey Drinkwater, purchasing agent speaking. May I help you?"

Hilda noted the look of deep concern on Harvey's face.

"Yes...no. Yes, yes. No, no. No, thank you." Negotiations could be tough. But you always had to remain polite to resolve conflict.

"Why? Because I already have one. Thank you anyway." Give them a reason. Use persuasion and logic. Break down the stubbornness on the other side of the negotiating table. Harvey's forte. Mind-wrestling pesky salespeople was child's play.

"No...no! No, I don't want one. No, really, I don't. Why? You asked me that already. Because, I don't really need one. But thank you for calling anyway. Good bye." Harvey hung up. What was he going to do with another credit card? He had forty-seven already.

Harvey didn't really have an office at the Zipper Emporium. He didn't really have a cubicle like the ones he saw in the cartoons. He just had a desk, a chair, a filing cabinet and a phone; all tucked under the stairs that led to the storage loft, in the back of an old storefront selling zippers, under a sign that lied.

But he was ambitious. Someday he would have his own office. Fate dictated it. Yes, Harvey Drinkwater, he thought. After eight months of being a purchasing agent, you deserve your own office. Someday he would muster the courage to demand that Mr. Dortmann recognize the important role he played in the company and give him an office. After all, wasn't it Harvey who'd thought of the 'Idea'? The one that launched Dortmann's Zipper Emporium into the big leagues of the clothing industry.

Well, not really.

It wasn't Harvey's idea. But Harvey had played a part.

Wasn't it Harvey, after all, that fetched a coffee for the sales rep while he waited to tell Mr. Dortmann the 'Idea'? And wasn't it Harvey that kept the rep entertained while he waited? Showing him pictures of Harvey's business trip to Washington to the National Purchasing Agents Convention. Lopez on the steps of the Capital. Lopez at the Lincoln Memorial. Lopez at the Smithsonian (well, outside it because dogs weren't allowed in). Lopez outside the Bus Station. Peeing on a hydrant.

Harvey browsed the Business Section of *The Daily Oregonite* and another article caught his eye: an exclusive interview with Byron Mitchell, chairman of Globallica. This newspaper was definitely not to be pooped on. Harvey picked out a jam donut from the box on Hilda's desk, poured a coffee, winced at how hot it was, wiped the stain off his pants, poured some more coffee, and settled into the old oak chair for a scholarly read.

"Mr. Mitchell," the journalist in the article asked. "Tell our readers, what has been the key factor in Globallica's meteoric rise to the top of the Fortune 500?"

Harvey's eyes were drawn to the magnificent photo of Globallica's Chairman Byron Mitchell, a gray-haired, Caribbean-tanned aristocrat of commerce, sitting behind a French-polished mahogany desk, elbows resting on the desk's Italian leather top with its gold embossed inlay.

What an impressive sight, Harvey thought.

"People," Mitchell said in the interview. "People are, and always will be, our greatest asset."

The words of the chairman jumped off the page as if he were in the room there with Harvey. Harvey jerked sideways to avoid contact. Hilda wondered what he was cowering at.

"Without people, our great company wouldn't be the great corporation it is," the chairman continued.

"Please tell our readers more, Mr. Mitchell."

Harvey was glued to the paper. Well, his sleeve was glued to the paper. Because his jam donut was between the paper and his arm.

Mitchell continued, "When I merged Consolidated Remanufacturing And Packaging (CRAP) with Advanced Surgical Supply of Colorado (ASSCO), I combined the best two pension liabilities in the industry. With this brilliant stroke of genius, I forged Globallica into the powerhouse it is today, with my bare hands."

The chairman's words about forging were riveting. It stamped an indelible impression on Harvey. It was like nothing Harvey had ever read before. So concrete. Monolithic. Words straight from the mind at the top of the biggest corporation in America, onto the page in front of him, and into his puny life. Compelling stuff. It must be Fate. Because only Fate would have caused Harvey to read beyond the headlines. Without falling asleep.

"But Mr. Mitchell, surely it wasn't just that?" the interviewer continued. "Wasn't your company in the right place at the right time? Exploiting market opportunities? Tell us about the strategies you used to generate such huge growth in revenues and profits."

"Simple economics, really."

Harvey could sense Chairman Mitchell was toying with the interviewer at this point. The feeling just jumped off the page and bit him. Or was it the horsefly that flew in through the open window to dine on the jam on his cheek?

"Economies of scale. Leveraging our strengths. Crushing our competition under our boot heels."

Harvey recoiled in his chair. Economies of scale? Mr. Dortmann didn't even own a scale. Harvey had suggested it. Mr. Dortmann thought it was stupid. Sell zippers by the pound?

Chairman Mitchell took charge of the interview. "Look (nitwit)…Consolidated Remanufacturing made the most powerful box cutters in the world and ASSCO made the strongest surgical thread. They needed our designs. We needed theirs. Simple. A perfect fit. We helped them develop the best rectal scalpels in the business. They helped us corner the market on ultra-thin, semi-invisible package binding. The rest is history."

This was far more exciting than zippers. Growth in zipper technology was proceeding at a snail's pace compared to this.

Harvey was transfixed.

"You often refer to your 'secret weapon'," the interviewer continued. "Can you please tell our readers about it?"

"Well, it's not much of a secret any more, I'm afraid. Even *The Harvard Business Review* has written an article about it," Chairman Mitchell replied. "It's purchasing, of course."

"Purchasing!" Harvey exclaimed, jumping out of his seat, spilling coffee all over his mail. The donut and the horsefly were washed into the wastebasket. "Yes! I knew it. Purchasing!"

Hilda jolted out of her quiet coma. Her romance novel dropped to the floor in pain. "Yes, Harvey. You work in Purchasing. In fact you *are* Purchasing. We don't have any other Purchasing here. It's just *you*. You're Purchasing," she said, hoping Harvey's hysteria would not accelerate into warp-drive. Which could be a problem.

"No, Hilda. You don't understand," he said, tapping the newspaper. "The chairman of Globallica says that purchasing is Globallica's secret weapon."

Harvey turned around on the spot, clutched the newspaper tightly to his chest, threw his hands in the air, and offered the article up as a gift to Fate.

Fate refused. For now.

"Purchasing! I knew it. I just knew it. Purchasing *is* important. Wait until I tell Mr. Dortmann. I've been telling him that all along."

"Be my guest," said Hilda, groping under the desk for her book.

Harvey rushed out of the back room into the front of the shop. "Mr. Dortmann! Mr. Dortmann!"

"Harvey, please. Can't you see I'm with a very important customer? You'll have to wait."

"But, Mr. Dortmann?"

"Harvey! I…said…*wait*!"

The elderly shopkeeper shielded his customer from the annoyance that had just erupted like a small geyser from the shop's back room.

Harvey's chin dropped to his chest. He bundled the newspaper under his arm and trundled out into the street, dejected. *Mr. Dortmann never understands,* he thought. *I'm wasting my time trying.*

The clang, bang of jackhammers rang like Quasimodo's church bells, announcing the arrival of the Globallica Tower to Ocean City's skyline. The noise drew Harvey down the street, mesmerized by the enormity of the site and the rising skyscraper, a building that would someday dwarf the derelict old warehouses and rundown wharves on Ocean City's waterfront.

What if? he thought. *What if?*

No, it was absurd. Mr. Dortmann was right. Smaller was better. That's why Mr. Dortmann only had one shop. If he had two shops, Mr. Dortmann had said, he would probably end up hiring another person. Like Harvey. And it would be too expensive. Mr. Dortmann was very wise.

Harvey unfolded the coffee-stained newspaper and pressed out the crumpled article with his fingers. He would save it. In fact, he would save every article he could find about Globallica. He would create a scrapbook. Tonight, Lopez would have to poop on the sports pages.

CHAPTER TWO

One year later

Lopez was not sympathetic. In fact Lopez was never sympathetic. About anything.

I should have had a cat, Harvey thought. Now there was an animal that could at least pretend to be sympathetic. Or was it boredom? Harvey could never tell about cats.

"Lopez," he said, just before tucking the two of them into bed. "You just don't know how stressful it is to work at the Zipper Emporium."

The little Chihuahua grumbled. Lopez had heard it all before.

"The office is small and cramped. And the work is absolutely overwhelming. I mean, if it wasn't for Hilda helping me, I don't know how the purchase orders would ever get out."

Lopez was simply not sympathetic. He muttered like he always did when Harvey whined.

"Of all people, Lopez. I thought you would understand. It's a dog's life."

Oh, no it wasn't. Not the time Lopez visited Dortmann's Zipper Emporium. He never saw Harvey crap on the floor. He certainly didn't see Harvey lick his balls in public.

"I don't think I can take it anymore. I need to find another job, Lopez. It's no good. I'm getting nowhere in the zipper business. It's just too small. I've outgrown it."

Harvey pulled the sheets and blankets over the little dog and settled into the pillows with him. "Tomorrow, I'm determined to find another job," Harvey mused. He kept repeating the phrase over and over as he dozed off to sleep, oblivious to the little mutt's mutterings. "Tomorrow, I'm determined to find another job…zzz…"

After a year of diligent construction and fourteen deaths, the Globallica Tower had risen to dwarf everything around it. It pierced the ever-present clouds of Ocean City like a stairway to corporate heaven.

Harvey had a dream.

And what a dream it was. Warm milk before bedtime did it every time. A smile emerged on Harvey's face. Even Lopez's snoring could not awaken Harvey from this night-time bliss.

It was a pleasant dream. To start with.

Harvey stared through the curls of vapor rising from the surface of his coffee as he sat by his window at Dortmann's Zipper Emporium. Outside, an edifice of metal, glass and concrete blotted out what little sun had ever shone into his life. The dream transported Harvey through the Emporium's window to the foot of the giant Globallica Tower. Harvey looked up at the bold bronze letters perched over its façade, a sign that proclaimed, 'People are Our Greatest Asset'.

Harvey made his grand entrance into Globallica's lobby. A buxom blonde, dressed like a belly dancer from the Arabian Nights, greeted him with "Good Morning, Mr. Drinkwater," as she handed him a fruit basket and *The Wall Street Journal*.

Harvey floated across the foyer on the wings of a cloud, the crowd parting like the Red Sea, deferring to his presence with a pleasant "Good Morning, Mr. Drinkwater" before he ascended the elevator, arriving at his spacious office. It was paneled with the finest Canadian tiger maple with matching desk and credenza. His secretary poured him a glass of forty-five-year-old Scotch from an imported Irish crystal decanter taken out of the illuminated bar behind his antique Corinthian leather chair.

In his dreams, the smell of leather drove Harvey crazy. In his bed, Lopez wriggled his bum closer to Harvey's warm nose.

Tinkling the designer ice cube against the side of his glass, Harvey sauntered towards the floor-to-ceiling smoked glass window in his Globallica Tower office. It offered a panoramic view of downtown Ocean City. The view was as he imagined it might be if the grey blankness ever took a holiday. Far below, Harvey could faintly make out the red-bricked structure of his former employer, Dortmann's Zipper Emporium.

Executive Harvey Drinkwater's realm was vast. His authority was absolute. He'd made it to the pinnacle of success. He could even hold down his liquor.

In his dream, Harvey leaned forward to take a better look at his old employer's humble establishment, a tiny shack amongst ant-like pedestrians. As he did, Harvey fell head first through a space where no glass had ever existed, plummeting one hundred and forty-seven floors. The whiskey glass was still in his hand as the street rushed up towards him, ice-cubes in a race with a stream of amber liquid to see which one would hit the pavement first.

Just as his body was about to enter Dortmann's Zipper Emporium via the air conditioning ducts on the roof, Harvey woke up in a cold sweat.

"Oh, Lopez!" Harvey said, bolt upright in bed, feeling strangely warm below his waist. "What a nightmare I had!" His hand slipped down under the covers. The ends of his fingers came back more than slightly damp.

"Lopez! Did you pee on me again?"

Harvey made a mental note to buy a cat.

CHAPTER THREE

Yet another year passes in Harvey's dreary life

A frigid, gray overcast winter had turned into a chilly, gray overcast spring. A few months later and summer beckoned. Harvey could look forward to a change. The weather forecast was warm. And gray.

It was getting worse.

The zipper business rose and fell.

Lopez had hemorrhoids.

What else could go wrong in Harvey's life?

Harvey stepped out of the train station and bought his paper from Mr. Fortinelli like he always did. At least one thing in Harvey Drinkwater's meager life could be considered positive. He trudged into work Monday morning with dry shoes. It appears that walking with your head pointed down at the sidewalk had its advantages.

A nasty gust of wind had followed him from the train platform to the back door of the Zipper Emporium. Fate had stood on the sidelines for far too long. It was time to step out of the shadows and into the gray, overcast sky.

Harvey slammed the door behind him, waking Hilda from her early morning nap.

"Did you see the fireworks Saturday night?" Hilda asked.

"What fireworks?"

"The First Anniversary Party for the Globallica Tower?"

"I'll buy the souvenir book. And look at the pictures," he mumbled, dejected.

"Oh, Harvey. Cheer up, for goodness sake. What's wrong with you these days? You've been in a funk for months."

Harvey uncurled *The Daily Oregonite* and spread the paper over last week's coffee stains. Less than two hundred yards from where he was sitting was the awe-inspiring Globallica building which featured prominently on the first page of *The Daily Oregonite's Special Anniversary Supplement*.

Harvey Drinkwater sighed. He cut out the photo for his scrapbook. His dreams consisted of yellowing paper and dabs of glue.

Just then, that nasty wind with its tormenting gusts—the breath of Fate that had chased him from the moment he stepped out of the train—blew through a crack in the window next to Hilda. Fate grabbed the newspaper clipping from Harvey's desk, lifted the scrap into the air and sent it wobbling, end over end, to the floor.

This was the day Harvey began to believe in Fate.

The newspaper clipping landed sunny side down.

Harvey froze like a video on 'Pause'.

"Oh, no, Harvey. You're not going into one of your transfixion fits again, are you?" Hilda exclaimed. "Harvey? Harvey?...*Harvey!*"

Hilda filled a foam cup full of ice cold water from the water cooler, tugged on Harvey's belt and poured the water down the back of his pants. This worked every time without fail. Harvey's sneakers began to fill up. His head jolted back. He saw the ceiling for the first time in months. He returned to his former self, which was not such a big chasm to cross.

Was it a miracle? Was it Fate? Possibly. It was definitely a gust of wind and an ice cold cup of water.

"I'm so excited, I think I've wet myself."

"No, Harvey. I wet yourself," Hilda said, relieved she didn't have to invent another yoga posture to explain Harvey's transfixion fits to Mr. Dortmann. "Oh, Mr. Dortmann, isn't Harvey clever? He's learning the crouching leper, leaning iguana position."

"Oi, vey," Mr. Dortmann would say, shaking his head.

"Hilda, look at this," Harvey bleated, handing her the clipping as if he'd just found a lost copy of the Declaration of Independence.

She put on her reading glasses.

"I know, Harvey. It's fireworks. I was there, remember?"

"No, Hilda. Not *that* side. *This* side."

She turned the raggedy-edged snippet over:

Your Future At Globallica Begins Today

The World's Greatest Corporation

Seeks The Brightest And The Best

We Are Recruiting Experienced People

For The Following Positions:

Janitorial Arts Consultants

Drinking Water Transportation Specialists

Snow Shovellers

Assistant Purchasing Agents

"Look, Hilda! *There*. See? Assistant Purchasing Agents. And they want experienced people!" Harvey chirped.

"The brightest and the best?" Hilda twittered.

"That's me, Hilda. I'm all over it like a big dog."

Harvey grabbed his coat from the hook behind his desk and proceeded out the door.

"Where're you going, Harvey?"

"Home, Hilda."

"Home? You just got here. You go home and Mr. Dortmann will fire you."

"He can't."

"Oh yes, he can."

"He can't, Hilda."

"Oh yes, he most certainly can."

"Oh no, he can't. Because I quit!"

Hilda knew where this conversation was going. The same place Harvey would if he quit. Nowhere.

"Goodbye, Hilda. My future awaits me."

"Goodbye, Harvey. See you tomorrow."

"I don't think so, Hilda."

"I *do* think so, Harvey."

"Oh no, you don't."

"Oh yes, I—," Hilda bit her lip. It happened every time. That's why she wore red lipstick to work.

The door glass rattled as Harvey made his grand exit past a perplexed Mr. Dortmann. "Where's Harvey going?" the shop owner said to Hilda.

"Home."

"Home? Is he sick?"

"No," Hilda said, refraining from editorializing. She was buying precious time. For what, she didn't know.

"Then, why is he going home?"

"Um…to change his pants, Mr. Dortmann. He wet himself."

"Oi, vey," Mr. Dortmann said, shaking his head. "Not again."

CHAPTER FOUR

Harvey looked up at the massive Globallica Tower. The clouds began at the 130th floor, passing by the building like floating cotton pillows. He could faintly see the angels on the outside at the very top of the 147-storey skyscraper. The angels dangled on gold chains, flying through the air with trumpets as they encircled the building's top floor on a purpose-built monorail.

It was another spectacular reason for wanting to work at Globallica.

They had angels dangling from the roof.

Chairman Mitchell had said in his latest interview for *The CEO Worshipers Journal*, the sight of trumpeting angels revolving outside his office window all day long made him a wiser man.

Someday, Harvey would have an office with angels dangling outside. But first, he had to figure out how to get into the building. Harvey knew this was a test. If you can't get in the building then you aren't smart enough to work there. The first barrier were doors with stainless steel handles as big as firemen's poles. He made it through with help from one of the hundreds of people going into the building like a migrating herd of caribou.

Inside the Globallica Tower, there was such energy. And he was only in the foyer. And what a massive foyer it was! Harvey imagined a thousand years from now people would dig up the ruins of Globallica's building to determine what kind of imperial structure had been built on the waterfront of Ocean City. Was it a Congress of the People? A Temple? What Gods were worshipped in the hallowed halls of marble and stainless steel? Fountains like Niagara Falls. Tropical palms.

Wading pools with Oriental carp. Well, the carp and the trees would be dead by then, but everything else would be perfectly preserved after those thousand years. What a legacy!

It was an honor just to be in the foyer.

But there was a problem. Once inside, the hurly-burly mass of people crisscrossing the glossy floor were entering revolving glass doors using security cards. Harvey felt as if he were a goldfish in a bowl. Or a carp in a pond. He looked up at the roof of the foyer's glass-paneled atrium, looked back at the glass-fronted entrance, then looked across at the glass revolving doors whisking people into the largest corporation in the world. He felt strangely alone in a crowd.

Then his chance came.

It was Fate.

And she was pretty.

She dropped her security card.

It wasn't surprising. It must have been very awkward to talk on a cell phone, type into a laptop, eat a donut and do the Sunday crossword at the same time as carrying a briefcase, file folders, a workout bag and a cup of coffee.

Harvey admired her skills. He probably would have dropped the security card doing only one of those things. Come to think of it, he would have dropped the card without doing any of those things.

But he was glad she did. And she was glad he didn't.

And that's how they met.

Penelope Warren and Harvey that is.

"Thank you," she said as he picked up her card. "You're such a gentleman."

Harvey blushed.

She swiped her card and entered a revolving door. Harvey followed when the next opening arrived but the door jammed shut. Only one person at a time was allowed through.

What was he supposed to do now?

It was fortunate that Harvey came two hours ahead of his interview, so he could figure out how to get in. He didn't want to leave a bad first impression. But after an hour and a half, he was concerned he would. And he would be late.

It was also fortunate the man wasn't hidden by plants. If he'd been hidden by plants, Fate would have sent Harvey home. But the little bespectacled man was sitting out in the open, behind a simple metal desk. A two-story monolith of gray bare concrete towered behind him. There was no sign above his desk. The man looked as lonely and as lost as Harvey. Harvey thought he needed some company.

"Can I help you?" the man asked with the look of a whipped puppy.

"Yes," Harvey replied. "Help is exactly what I want. I have an appointment with Human Resources at 9:00."

"Phones are over there," said the little man, hunched over his newspaper. Harvey looked but he couldn't see any phones.

"Over where?"

The man pointed. "There."

Harvey squinted. There was a glass box with red metal edges and a fire extinguisher in it. It wasn't a phone.

"Where?"

"Oh, all right. I'll show you."

The little man pushed his chair away from the desk, holding his head stiffly as he turned. His shoulders were hunched as if he were one of those toys that needed a key in the back to wind them up. The man passed by the glass box with the extinguisher. Beside it hung a tiny ear piece on a thin metal peg sticking out of the concrete. He handed the ear piece to Harvey and returned to his desk.

Now Harvey knew what an ear piece was. Hilda had one. She couldn't do her nails and talk on the phone without one. But at the Zipper Emporium, Harvey preferred to use the old-fashioned type of phone, the one you held in your hand or in the crook of your neck. A phone that came in two pieces attached to one another with a curly flexible cord. To Harvey, using an ear piece was like using chopsticks.

Many people could pick up a pea with chopsticks. Others got out a whittling knife to sharpen the end and stab the peas. Others starved to death. Ear pieces were kind of like that too.

Harvey did everything to make the ear piece work but suck on its end. Eventually sound ended up in the right part of his body. But that was the easy part.

"Please enter your employment number," a familiar voice demanded. It was the same female voice he heard when he had a question for the cable company when his TV went dead. He didn't know she'd quit the cable company to work at Globallica.

Harvey looked frantically at his printout of the email Globallica's Human Resources Department had sent him. There was no number on it whatsoever.

"We're sorry you're having so much trouble."

A number was definitely what the lady wanted.

"Please try again later."

"Wait. Stop," Harvey stuttered. "Ask me another question."

"Good-bye."

It was no use. She was gone.

Harvey placed the ear piece back on its peg. Was all hope lost? A man came up behind him and picked up the little ear piece. Harvey heard him say, "Two-four-nine-four-three. Five-seven-six-four-two." The man walked over to the revolving glass doors and they let him in.

Oh, boy! Harvey thought. *The secret code. Just like in the movies.*

He picked up the ear piece and tried to repeat what the man had said, but wasn't quite able to remember it all. He got stuck after 'Two'.

But the lady was very kind. This time she gave him some choices.

"Press or say 'One' if you're a contract employee."

"Press or say 'Two' if you're a bundled services employee."

"Press or say 'Three' if you're a resident supplier employee, technical."

"Press or say 'Four' if you're a resident supplier employee, non-technical."

"Press or say 'Five' if you're an ASSCO employee on temporary assignment prior to layoff."

"Press or say 'Six' if you're a Consolidated Remanufacturing employee on a career transition."

"Press or say 'Seven' if you belong to the Amalgamated Union of Crumpled Paper and Styrofoam Peanut Workers of America."

"Press or say 'Eight' if you belong to the International Association of Surgical Instrument Test Technicians."

"Press or say 'Nine' if you're a consultant."

"Press or say 'Ten' if you're hopelessly lost."

"Press 'Star-Pound' to repeat this menu in Swahili."

The last one sounded intriguing. But Harvey said 'Ten'.

"Thank you. Employment number, please?"

"Two four… um, five? Six?"

"We're sorry you're having so much trouble. Please try again later."

Two more attempts and the nice lady—who never got mad even though Harvey used some words he heard Mr. Fortinelli say when someone stole one of his newspapers without paying—finally said, "If you did not find your selection, please go to Reception."

Reception? There was only a lonely little man at a metal desk.

Harvey looked around. The hurly-burly had gone. There was no more hurly-burlishness to be seen anywhere. While Harvey was scrolling through the list with the nice lady on the phone, the lobby had emptied. He and the little man were alone, on a desert island of polished marble, granite and palm trees.

But they were not alone. Behind the little man at the desk was a cat. And a sleeping bag.

"Reception?" Harvey asked the man.

"Yes?"

Harvey pushed the paper he'd been sent by Human Resources under the little man's nose and hoped for the best.

"Just a minute. Take a seat."

"Seat?"

"Take... a... seat."

There was no seat. Just like there was no phone.

This was another test, Harvey thought. There was a seat. And Harvey was supposed to find it.

The little man at the desk rolled Harvey's email into a tube shape, tied it with an elastic band, put the tube of paper inside a bigger clear plastic tube, and stuffed that plastic tube up an even bigger plastic tube that ran up the full height of the concrete wall. The tube with Harvey's email was sucked up with a loud *Ssss-Rupp,* rocketing up from the ground floor through the atrium's glass roof until it vanished.

Harvey found the seat. Way over on the other side of the foyer, so far away the little man looked like he'd disappeared. And then Harvey waited. And waited. And waited.

Harvey was about to kiss the metal ductwork of Dortmann's air conditioning unit again when he was awakened by a commotion in the now-deserted foyer of the Temple of Industry.

An extremely well-dressed man—about forty, impeccably coifed hair , gray-pinstriped suit, crisp white shirt and red tie— was yelling at the top of his voice at a revolving glass door. Harvey could understand why. The door was not revolving.

Behind the man stood a tall, buxom young lady wearing a black skirt and white blouse. She had shiny bleached-blond hair, bright red lips and eyelashes that looked like two spiders had nested on her face. She was holding a fruit basket and *The Wall Street Journal.*

The man got out his cell phone and verbally abused it.

"Jennifer, let me in. I lost my pass again."

A moment of silence.

"Jennifer, I don't have time to fill out those crazy forms. I just want *in*, damn it!"

Another moment of silence.

"Jennifer, what brain-dead asshole approved that procedure?"

More silence.

"*Me?* Well...yes...I know, I'm the vice president of Human Resources. But why would I be so stupid to approve something that applied to *me*?"

The young lady with the spicery eyes shuffled her tushy and snapped the gum in her mouth. The fruit basket must have weighed a ton. Harvey offered to hold it.

"I left it in the Financial office? They sent it to 'Lost and Found'?" There was a pause. "Yes, I lost it. Yes, they found it. That's no excuse. Jennifer, get your butt down here and let me in!" the man screamed into his cell phone. "I can't wait for that tube thing to bring my security pass. I've got an appointment with the chairman in five minutes. And I've got his Relaxation Therapy Consultant with me."

The young lady with the fruit basket smiled. She handed Harvey her business card. It had a picture of her wearing what looked to Harvey like a transparent swimsuit. Then she grabbed his crotch. Which was an unusual way to shake hands. Perhaps she was a foreigner and new to this country and its usual customs.

More silence from the man on the phone, then: "Thank you, Jennifer. You're so sweet and kind. Remind me to fire you...you dumb shit."

Air hissed through the man's teeth like a punctured bicycle tire. He turned around. The Relaxation Therapy Consultant was talking to a nerdy-looking young man with a bulge in his pants, holding a fruit basket.

"Jennifer's coming down to let us in. Who's that?"

"I'm Harvey Drinkwater. Pleased to meet you—"

Harvey extended his hand into open space where it stayed untouched. The revolving glass doors produced Jennifer. The man in the gray-pinstriped suit yanked the Relaxation Therapy Consultant by the arm. The Relaxation Therapy Consultant grabbed the fruit basket from Harvey on her way through the revolving glass doors.

Harvey was alone again.

Except for the little man behind the desk. With his cat and a sleeping bag.

Thud! Plonk!

That was a funny way for Fate to make an entrance.

Finally.

CHAPTER FIVE

The small tube that had fallen through the large tube attached to the concrete wall woke the cat. It was black and white and went by the name of Dennis. The cat, that is. Not the tube.

"Here's your security pass," said the little man, handing Harvey a crisp plastic card with a magnetic strip and a bar code on it.

Harvey approached the revolving doors with fear and trepidation. He didn't know how much more rejection he could take. Well, in reality, a lot more. So far the day was going quite well.

Harvey swiped the newly acquired card and closed his eyes. He gently pushed on the revolving door. It moved. He took a step. The door moved some more. Harvey was enjoying it so much he didn't want to leave. But eventually the revolving door insisted that he follow its movements and cross over to the 'Other Side'.

The 'Other Side' was a magical place. Well, in Harvey's mind it was. It was another foyer. Only this time with elevators.

Oh, dear God. Who was going to tell me about the elevators? he thought. Harvey looked for an ear piece on a peg on a wall. There wasn't one. Then he made a decision. He would try using the same elevator the man in the gray-pinstriped suit and the lady with spiders in her eyelashes who carried a fruit basket used. At least if he met them again he could ask for directions.

The elevator had an impressive title: 'Executive Suites'. It opened immediately with a simple swipe of Harvey's magical new card. Once inside, Harvey couldn't see any buttons to push.

Harvey looked around, perplexed.

Oh, no. I'm lost in an elevator, he thought.

But a nice lady's voice rescued him, saying, "Which floor?"

"Human Resources," said Harvey confidently.

"Taking you to...Human Resources," the lady said, from somewhere in the air above him. Harvey looked around the elevator, but he was sure he was alone.

The numbers above the door whizzed by ten floors at a time. Harvey felt the beef jerky he had for breakfast prodding on the side of his stomach. His mother had told him to chew his food. But he wouldn't listen. Now she was dead.

The elevator slowed down as it approached the 135th floor, stopping gently before opening its doors. The phantom lady announced, "Human Resources."

Harvey couldn't believe what he was seeing as he stepped out of the elevator. In front of him was a beautiful teak counter, several extremely comfortable looking armchairs, and an even more beautiful girl sitting behind the counter, filing her nails. She looked vaguely familiar. The word 'Jennifer' on the nametag was definitely a clue.

Behind Jennifer, glass walls curved around the elevator foyer in a complete circle. Harvey felt like a fish in a bowl again. He knew he should have learned how to swim. Beyond the glass walls was what appeared to be an art gallery, a fitness center with tanning bed and hot tub, a lounge with the kind of flatscreen TV that Harvey hoped he would win in one of those contests that came in the mail, and a putting green, complete with fountain, waterfall and sand trap.

Harvey approached Jennifer the receptionist and wondered if he was in the right place. "Which office is Human Resources?" Harvey mewed. "I have an appointment at 9:00."

"Well, you're here," said the pretty young girl.

"I'm here? But which office is it?" he asked, looking behind her into the kaleidoscopic maze of rooms that didn't seem to have anything do with being offices.

"You're here in Human Resources," she said, glancing up at the person gaping at her like a startled chipmunk.

"All of *this* is *that*?" He pointed at the golf green and big screen TVs.

"All of *which* is *what*?" she replied.

"Human Resources?"

"It most certainly is. Because what is here is everywhere there," she said, jerking one of her thumbs over her shoulder.

"You mean everything *there*, is, well, um—"

"Human Resources? Yes."

Harvey had just gone around in circles without going anywhere. He still wasn't sure where 'here' was, so he asked again in a slightly different way. "Is Human Resources exactly where I'm standing?"

"Yes," she said, continuing to file her nails.

"Is the Human Resources where I'm standing exactly the Human Resources where I am supposed to be?" he asked.

"Well, that depends on where you're supposed to be."

"I'm supposed to be in Human Resources."

"Well, you're *here* then, aren't you?"

Dizzy, Harvey sat down in one of the big comfy chairs. The elevator doors opened. Out popped the man in the gray-pinstriped suit with the cell phone—the one who was annoyed, but was still allowed to pass through to the 'Other Side' anyway. This time, there was no lady with spiders in her eyelashes carrying a fruit basket.

"Jennifer, when's my next appointment?" he said, flying by the desk.

"2:00," the beautiful girl said.

"Great. I'll get some putting practice in."

Jennifer pushed a button on the desk. *Buzzzzz.* And with that, the man in the gray-pinstriped suit disappeared through the glass door behind her. Well not really 'disappear'. The door was glass and so was the wall. Harvey could see the man stripping off his tie and jacket and slinging them onto a Corinthian leather chair in an office with a tiger maple credenza. This looked vaguely familiar to Harvey.

Harvey approached the girl at the counter.

"My appointment is at 9:00," he whimpered.

"Name?"

"Harvey Drinkwater."

"I don't have a 'Harvey Drinkwater' on his calendar."

"But I'm *here*—"

Jennifer shot him an icy cold stare. It was a look of 'we are not going there with *here*.'

Harvey opened his mouth. "I know you're *here*, but—"

She leapt up from her chair and poked a finger towards the gaping hole in his face. "No, Mr. Drinkwater. No more *here* and no more *there*."

"But—"

She pushed the button on her desk again and the vice president of Human Resources missed his putt.

"You're 9:00 appointment is here," she said over the intercom.

"What 9:00 appointment?" he asked, shaking his putter in the air.

"The one at 9:00," she said. "With Harvey Drinkwater."

"I have an appointment with *who*? Send him in, I guess."

Buzzzzz. The glass door behind her opened magically.

"Jennifer?" The man said as he teed up his next putt.

"Yes, Mr. Gerson?"

"Didn't I fire you?"

"No, Mr. Gerson. That was your last secretary."

"Take a note, Jennifer. Put firing you on my calendar."

"Yes, Mr. Gerson."

The pretty young lady smirked, pointed Harvey to the glass door behind her, and went back to filing her nails.

Harvey crept into the opulent office, making sure he didn't tread on anything he wasn't supposed to tread on, bump into anything he wasn't supposed to bump into, or drool on anything he wasn't supposed to drool over. He slunk into a cozy Corinthian leather chair opposite a rather large tiger maple desk.

"Get out of my chair!" Bob Gerson, VP of Human Resources barked as he entered.

Harvey leapt out of the chair like he was leaping across the puddle next to Mr. Fortinelli's newspaper stand.

Bob Gerson removed the gray-pinstriped Armani jacket off the back of the chair and brushed away the creases Harvey had made. And the drool.

"Sit," he ordered.

There was no other chair.

Harvey sat cross-legged on the floor. And wiped his mouth.

"So?" the man said.

"So?" Harvey replied.

"So why are you here?"

"It's about the job."

Gerson slunk into the leather chair. He leaned forward and whispered, "You know about the *Job*?"

"Well, yes. It was in the newspaper."

"In the *newspaper*?" The VP leapt out of his chair. "Are you sure? So *soon*?"

"Yesterday."

"*Yesterday*?"

Harvey nodded.

"Yesterday? Are you sure?"

Harvey nodded again.

"Yesterday?"

Harvey felt like one of those dogs sitting in the back window of a car, nodding uncontrollably.

"But how could it be?"

"They printed it?" Harvey queried.

"Jennifer…"

"Yes, Mr. Gerson."

"Get me yesterday's paper."

"Yes, sir."

The pretty young lady returned with a paper from the glass coffee table next to the comfy chair that Harvey wished he was still sitting in. He was getting a crick in his neck looking up at Mr. Gerson from his spot on the floor.

Mr. Gerson plopped the newspaper on top of the polished tiger maple desk and frantically swiped the pages. "Crime reports? No, not there. The Business Section, perhaps? No. Ah! I bet it's in the Obituaries…"

In between each flick of the pages, Harvey Drinkwater received an icy cold stare from the VP of Human Resources. Harvey was developing a lump in his throat. Or was it the beef jerky coming up?

"OK, smart ass. Where is it?"

"It?"

"The *Job*?"

"It's here," Harvey replied.

"Here?"

Mr. Gerson didn't know it. But he didn't really want to go there with *here*. And to be honest neither did Harvey. One more dizzy spell and he would upchuck the beef jerky all over Mr. Gerson's newspaper. Or worse.

"In Globallica," Harvey said.

"You did the *Job* in Globallica? Right *here*? In Globallica?"

"Well, not yet. But I hope to…"

"*What*? What the hell are you talking about?"

Harvey stood up, flipped two pages of Mr. Gerson's newspaper and pointed to the help wanted advert. A piece of beef jerky bobbed in the back of his throat. Harvey said, bleating, "Assistant purchasing agent?"

"How did you get up here?" Gerson leaned forward and pushed a button on his desk. "Jennifer…how did this guy get up here?"

"He said he had an appointment."

"I had an appointment," Harvey added, just to clarify.

"Where?"

"Here."

"*Here*? As in 'right here'?"

The beef jerky was cocked and loaded.

"Purchasing doesn't do its interviews *here*."

"They don't?" Harvey mewed.

"No."

"But it's past nine o'clock. And I'm late. Very, very late."

"They do their interviews at 9:00PM. At *night*."

"They do?" Harvey mewed again.

"Yes, they do."

When he got the email, Harvey thought it was a typo. Who did interviews at 9:00PM? Globallica Purchasing, apparently. Harvey swallowed his beef jerky again. This time it was nice and soft. But it had a bitter aftertaste.

"*Get out!* And I don't want to see your sorry ass up here again or I'll fire you. Jennifer, take a note to fire Harvey Drinkwater."

Well, that went very well, Harvey thought, as he tip-toed carefully past the Ming vases, exited through the glass door past Jennifer, and made his way to the elevators. *I met a vice president of Globallica. And...I'm not late after all.*

CHAPTER SIX

For the first time in years, Harvey had unscheduled free time. He couldn't go back to Mr. Dortmann and the Zipper Emporium because he'd quit. He couldn't stay in Globallica's lobby because it was extraordinarily boring. Just a little man and a cat. Plus the seat was uncomfortable. So he left Globallica's skyscraper and took in the cultural sights of Ocean City to while away the time before his interview.

The Museum of Sardines.

Harvey Drinkwater never realized how much historical panache had been crammed into such a small space. The history of sardine processing was fascinating. The gallery of antique can-openers was awe-inspiring. And then there was the plaque commemorating the day Ocean City set a Guinness World Record: the most simultaneous wheelies by a group of motorcycles—four hundred and ninety-five. Set when the Hell's Angels chose Ocean City for their 'Rumble in the Surf' convention in 1979. It was a thin year for Guinness World Records.

And there was the magnificent Arthur P. Stottlemeyer Memorial Park right across from the Globallica Tower.

Arthur P. Stottlemeyer was the Founding Father of Ocean City. In 1849, he'd been washed up after a shipwreck near a whale de-boning station called 'Big Buffalo Knuckles' by the Indians. Nearly dead from the relentless pounding of the ocean's waves, Arthur P. Stottlemeyer was rescued by a band of immigrant European gypsies that had taken a wrong turn out of Abilene, Texas on their way to New York City and had been stopped at the ocean's edge in their fruitless search for the Big Apple, two thousand, nine hundred miles behind them.

Stottlemeyer and the gypsies were pioneering entrepreneurs and soon found they had a common interest: making money. They formed a company to terrorize passing wagon trains using an old gypsy prank, sneaking into the homesteaders' camps at night and tying dead fish to the undersides of their wagons. The next day, the smell of rotting fish and the swarm of flies it created, nearly sent the pioneers mad. They suspected each other of having hygiene problems. The ruse drove the pioneers to find comfort in Arthur P. Stottlemeyer's mobile mental health service and group therapy clinic, one of many monopolies Stottlemeyer and the gypsies had created in Big Buffalo Knuckles.

The wealth produced by Arthur P. Stottlemeyer and his gypsy friends fueled the growth of the tiny settlement for the next thirty years. Then in 1879, someone named Sam discovered you could eat sardines. If you knew how to catch them. And he did. The gypsies scammed the rush of migrants to Sam's expanding sardine processing plants on Oregon's coast. The economic boom accelerated until Big Buffalo Knuckles became today's thriving metropolis of Ocean City. The city's culinary fame, especially its prized sardine ice cream sundaes, put the 'Jewel of Oregon' on the tourist map.

Notwithstanding the richness of Ocean City's cultural heritage, Harvey Drinkwater did what every jobless person in America did given their unfortunate circumstances: he curled up on a bench in the park and fell asleep in the sunshine.

The sun had set and Harvey was in danger of being late for his 9:00PM appointment with Globallica Purchasing when Fate intervened. He was awakened by one of Ocean City's finest. A gentle nudge from the policeman's electric cattle prod and Harvey was 'up-and-at-em' to tackle the world's problems.

Harvey returned to the Globallica Tower, its lights shining brightly through the foggy gray night. Once inside Globallica's hallowed but empty foyer, Harvey couldn't see anyone to help him find his way. The little man, the cat and the sleeping bag were gone.

The lobby was dark except for whatever moonlight filtered through the fog outside the building into the foyer. And then Harvey saw it. A curl of smoke rising from within the grove of palm trees. Venturing carefully into the urban jungle, Harvey discovered the little man and his cat around a small campfire, toasting marshmallows.

"Hello? Excuse me."

The little man felt the end of his marshmallow, stuck it back in the fire to cook some more, and looked up at the person intruding on his privacy. "You again. What do you want this time?"

"I'm lost again. But I still have my pass. I have an appointment in Purchasing. And I don't know where to go."

The little man re-checked the marshmallow. It was done. The cat licked its lips. A mangy tail wagged in anticipation. The marshmallow was broken into two gooey pieces. The cat devoured half of the treat. The man consumed his half, leaned forward, rose like a toy with a key in its back, and beckoned Harvey to follow him.

"See that glass tunnel up there? The one leading out of the building?"

Harvey squinted. In the twilight, he could just make out on the other side of the security doors, a dimly lit glass portal high above the forest's canopy, situated at the top of a long escalator. "Yes, I see it."

"Follow it. It goes to Purchasing." The man turned and shuffled back to his campsite, his cat and his bag of marshmallows.

Harvey was very grateful but sad. The little man had helped him, perhaps not as politely as Harvey would have liked, but he had helped him. Why was the little man camped in the palms? And more importantly, why did the cat like marshmallows? Troubling questions indeed. Harvey risked being late, but these questions needed an immediate answer.

"Is this where you *live*?" Harvey asked.

"Yes. What's it to you?" said the little man.

"Well, I'm sorry to bother you. But why do you live *here*? You have a good job, don't you? There must be other places to live, aren't there?"

"Maybe. But I don't want to live in them. Not anymore. I'm happy. Dennis is happy. Now go away."

"What's it like working for Globallica?"

"I don't work for Globallica."

"You don't?"

"No. I work for Luigi's Security, their contract security firm. I used to be a vice president."

"A vice president? Of Luigi's?"

"No, of ASSCO. You know, the company that merged with Consolidated Remanufacturing to form Globallica."

Harvey nodded. His knowledge of Globallica's history was profound. It had to be. When he'd run out of scrapbooks, he'd plastered his bedroom's walls with newspaper clippings and magazine articles about Globallica. Every night he stared up at a Fortune article pinned to the ceiling above his bed, the one analyzing Consolidated's merger with ASSCO. Harvey could recite the article like it was Shakespeare.

"Have you read about the 'Merger from Hell'?" the man asked.

Harvey winced. "No? But, um… I think I've seen the movie."

"Consolidated screwed me and every other ASSCO executive out of every bit of money we had. Some sharp Harvard MBA weasel who's now the VP of Human Resources worded the deal so we ended up with nothing and those slimeball Consolidated executives got everything. It was in the fine print. The fine print we didn't read before we signed the deal."

"But you're still *here*?"

"The fine print. We had to stay on as consultants. For five years. But they didn't say doing *what*. This is my third year as a contract security guard. And I can't afford to pay any rent. So I live here."

Tears formed in Harvey's eyes.

The little man stood up and put his arms around his new friend. "Hey, I'm the one who should be crying, not you. But I'm not. Someday, someone will make it right for me and my cat Dennis. Don't worry. This isn't a Greek tragedy. I'll be okay. You're young. But if you don't mind me giving you some advice, don't make the same mistakes I made."

Harvey thanked the little man but he was pretty sure he'd made enough mistakes already. "I have to go now. By the way, what's your name?"

"George Thaddeus. Just call me George."

Harvey turned his back on George the security guard and his marshmallow-eating cat, Dennis. The magic in Harvey's newly acquired plastic card swept him through Globallica's security system like Dorothy being whooshed from Kansas into the Land of Oz. Harvey ventured forth on an epic journey of discovery—through the revolving doors, then from the bottom of the escalator to the top of the escalator, and then into the glass walkway that connected the Globallica Tower to the building next door.

Harvey recognized the building at the end of the glass walkway. It was one of many derelict warehouses along the harborfront that looked like they would fall down in a strong ocean breeze. This warehouse had been a factory that used to grind sardine fish scales and put them in pepper as filler. The warehouse had once been protected by the Ocean City Historical Society as a building of significant historical value but apparently was now owned by Globallica.

On its weathered brick sides, faded white and yellow letters from old advertising slogans sang out with ghostly messages from the early 1900s:

MAMA GYPSONI'S
MIRACLE WART REMOVAL CREAM
AND INTESTINAL SUPPLEMENT

EXTRACT OF SHARK'S BLADDER
SAY GOODBYE TO INCONTINENCE

And the famous:

IF IT'S NOT A STOTTLEMEYER
IT'S NOT A HEAD CHEESE SANDWICH

The derelict warehouse was no longer a derelict warehouse. It was a derelict warehouse with a glass tunnel connecting it to Globallica—the same glass tunnel that Harvey Drinkwater walked through, two stories above the road below. The further he walked, the darker the tunnel got. The glass roof leading up to the warehouse's entrance had been painted over until it had been completely blacked out. Cobwebs dangled from the arched ceiling. Cryptic messages in blood-red, graffiti-styled letters were written on the black-painted glass panels:

SAVE GLOBALLICA OR SAVE YOURSELF
SAVE OR TURN BACK!

THE PEN IS MIGHTIER THAN THE SWORD
UNLESS THE SWORD IS STUFFED UP YOUR ASS
GET YOUR PEN AND CHECKBOOK READY!

ALL WHO ENTER HERE PAY WITH THEIR SOUL!

This was great. Harvey had heard about companies that let their employees celebrate holidays at work. Mr. Dortmann was too serious and didn't approve of it. But Harvey hadn't heard of anyone celebrating Halloween so early…in July.

At the entrance to the derelict warehouse was a man in a dark brown monk suit, drapery cord wrapped around his waist. He sat on an uncomfortable looking stool. As Harvey approached, the monk stirred from his slumber, his face hidden by the hooded cowl of his robes, his hands buried inside oversized cuffs.

"Which supplier dares enter the Chamber of Savings? I am Arkon, Keeper of the Keys to your Hell."

Boy, was he good. Harvey loved scary movies. He and Lopez would cringe under the covers sharing a bucket of popcorn, peering out at the TV in his bedroom. The scarier the better. Why did that girl always go into that creepy, empty old house *alone*? Even Harvey wasn't that foolish. But then again, he was now alone in a derelict warehouse, with a maniacal monk who sounded like Freddy Krueger. And there were no witnesses.

"H-H-Harvey D-Drink-wuh-wuh-water…," Harvey replied in the most confident voice he could muster.

The monk spotted the plastic card flapping in Harvey's nervous hand. Arkon snatched the card from Harvey and swiped it into a card-reader. A computer screen flashed in the monk's face, the ghostly gray of the monitor's flickering light falling on the man's wrinkled cheeks. "Hmm, a fast-track employee. Oh, and you said, Harvard?"

"No. H-H-Harvey."

"MBA?"

"NPA Convention. Washington 1999."

"Huh?" the monk said. "Why are you here?"

Harvey's knees knocked. "I want to work in Puh-Puh-Purchasing…"

"What do you want to do in Purchasing?"

"Assistant puh-purchasing agent, Mr. Arkon, sir."

The monk named Arkon slapped his head. "Now I understand what's happening! Disguising yourself as a fast-track lateral developmental transferee? I should have known."

Harvey had broken a lateral something once before. It required a cast.

"Getting a view from the bottom of the organization, eh?" Arkon remarked as he looked back at the profile generated by the security card of a Globallica executive from HR—the card that had fallen down the side of a gray concrete wall inside a plastic tube.

"Good idea," Arkon smirked. "Networking with the rank and file before cutting their jugulars? Textbook. I'm impressed."

"Y-yes, if you s-say s-so, Mr. Arkon, s-sir."

"Well, come back tomorrow morning. Ask for Bunny. She'll get you started."

"You mean I have a job?"

"You already have a job." Arkon re-checked the information on Harvey's security card. *What was someone from HR doing on a developmental transfer into Purchasing?* he wondered. Whatever it was, Arkon was not about to argue. "We open the Purchasing Office at 6:00 AM sharp."

Harvey launched himself upwards. He splashed down into the puddle that had grown out of his pant leg. It was the warmest thing he'd felt since making contact with an electric cattle prod in the park.

Harvey Drinkwater was now an assistant purchasing agent at Globallica. And he didn't even need to go through the agony of an interview to get the job.

CHAPTER SEVEN

As Harvey strode into Globallica on his first day of work, he wondered if the company would mind if he took a few cuttings from the gardens in the lobby. In his excitement the day before, he'd forgotten about Lopez. Give the little dog credit. He hadn't peed on the floor. But all the potted plants in Harvey's apartment were now dead.

A book on *Dog-friendly Horticulture* would have to take a back seat to the other books on Harvey's growing list of educational priorities. *Ear Pieces for Dummies* was a must. *The Idiot's Guide to Elevators* perhaps. And *Frankenstein*, to get in the mood for work. He'd tried reading *Quantum Physics for Purchasing Professionals* but couldn't get past the first paragraph without falling asleep.

He checked his watch. It was 6:05AM. He was late. He raced up the escalator and sprinted down the glass tunnel towards the door marked 'Purchasing' with the dire warning signs above it. Mr. Arkon was not there.

Harvey paused. Which was the wrong thing to do.

A sudden pounding of feet broke the silence behind him. Harvey was swept inside the derelict warehouse by the rush of purchasing agents pushing and shoving each other like rats surfing a flood in a storm sewer.

Beyond the main entrance into Purchasing was a small foyer with musty smelling carpet and signs pointing in all directions: 'Stainless Steel', 'Cotton Balls', 'Sterilizing Fluid', 'Cardboard', 'Non-Metallic

Packaging Materials', 'Twine' and a host of others, including the cryptic, 'Miscellaneous Commodities'.

Harvey saw everyone swiping their employee cards through card swiping machines to access yet more sets of glass security doors. It seemed like the right thing to do. So he picked a door and did it. No luck. He tried another, same thing. He waited and waited. The foyer emptied. Harvey would add 'déjà vu' to his list of new beliefs, after Fate.

Then a pretty young lady exited one of the doors, looked at him and said, "Bob?" She seemed vaguely familiar.

Harvey looked around. He was alone. There was no one with him. So therefore, there was no one named Bob.

"Bob Gerson?" she asked, staring straight into Harvey's eyes.

Harvey gulped. "I'm Harvey Drinkwater," he said.

"Oh, I see. Working *undercover*, eh?" The pretty young lady winked. "Nice idea, Mr. Gerson. Oh, sorry. I mean, Mr. Drinkwater."

He liked this place already. They were so friendly.

"Well, Mr. Drinkwater," she said, winking again. "Welcome to Purchasing. My name is Penelope Warren. Aren't you the kind person who helped me through the doors the other day?"

Harvey blushed. "And you're the person who can eat a donut while talking, texting and doing a crossword puzzle? I was very impressed. I wish I could do that."

"Follow me, Mr. Drinkwater. I'll show you to your cube."

Cube? As in 'your own cubicle'? Harvey Drinkwater was living a dream. He was so excited. *His own cubicle!*

Penelope Warren ushered Harvey through a set of double-doors under a sign that said, 'Miscellaneous Commodity Purchasing'. There was an incredible buzz about the place—a sea of people in constant motion, clacking away on keyboards, chattering away to each other like excited chipmunks, roaming the aisles with cell phones while laden down with piles of file folders.

Harvey had entered purchasing nirvana.

Purchasing's Olympus. A buyer's Disney World.

"Welcome to the Department of Miscellaneous Commodities," said Penelope.

"What's a Miscellaneous Commodity, Miss Warren?"

"You'll see. And please, call me Bunny."

"Bunny?"

"Yes, Bunny. I've been called that ever since high school. Everyone I work with here calls me Bunny, too."

"Will I be working for you, Bunny?"

"Oh no, Harvey. Not exactly. I'm an assistant purchasing agent like yourself. We'll be working together. We always help each other. It's the only way to preserve our sanity."

Harvey couldn't agree more. Every time Hilda grabbed his pile of invoices, he insisted it was his turn to do them. But she wasn't a team player. In fact she could be very rude. "Over my dead body," she would say.

"You'll be an assistant purchasing agent to Darcy Gillemott. She's the senior purchasing agent in charge of the section you'll be working in. She has an interesting deck."

"Deck? She's got a deck in her office? A wood one? With a barbecue?"

"No, silly. Her buying 'deck'. That's the commodities she buys. All kinds of interesting things. She'll tell you. I work for Angus McCalliwag. Now there's an easy deck. At least for Angus. What a breeze."

"What does he buy?"

"Ammunition and rocket fuel."

"Ammunition?"

"It's a long story." Bunny sauntered through the main aisle, Harvey in tow. "Everyone here works for Kendall Swick, the Director of Miscellaneous Commodities Purchasing. I'd introduce you to him but he's not in today. He's at a supplier trying to get savings. It's just as well. It'll give me some time to train you before Kendall piles on the work."

Looks like boredom will be a thing of the past, Harvey thought.

Penelope grabbed Harvey by the shoulders and steered him behind a cubicle wall. "Watch out. Here comes Todd."

"Todd?"

Todd Hertle appeared to be Harvey's age, mid-twenties, but that's where the similarity ended. He had a thin face, wore thick glasses and had a funny little body. When Todd walked, it looked like he was going in two different directions at once. The top half was not totally synchronized with the bottom. Even when he was standing still, it looked like he was moving. To call him hyperactive would not be a sufficient description; looking at him darting in and out of the desks and cubicles was like watching a video on fast forward.

"Sorry, Harvey. There's no way to avoid him. Brace yourself."

Harvey clung to the edge of a printer as he and Bunny tried not to make eye contact with Todd.

Too late.

"Well, fellow slaves," Todd chortled. "Rumor is the Pretzel Makers will be scouting our department tomorrow for a Drill Down. Buckle up for safety, boys and girls. Who's your new boyfriend, Bunny?"

"Harvey Drinkwater, this is Todd." This time someone actually shook Harvey's hand when he stuck it out. "He's going to work for Darcy."

Todd sucked air through his teeth. "Oo...for Darcy? Tough assignment, Harvey. Don't envy you. No, siree. Z-COTs are wicked to buy. I filled in when Darcy Gillemott was on vacation. What an experience, I tell you. Wouldn't like to do it full time. No way. It's a wonder Darcy isn't barking like a dog by now."

Harvey's brain cells were on overload. Todd was speaking a language that sounded like English but might be a cross between Chinese and Klingon. Why did they drill holes in pretzels? And when

Todd mentioned evil-barking zebras, or something like that, Harvey thought a brain vessel had popped inside his head.

"Take it easy with Harvey, Todd. It's his first day."

"Sorry, Bunny. Don't forget the International Video Conference tomorrow morning. It's your turn to go 'Live with Kendall'. I'm counting on you. Don't let me down."

"Don't worry, Todd. I'll be there. But if DragonForce's gang comes around just before it starts, you might be out of luck."

"I hate it when that happens. Nice to meet you, Harvey." And then Todd was off, like a spinning Tasmanian Devil from a cartoon, leaving Harvey with the beginning of a severe headache. There was too much to remember. He even forgot the questions.

"Bunny. I'm lost."

"Well, you're here."

Harvey wasn't about to go there with 'here'. He wanted to stay right where he was and figure out what was 'up' and what was 'down'. Dragon-farting, pretzel-eating zebra coats were more than his simple little brain could absorb in one sitting.

"Do I need a night school course?" he asked Bunny, his voice desperate for help. The last night school course Harvey took was a disaster. Soapstone carving was just not for him. His walrus looked like a worm with a thyroid condition.

"Huh? Why?" she asked.

Sweat beaded up on Harvey's forehead. His complexion was pale. Like someone about to faint. Which is exactly what Harvey was about to do.

"Oh, I get it," she said, realizing Harvey's dilemma. "The terminology? It's like that everywhere inside Globallica, Harvey. We use acronyms for everything. You'll catch on."

Harvey made a mental note not to eat beef jerky for breakfast again. If every day was going to be like this, then he had to limit his chances of repeating his food. Tomorrow he would try muesli.

"Todd's a character, isn't he?" she said.

"Yep, that's one way to describe him. And then there's a Pretzel Maker. What's that?"

"Oh, they're bad news, Harvey. Find a place to hide if someone spots them. You'll know it when it happens. Believe me."

At this moment, Harvey would believe flying pigs might abduct him and take him to Kansas if Bunny Warren told him it was true. He was totally dependent on her, like a leech on someone's leg.

"And a Z-Coat?"

"You mean a Z-COT? I'm afraid Darcy's going to have to explain that one. I'm not too sure myself."

"And 'Dragon Fart'?

Bunny Warren laughed. "You mean 'Dragon*Force*'?"

"Um, yes…both sound dangerous."

"They are. Or should I say, *she* is. Katrina Borchevski. One to be avoided. The Devil's apprentice. Arkon hired her after an executive recruiting drive in Russia. She calls herself DragonForce."

"I've met Mr. Arkon already. He was nice. A bit spooky. But nice."

Bunny Warren frowned. A demented old man in a monk's suit was not her idea of nice. "He's just called Arkon around here, Harvey. Not *Mr.* Arkon. We don't refer to any of the executive directors by their first and last names. They just have one name. That's all."

"My dog has only one name, Lopez." Harvey pulled out a picture.

"Cute dog. I know it seems strange, but when someone is promoted to executive director in Globallica Purchasing, they change their name. To just one name. A name they use to project a certain kind of, well…persona, I guess. It's considered a perk of the job."

"One name? Any name?"

"Yeah, anything they want. Something real. Something imaginary. Anything at all. It's a real competition between the executives to outdo each other. Most of it is made up, like DragonForce and Arkon. Sometimes it's a real name."

"But why change your name? I'm happy with the one I've got."

"It's a power trip, Harvey. These executives get to a position that is so high up, they feel they're looking down on us little people like gods. It's part of the culture around here. Don't ask me how it started. It's always been that way. They choose a name to suit the personality they want people to believe they have. A mythical creature to be feared. A romantic hero. A powerful general. Greek and Roman gods. Dungeons and dragons. Chips and dip. Who knows where they dig up these weird names? Globallica Purchasing even hires consultants to help them choose names. It's that important to their future careers."

"It is? What about Mr. Swick?"

"You can call him 'Dork' if you like."

Harvey took out a small notepad. He wrote down, D-O-R-K…

"No, Harvey. I'm just kidding. Kendall's not high up enough for the name game. Thank God. It's the next level above him…executive director. When you get to that level it gives you the right to choose a name. Kendall reports to Executive Director Bjorn."

"Bjorn?"

"Executive Director of All Commodities. Yup, Bjorn. A legendary Norwegian probably. A famous Viking rapist or something like that. He used to be a regular guy like us. Name was Dag Hakanberg. Started in Globallica's Oslo office. He was nice when he was an assistant purchasing agent like you and I. But now he's an executive director, watch out. Promotion sure changes them."

"Bee-Yorn?"

"A lot to learn, Harvey."

Harvey was confused. He understood the concept of one name as it applied to dogs. He just had to take an existential leap forward to apply it to human beings. He would practice. Leaping. In the park by his apartment. He was determined to be a good assistant purchasing agent, no matter what the personal cost.

***

Todd Hertle was not the only one who spoke in a foreign language. Angus McCalliwag had a very strange way of speaking English. He said he had a Glaswegian accent. Harvey had never met anyone from Glaswegia before so he had to take his word for it. When Angus spoke, it was somewhat musical. It sounded like he was rapping, with the occasional pause to spit up phlegm.

And Harvey didn't think Angus heard a word Harvey said. No matter how many times he reminded Angus that his name was Harvey, Angus kept calling him 'laddie'. Harvey made a mental note to take a night school course in the Glaswegian language.

"Bunny tells me you buy… ammunition?"

"Ach aye, me laddie. It's a long story," Angus replied, adjusting his kilt. Angus was as tall as a moose and just as lanky. His ginger eyebrows bounced up and down his face as he talked. "Sit yer wee tushie doon and I'll tell yee about it."

"Oh no you won't, Angus," a woman's voice interjected. "We've got work to do. And if this is Harvey Drinkwater, he'd better get started right away."

Darcy Gillemott was an imposing woman. At least Harvey thought she was a woman. She was very tall, flat-chested, broad-shouldered, had wispy hair and a thin moustache, the kind Harvey tried to grow once to look cool. Hilda Ausfahrt told him he should shave it off because the laughing hurt her hernia.

"Harvey," Darcy said. "Take these and read them."

Harvey now had his own stack of file folders.

"Then input this week's data and prepare the Z-COT report. I have to go to the Savings Board this afternoon. Bunny can help you get started."

Darcy took a few strides with her long legs and was gone.

"Well, you've officially arrived," said Bunny, pointing Harvey into one of the cubicles outside Darcy Gillemott's office.

Harvey looked around the cubicle and that warm feeling returned. The cube was not much bigger than his desk under the stairwell at the Zipper Emporium. But it was modern, clean and private. And Harvey couldn't be happier. He plunked the pile of file folders on the desk and sat in his new chair. It was like a pilot's seat with levers and buttons and armrests that moved in and out. He started fiddling with them and nearly catapulted into the waste basket.

"Harvey, don't get too comfortable," Bunny warned. "You have an appointment with Olive Olympios in half an hour. And you absolutely *cannot* be late. I'll come back for you."

Bunny left him to absorb his strange new surroundings.

Harvey took the first folder off the top of the pile. It had a neatly printed label: *Honey Bee Production Statistics for the Pacific Northwest*. The next one said: *Stray Cat Trends in Arkansas*. Then there was: *Climactic Conditions in Ecuador* and a cryptically titled one labeled: *The Peruvian Project*. Another one ominously called: *Nitrogen Content of Rhinoceros Manure*.

At the very bottom of the pile, there was a folder with the simple title: *Dirt*. It was the only folder that was empty.

Harvey opened *Honey Bee Production Statistics for the Pacific Northwest* and flipped through pages and pages of numbers and graphs. He thought quantum physics was more interesting. Soon Harvey's head was sitting sideways on the pile of folders, his drool dripping from one folder to the other until it formed a foamy pool on the top of his desk.

"Harvey!"

Harvey's head jerked upright and his eyes burst open.

Bunny stood over him. "Harvey, we're late. Get up. We have to go. If Olive's not in a good mood, we're in big trouble."

CHAPTER EIGHT

Olive Olympios was a fierce-looking woman in her late fifties who had the body of a wrestler, the expressions of a taste tester at a lime juice factory and the disposition of a castrated hornet. If you combined her physical appearance with her authority and job responsibilities, you might mistake her for a genetic mutation between a Swiss banker and a mass murderer. Her job title was Personal Productivity Manager.

Olive controlled access to Purchasing's computer systems, passwords and login ID's; the distribution of computers and cell phones; and the ordering of office supplies. Being late for an appointment with Olive Olympios was like spitting in the face of the Spanish Inquisition.

"Mr. Drinkwater, I service two hundred and sixty-seven people. You are number two hundred and sixty-eight. When you have an appointment at 9:37:24, I expect you to be here. You have been allotted two minutes and thirty-five seconds to be assigned login ID's and to file your initial stationary requisitions with me. You are one minute and forty-eight seconds late, which leaves me only thirty-six seconds to instruct you in departmental procedures, of which I have used twenty-three seconds so far. Which basically means, I only have enough time to re-schedule you for another appointment which will be—" Olive took a deep breath and scrolled through her electronic planner which had the processing power of a Silicon Valley server farm. "In two months, three weeks, seven days, two hours, four minutes and thirteen seconds from now, assuming you start work the same time I do, which is at 5:28 AM. Good day, Mr. Drinkwater. Next!"

And with that, Harvey's audience with the Department of Miscellaneous Commodities' Personal Productivity Manager was over. And he did not have login IDs.

"Don't worry, Harvey," said Bunny. "I know someone, who knows someone, who has a girlfriend in IT, who might be able to hack into the computer system and give you a temporary ID. I'll make a few calls. In the meantime, pretend you have access. And act like you know how to input data. At least until Darcy Gillemott goes on leave."

"She's leaving?"

"Well he…um, I mean *she*…is having an operation."

"Is it serious?"

"Well it's sort of a male problem…oops, I mean a female problem."

"Oh. She's going to be all right, isn't she?"

"He'll be…um, she'll be…fine. When he becomes a she."

"She's a he?"

"Yes, she's a 'he'. He'll be a she soon, but right now he's still officially a 'he'. Then when he returns, he'll be a she. Officially. But not before."

That was it. Harvey would join Beef Jerky Anonymous and swear off the spicy sticks forever. If he was going to get dizzy like this, he needed something that would stick to the sides of his stomach and not come up for fresh air. Harvey was now a committed muesli-eater.

"I know what you're thinking," said Bunny, noticing his queasiness.

"You do?" Harvey wondered if muesli caused your breath to smell when you repeated it. That's what he was thinking.

"Yes. You're thinking, why is Darcy Gillemott having a sex change operation, aren't you?"

Whooahh, Nelly, Harvey thought. Going from breakfast preferences to sexual preferences was an existential leap that even Harvey wasn't trained yet to perform without risking personal injury and having lateral damage. "No, Bunny. I wasn't."

"Okay, Harvey. Look, you've been bombarded with all kinds of stuff. This is just your first day. And I think you've coped well. I'll leave you alone for a little while and check in on you later, okay?"

"Sure."

Harvey Drinkwater needed a mental rest. Things were happening fast. His priority list had been re-arranged and his schedule was filling up. He needed to buy a dictionary to find out what a Z-COT was. He had to practice pretending to input data into a computer he didn't have access to. He needed to schedule a meeting with Angus McCalliwag to understand why Angus bought ammunition (there were lessons to be learned from that no doubt). And finally, he had to wipe the drool off his pile of file folders.

But of more immediate concern was the subject of the curious old man sitting alone in Darcy Gillemott's office. He'd been there when Harvey arrived in the office and hadn't moved since. The old man was wearing tattered blue-jean overalls, a plaid shirt and one of those farmer's baseball caps with mesh air holes which sat on his head like an upside down bowl. Screen printed on the front of the cap was a logo that read *Ocean City Seed Mill*.

The man was in his late sixties or early seventies, silver gray hair, gray moustache and gray eyebrows, weathered wrinkled face, dirty fingernails still soiled from laboring in the fields. He had a toothpick in his mouth which he chewed relentlessly—that slight movement and the blinking of his eyes were the only things indicating the old man was still alive.

Harvey flicked through the files in front of him, occasionally looking into Darcy's office to see the little man chewing his cud. Eventually the man looked at his watch, picked up a brown paper bag that had been sitting beside him—Harvey surmised it contained his lunch—and left Darcy's office in a slow shuffle consistent with the man's age. The man disappeared from view down the corridor.

Harvey was puzzled.

The same way he was puzzled about the contents of the files stacked in front of him. Each folder had the stamp 'Z-COT' on it and had the same name 'Takata Hoshimei' inside as a contact.

Fate had a way of entering Harvey's life at random but opportune moments. The phone rang. Harvey answered it—after all, it was his phone, in his cube.

It was Takata Hoshimei. "Ah, Drinkwater-san. Miss Wallen said you be in."

Wallen? Harvey didn't know a Miss Wallen.

"Okay," Harvey answered.

"I need you come see me tomorrow, Drinkwater-san. We need you buy more cat litta. We run out. Okay, Drinkwater-san?"

"Okay," Harvey said, much less confidently. This sounded like an emergency. Cats without enough litter were not to be fooled with.

"Sayonara, Drinkwater-san."

Then the line went dead. Kind of like Harvey's brain. Unfortunately for him, the Department of Miscellaneous Commodities didn't allow a brain to run down until it was completely dead, just in intensive care and on life support. In Purchasing, there was no time for idleness. Unfortunately. For Harvey. Rigor mortis was preferable to what happened next.

Todd Hertle returned. "Reports."

"Reports?" said Harvey.

"Reports, Harvey. Yes, reports. Savings reports. That's what it's all about in Purchasing, Harvey. Savings. And Savings Reports. Reports on savings. You have them done, don't you?"

"Reports on what?"

"Oh, Harvey, Harvey. Reports on…dumby, dumby, dumby, ta da!" Todd gestured like a Las Vegas comedian with a top hat and tails. "Savings, Harvey. Savings, savings and *more* savings."

Todd adjusted his glasses with thick lenses so his eyes appeared ten times bigger than they were instead of only four times bigger. "You have savings, don't you?"

"Savings on what?"

"Exactly. *What* is exactly what I want savings on," said Todd confidently.

"Well, I don't have any, Todd. I think. But I'm not sure. Exactly. I think."

"Oo-kay. We'll count that as 'No Savings' today, shall we?"

"Oo-kay, Todd. Sounds good to me. Sorry. Maybe tomorrow? I guess."

"That's how it works, Harvey. You're catching on fast. Tomorrow, I'll check in again. And maybe...maybe, we'll have a teensy, weensy little bit of savings to report? Maybe? You won't let us down, Harvey, ol' boy, will you?"

Harvey gulped. He was more comfortable with Olive Olympios. At least he knew exactly where he stood. She was pissed off. He was screwed. It was simple. Todd Herle made life complicated.

"Oh Todd, lay off the poor guy. It's his first day," Bunny Warren said, returning. She was a life saver. Harvey could resume being a leech, a role he was eminently qualified to perform. "Besides, Todd," she continued. "Ho Gung wants you. Something about a Logic Master coming to Kendall's next staff meeting."

"A *what*?" Todd's lower body danced about like a four-year-old that needed to go to the bathroom. "Is Kendall *nuts*! Inviting a Logic Master to his staff meeting? What hare-brained idiot told him to do that?"

"Well, Todd...I think *you* did."

"Bunny, please. Don't do this to me. I did not, most definitely *did not*, invite a Logic Master to Kendall's meeting. Ho Gung might be crazy enough to do that. But not me."

"Well, it was indirectly your fault, Todd. Don't you remember the last staff meeting? When you said that submitting Sun Ho Gung's

Baby Formula Proposal to the Savings Board was like trying to defy the laws of gravity? It was not only stupid, it was illogical. Remember?"

"Oo, yes, well—"

Todd Hertle's voluntary muscle movements were now accompanied by a host of involuntary ones.

"Then you got up out of your chair, pranced around the room, and re-stated that thinking the Baby Formula Proposal will fly is like waking up in the morning and pretending gravity doesn't exist. Remember that, Todd?"

"Oo, yes, well—"

At this point, you could have plugged Todd Hertle into Ocean City's power grid. He was generating enough nervous energy to eliminate a year's worth of brownouts caused by the Globallica Tower's insatiable appetite for electricity.

"Then to cap it off, you leapt like a ballerina through the conference room, singing, 'It's illogical... it's a-stupid...' to the tune of 'It's a-wonderful, it's a-marvelous...' Remember, Todd? Todd? Todd! Are you okay?"

Todd Hertle was well and truly whipped into a trance-like state. Todd's glasses had steamed over. He turned and bounced off the partition wall, mumbling incoherently. His hands moved like he was playing air guitar. Harvey was envious. He always wanted to play air guitar but didn't have time for lessons.

"Harvey, help me get Todd back to his cube. The thought of a Logic Master at our next staff meeting is obviously too much."

The two corralled Todd Hertle like a runaway steer and herded him into a cube three rows down. Todd Hertle reclined in his chair, looking like one half of a wrestling match.

Harvey Drinkwater wasn't afraid to ask questions. He was afraid of hearing the answers. "Bunny, what's a Logic Master?" he squeaked. "Do they make pretzels too?"

"Oh, Harvey. I really feel sorry for you. You have so much to learn. Things like this shouldn't be happening on your first day." Bunny Warren's words were pleasant and soothing. "I tell you what, Harvey," she said. "Go down to the coffee station and get us a cup of coffee while I make sure Todd's all right."

"Oo-kay," said Harvey as he moved like a robot in the direction Bunny pointed him. On his way, Harvey passed by a wall covered in cherry-framed, poster-sized photographs. In each one, a smiling person handed what looked like an oversized check to another smiling person who looked like they were a model for a Giorgio Armani suit advert. He recognized one of the faces holding a check. It was Angus McCalliwag.

The coffee station was at the end of the hall. Amazingly, Harvey was able to pour two cups of coffee without spilling them more than once. He made his way back past the photographs, pausing to look at Angus' smiling face.

Angus' office was next to the wall of photos. "Aye, laddie," the tall ginger-haired Scot said. "Tha' was a prood day indeed."

"Are you getting some kind of reward?" Harvey asked.

Angus laughed. "Nay, laddie. Yee wee friend here—*me*—was doon' tha rewardin'."

Harvey cocked his head sideways and twitched. The man in the photo with Angus was stocky and short, in his late sixties and had a mane of silvery hair that looked like it could withstand hurricane force winds without mussing up.

Angus noticed Harvey's confusion. "Tha' overgrown tart there is Talus, the vice president of Purchasing. He's our equivalent of tha Loch Ness Monster. He surfaces only once in a wee while. And yee have ta snap a selfie to prove tha slimy creature even exists."

Harvey grimaced. The thought of having a creature like the Loch Ness Monster roaming the halls of Globallica in an Armani suit gave him the willies.

Bunny joined them. "Over here is Sun Ho Gung before his nervous breakdown. And here's Darcy."

Harvey didn't recognize Darcy Gillemott. The photo showed a beefy man with bushy sideburns and a goatee handing over a check to another man, not the same one Angus referred to as Talus. Someone else.

Bunny noticed Harvey's confusion. "Yes, that's Darcy. Before hormone therapy."

"And who's this?"

The man receiving the check from Darcy resembled a Scandinavian Olympic cross country skier; tall, blond, blue-eyed, slim, wiry.

"Aye, laddie. Tha's Dag Hakanberg. Tha's our Bjorn."

"The rapist?"

"Wha, laddie? Aye, the Viking's doon a bit o' pillagin' in his time. Ya might be right about tha."

"Angus, that's no way to talk about Bjorn," Bunny said. "Ignore Angus, Harvey. Let me explain what all these photos mean. Talus chairs the Savings Board. All the executive directors like Bjorn, DragonForce and Arkon report to him. When big savings are made from suppliers, we have our photo taken with the executive directors. It was an honor to have his picture taken with Talus despite what the old Scottish fart thinks."

Rows and rows of photographs lined the wall to the coffee station. So this was what purchasing was all about. Making savings. Handing over a check from a supplier. Getting your picture taken. This was 21st century purchasing in action and Harvey was smack dab in the middle of it.

"Harvey, let's go over your Savings Report for tomorrow," Bunny said. "I'll show you how to report savings when you don't have any."

Harvey looked puzzled.

"It's easy."

"Oo-kay," said Harvey. Confidently.

CHAPTER NINE

Lopez understood. It was difficult, but he understood. Well at least Harvey thought he understood. The first day in a new job was always difficult. Not easy. Making new friends. Wiping drool off files. Learning new languages. That was the part Lopez seemed to understand the best. Drooling.

Bunny Warren had tried to explain. It wasn't easy for Harvey. But she seemed to take it well. She kept waving her hands in front of his eyes to make sure he was still there. Which he was. Just about.

Yes, as that first week progressed, Harvey Drinkwater learned a lot.

He learned that Logic Masters attended meetings to make sure decisions were logical, because it wasn't logical to think that logic would necessarily be a part of decisions. And he learned that—more often than not—a Logic Master's judgment was less logical than the logic they were judging.

He learned how to write a Savings Report when there weren't any savings to report. But there could be savings to report if someone hadn't interrupted to ask for a Savings Report.

And he learned how to access a system that was inaccessible, to input data that was irrelevant.

Regarding the mysterious Z-COTs, he learned that Bunny didn't know what she was supposed to know, because no one knew that she didn't know. And what he didn't know was that he was supposed to know it too, even though she didn't. Which was a problem. Because he didn't know there was a problem. And neither did she.

And he learned that the dictionary he bought didn't define what a Z-COT was. It had zygote, zip code, seacoast, baby cot, Z-cars, tai chi and Cote d'Azur. But no Z-COT. It had taken Harvey six hours to determine that simple fact. But at least the dictionary was more interesting to read than quantum physics.

But one big mystery remained. Why was there an old man with a ventilated baseball cap sitting in Darcy Gillemott's office at the same time each day, doing the same thing? Which was essentially nothing.

Once again, today, Harvey could look out of his cube and see the man doing what he did yesterday and the day before that. Which was chewing the cud. Calling it nothing would be insulting if you were a cow, since doing what the man was doing would be considered doing something for a cow. So in this case, something was not better than nothing. It was equal to it.

Harvey had left his cube and approached the entrance to Darcy's office to ask the man if there was something other than nothing that Harvey could help him do.

That was a big mistake.

Down the hall, a set of double doors burst open. Todd Hertle hurtled through them, screaming at the top of his lungs, "Pretzel Makers! Run!"

"Pretzel Makers?"

Everyone scurried for cover. They hid under desks. Opened storage room doors and vanished. Dove under conference tables. The smallest employees opened file cabinets and with great skill and agility acquired from a disciplined regimen of Pilates and a carefully monitored Mediterranean diet, were able to jump in to evade capture.

Harvey was unfortunately unable to appreciate how supremely important it was to hide your sorry ass when the Pretzel Makers swept through the department.

One thing was absolutely, unequivocally clear. It required no detailed explanations from Bunny or Todd or Angus. Harvey didn't need to take a night school course to learn it. It required no written training manual, visual job instructions, or really any intuitive understanding. Which was just as well. Because Harvey didn't have any of the above. But it didn't matter.

Harvey found out quickly why Pretzel Makers were called Pretzel Makers. They turned people into the shape of a pretzel. And they were very good at what they did.

By the time they were done, Harvey had a full appreciation for this unique skill. The Pretzel Makers were like the magicians he saw in the park who created dogs out of balloons for little kiddies. Twisting people without breaking bones was truly an art form.

Two trim, athletic young men transformed Harvey into their latest anatomical design: a Harvey-Drinkwater-sandwich with Globallica's newest assistant purchasing agent as the meatloaf.

Harvey also liked their uniforms. When he could see them. Most of the time he was counting the toes on his foot as it rubbed up against his cheek. The Pretzel Makers were immaculately attired: steely gray shirts with black ties, black dress chinos and black boots with silver buckles. On their breast pockets they had *Globallica Purchasing* embroidered in black and silver lettering. They wore armbands which were all black with a large gold-embroidered dollar sign within a diamond-shaped gold border. Whatever it was they wanted Harvey for, it must have been very important, because they had dressed up for the occasion.

The two Pretzel Makers whisked him away arm-in-arm, striding like those funny Olympic long distance walkers as they wiggled their hips. Bunny understood Harvey's predicament. They were kindly escorting Harvey to his cube to get his savings files but it was hard to find the appropriate file when your left hand was scratching your right ear from underneath your crotch.

Bunny emerged from her hidey-hole to help. "Psst, Harvey!" she said, out of sight behind a partition.

"Bunny, what's happening?"

"You've been 'selected' to attend the Drill Down. The Pre-Savings meeting."

"Is that good?"

"Not particularly."

"I didn't think so."

Harvey was catching on quickly.

"Who are you talking to?" said a third man, marching up the aisle. "Bunny Warren? I thought so. Come out, where I can see you."

"I think this is what you're looking for, Johann," Bunny said, entering Harvey's cube to locate the report she'd helped Harvey prepare the day before.

Johann Thorsveld, Squad Leader, Fourth Brigade, Presentation Expeditors, flipped through Harvey's report with a chilling nonchalance. This had been a 'clean kill'. Normally mechanical equipment with laser targeting had to be brought in to find suitable 'attendees' for the Pre-Savings Meeting.

"Okay, we've got it," he said to the two Pretzel Makers. "Let's go."

The two Pretzel Makers dragged Harvey down the hall. Bunny felt obliged to follow them. Harvey might be working undercover but screwing up a Pre-Savings Meeting was not a good idea.

"Bunny, what's a Pre-Savings Meeting?" he whimpered as he was frog-marched out of the office.

Bunny explained as best as she could, given Harvey's head was bouncing off his knees. Pre-Savings was a meeting to predict possible savings if it were possible to predict savings at all. Most of the time, Pre-Savings Reports from assistant purchasing agents like Harvey were indeterminable drivel. But that was okay because the Pre-Savings Board didn't have a clue what the reports were trying to say. And as long as you were able to say something, then something was better than nothing. Or equal to it, yet again.

As soon as Harvey was dragged into the conference room where the Pre-Savings Board was convening, it was his turn to present. Harvey proved he had a genuine talent for saying nothing disguised as something. It just seemed to come naturally for him. It must have been in his genes. It was clear to the Pre-Savings Board from his presentation that Harvey had the right qualities for a fast-track career at Globallica.

"Honey bee production has numbers...um," Harvey explained with a climbing passion in his voice, "which indicate that the quantity of honey bees has neither risen nor fallen since the last time honey bee production numbers were counted."

He continued, "Stray cats in Little Rock are to Little Rock what honey bees are to Seattle. Which is to say... that we've run out of cat litter. Apparently. Unfortunately. According to... according to...," Harvey thumbed through his files to remember the name of the nice little Japanese fellow he'd talked to on his first day. Which was a waste of time. Thumbing that is. Bunny closed the folder and read him the label on the outside.

"Takata Hoshimei...," she whispered in his ear.

"Takata Hoshimei. And the Peruvian Project should produce savings soon," Harvey added, taking pride in his newly found improvisational skills. Which was the wrong thing to do. Apparently.

"It *will*?" said Johann Thorsveld, the excitement in his voice infecting the room with energy. He jumped clear out of his seat. "The Peruvian Project?"

Harvey slunk beneath the conference table just as Johann launched himself on top of it. "Drinkwater, *savings*? When? How? And how much?"

The buzz around the room was electric. "Don't make anything up, Harvey," she whispered as she crouched under the table and pulled him out. Bunny had a scornful look on her face. "Johann is like a shark in water. He can smell blood."

Harvey looked at his arms and legs. He wasn't bleeding. Bruised, but not bleeding. The Pretzel Makers had made sure of that. They were very skillful at what they did.

Changing the subject to the growth statistics of hybrid tea roses in rhinoceros manure was no longer possible. The feeding frenzy had started. Harvey was lifted unceremoniously and put in 'The Stool' in the middle of the room. 'The Stool' was a specially designed piece of hard wooden furniture underneath a bank of high wattage track lights, hot enough to singe someone's eyebrows.

The room's perimeter lights dimmed, leaving a quivering little man in the sole spotlight. Sweat flowed off Harvey's forehead and dripped down the tip of his nose. Johann Thorsveld emerged from behind the conference table and whacked a wooden pointer against Harvey's thigh. "So Mr. Harvey... Drinkwater...."

"Y-y-yes," Harvey replied. "Th-that's m-m-me."

"You have savings, don't you? Stop trying to hide them."

Harvey gulped. He was getting good at gulping. Initially, it hurt his throat. But now, using the proper breathing technique, he could gulp without much pain.

"Possibly." Harvey knew it wasn't a possibility. It was a lie.

"You're lying."

Yes, Harvey thought. *Yes, I am.* But lying seemed like the right approach. Especially when a snazzily-dressed but menacingly-uniformed man hovered over you with a stick and when you could smell your eyebrows reaching the point of spontaneous combustion. "I th-think it w-will p-produce s-savings in...um..."

"Don't think, Mr. Drinkwater. *Know.* And tell the truth this time."

Harvey looked around the room. Bunny had buried her hands in her head. The other unfortunate fools— the ones who like Harvey had been unable to escape the grasp of the Pretzel Makers— looked at Harvey as if he were some kind of Messiah defying his heathen captors before being fed to the lions.

"In...in..."

Johann whacked the hickory stick against his thigh. His eyes widened, producing an almost electric glow from deep inside his pupils. "In? Yes? In? Come on. In...?"

"In…" Harvey grimaced. He knew he was in trouble. How much more trouble could he get himself into if he just made up a number? They made up names for themselves. Why couldn't he just make up a number? What possible harm was there in that? he thought.

"In…in…in *two* weeks."

There. It was done.

He'd given them a number.

What a relief. That wasn't so hard after all.

"In *two* weeks!" exclaimed Johann, joyously.

"In two weeks?" sobbed Bunny, inconsolably.

"In two weeks," repeated Harvey, confidently.

"Excellent, Drinkwater. See, you cowardly worms. Savings are not only possible in Miscellaneous Commodities but Mr. Drinkwater here will deliver them. In *two* weeks. Well done, Mr. Drinkwater."

Johann Thorsveld leaned over the quivering mess occupying 'The Stool' and whispered quietly in Harvey's ear, "In *two* weeks, Mr. Drinkwater? Yes, in *two* weeks and not a minute more. I will look forward to seeing your Savings presentation. In *two* weeks."

Thorsveld's chuckling reminded Harvey of those late night black and white horror films he and Lopez enjoyed so much. At least until the part where the hero's innocent sidekick was eaten by werewolves. Lopez usually played that part. Innocent sidekick that is. But not this time.

***

When he returned to the office, Harvey got some immediate praise for his fine first appearance at the Pre-Savings Drill Down.

"Yee poor frigging sod," muttered Angus.

"Totally gruesome, dude," said Todd.

"We're screwed," observed Bunny.

But his outstanding performance allowed him to get login IDs in world record time.

"You're going to need them," volunteered Olive Olympios, wiping a tear from the corner of her eye.

CHAPTER TEN

Eventually Kendall Swick's wide Hawaiian tie would come back into fashion. Hopefully before his heirs donated it to the Smithsonian along with his tight-under-the-arms, blue polyester suit. He straightened his tie and slicked down the large flap of black-dyed hair that originated from just above his left ear and stretched over his bald head to his right ear. Perfection was his goal. He had to look just right for the International Video Conference. Kendall Swick took a quick look in the mirror and made a note in his digital planner to buy more hair dye. Attention to detail was the hallmark of the successful manager. Not everyone was capable of attaining that pinnacle.

At the other end of Kendall Swick's office was a bank of flatscreens, four high and three wide, with nameplates showing the locations where Kendall's overseas buyers worked: Bangkok, Adelaide, Osaka, Karachi, Saskatoon, Nuevo Laredo, Reykjavik, Lima, Brussels, Frankfurt, Hamburg, Bologna.

Harvey knew some of these were cities. The rest were either vegetables or luncheon meats.

Todd Hertle spotted Harvey peering into Kendall's office. "Harvey, ol' boy. Just the man I need." Harvey was developing a nasty habit. Not from the muesli he ate at breakfast but from lingering too long in one spot without moving.

"Bunny has let me down again," Todd said. "She knew this morning was 'Live with Kendall' and it was her turn. But I can't find her. So Harvey, I need your help. You'll have to sub-in for her."

Before Harvey could say, "No thank you, Todd. It will likely upset my stomach," he was yanked out of Kendall Swick's line of sight and dragged across the aisle. Todd pushed Harvey towards a large metal door with a sign that said, 'Danger. Keep Out. Radioactive Biohazard. You've been warned.'

The sign caught Harvey's attention. But its message didn't matter to Todd. The door was opened with a brusque yank and Harvey was tossed inside.

Harvey looked around. Floor-to-ceiling metal racks loaded with video equipment. Shelving with tote boxes full of odd-looking clothing and wigs. A hyperactive Todd Hertle completed the ambiance.

Todd frantically pushed buttons on a touchscreen control panel, picked up a clipboard and ran down a list which contained names in one column and dates in another.

"Let me see," he pondered, deep in thought. "Who hasn't presented in a long time?"

An alarm clock rang. It startled Harvey. Being startled was now a common occurrence in Harvey's new work life. But nothing startled Todd Hertle. One person's 'startled' was Todd's 'transcendental meditation'.

"Two minute warning, Harvey," he instructed. "We've gotta go. Gotta go. Gotta *really, really* hustle now."

Harvey looked around. Go where? They were in a very small, cramped room with more electrical cords than a rock concert.

"Ah, this one," Todd said, picking a tote box. "Yes. Haven't used this one for a long time: Jack Daniels."

"No, Todd. I can't hold that down. Especially on top of muesli."

"No, Harvey. In two minutes, you'll be 'Jack Daniels'. He's our purchasing agent in Nuevo Laredo, Mexico. Your buyer's deck consists of cactus seedlings and blue agave tequila. Here's your script."

Harvey was handed a single sheet of paper.

"Hold on, I'll get your costume." Todd produced a striped poncho and a blue velvet sombrero and then the final touch, a fake moustache, was stuck on Harvey's top lip. "Just read the script exactly as it's written, Harvey. Trust me, you'll be fine."

The croaky, high-pitched voice of Kendall Swick came over a set of speakers inside the room. "Todd, are we ready for the video feeds?"

"Yes, Kendall. I have Bangkok and Karachi connecting." Todd punched 'play' on the appropriately-labeled video streaming hardware feeding the flatscreens. "Lima and Brussels next." Not vegetables obviously. "Hamburg is down, Kendall. I'll call IT to reconnect."

"Not again," whined the voice over the intercom.

Harvey read through the mustard-and-relish stained script that Todd had thrust into his hands. "This doesn't make any sense, Todd."

"Great, Harvey. You'll pull it off perfectly. Kendall," he continued, "I have the other channels up. Saskatoon, do you read me?"

Todd pushed 'play'.

"Reykjavik, are you there?"

Another 'play' button was pressed.

All the remaining video feeds were on 'play' except Nuevo Laredo. A beat up old video camera was mounted on a tripod at one end of the room. A green screen was behind it. Todd grabbed Harvey by the shoulders, moved him dead center in front of the camera and said, "OK, Harvey. I mean 'Jack Daniels'. Time to get into character. You're on in—" Todd counted down with his fingers. "Five, four, three, two, one...and...*action!*"

"Boo-anus dee-us, see-nee-or Swick," Harvey read, exactly as the phonetically written script called out. The moustache tickled his lip as he spoke. "Theese is Jack Daniels from sunny May-hee-co."

Todd flashed an okay sign with his fingers, then turned off the video cam. "You were great, Harvey. Just great."

"That's it?"

"That's it for now. We'll let the other recordings run for a while. Kendall usually talks nonstop for at least twenty minutes before coming up for air. If he asks a question, I'll cue you and you'll jump right in. Should be over in a half an hour."

"But with all these monitors playing at once won't he have trouble talking over the noise?"

"What noise?"

"The noise on the screens, Todd."

"But there's no noise on the screens, Harvey."

"There isn't?"

"No. They're supposed to be that way, Harvey."

"They are?"

"They are."

"No one talks?"

"No one talks."

Harvey looked up into the ceiling. *Was there an echo in the room?*

"There's nothing on the screens?"

"Well, yes of course, Harvey. Our overseas buyers. At least stock footage of them...not saying anything."

"They don't say anything?"

"No."

Harvey plucked up the courage to ask that singularly piercing, insightful question; the kind of question he was learning to ask as part of his development as a world-class purchasing agent, "And why not, Todd?"

"Well, two reasons, Harvey. First, Kendall doesn't want them to talk. He wants them to *listen*. Second, we have no overseas buyers."

"We don't?"

"Not any more. Talus shut down the Overseas Division of Miscellaneous Commodities three years ago and fired all the buyers. But we have archive footage of them."

"And Kendall doesn't know the buyers are gone?"

"Nope."

"And why not, Todd?" Effective questioning again.

"Why does he need to know, Harvey? He's just the manager. It makes him happy to have overseas buyers. We're happy to oblige him. A happy Kendall Swick is a happy department, Harv. It's MBA 101, isn't it? Make sure your manager is happy. I thought you knew all that kind of stuff. From MBA school."

"But Todd. What happens if the real Jack Daniels finds out I've been impersonating him?"

"No worries there, Harv. Poor cl' Jack's dead. Stepped on a land mine on a trekking holiday in Iraq. Poor soul. We'll miss him. Our supply of cheap tequila from Mexico has dried up completely now he's gone. But it had to be him, Harvey. According to the schedule, it was his turn to be 'Live with Kendall'."

"But he's dead, Todd."

"Harv, consider what you did as honoring his legacy. And you were brilliant."

Impersonating a dead Mexican buyer did have rewards. Harvey could add some new qualifications to his resume: Spanish language skills, amateur dramatics, effective questioning.

Kendall's whiny, squeaky voice returned to interrupt them. "And what do you think of that proposal, Sinji in Osaka?"

Todd scrambled to find the Osaka 'video feed' and pulled the plug on that server. The 'power on' light went dead. Todd grabbed the mike and shoved a new script in front of Harvey. "Get ready. Jack Daniels again." Todd pointed to the paper. "Read from here."

Harvey looked at the script entitled: 'Responding to Kendall's Proposals.'

"Sorry, Kendall. Technical issues," Todd said into the mike. "But we've got Hamburg back." Todd pressed the appropriate 'play' button on the control panel. "Oh, dear. Osaka's gone down again. Don't worry. Mexico has a comment."

Mike on. Fingers up. "Three...two...one...*action!*"

Harvey was enjoying himself. He read the script, "May-hee-co can support that idea, see-nee-or Swick. If you like, we could pilot it here. If it flies, I'm sure the other regions will come on board with your bree-lee-ant-ee proposal."

"That's what I like to hear," Swick replied. "I hope everyone heard that. Mexico's taking the lead. Setting a good example. Just like Saskatoon last week. That's putting the 'Global' back into Globallica. Todd, e-mail Osaka. We don't want them to fall behind on this new direction because of a technical glitch."

"Right, Kendall."

"I guess that's all I have for this week," Kendall Swick said. "Same time next week. Goodbye."

With that cue, Todd threw a master switch cutting power simultaneously to all the servers. The International Video Conference was over.

"Quite a people person, isn't he, Harv?"

"Well, he inspired me, Todd. When do I start my flying lessons?"

"Flying lessons?"

That damn echo again.

"To pilot whatever he wants to fly, Todd. After all, a happy Kendall is a happy department. Geez, Todd. I thought you knew that stuff. It's MBA 101."

"Oo-kay, Harv. Whatever you say. I'll book you in."

***

"So how long will it take to reach maximum potency, Sunny?" Todd said as he looked at the teabag.

"About five minutes."

"No long term effects?"

"I've been drinking a cup of this tea every week since I was eleven and just look at me now," Sun Ho Gung replied.

"That's what I'm worried about."

The teabag had a string with a little label attached. The label said, *Sweet Dreams on the Yangtze*. Todd sniffed it. The foul odor the teabag emitted smelled like dried toe-jam from a Vietnamese pot-bellied pig.

"The smell gets a bit better after the tea is brewed," Sun Ho Gung said. "But mustn't let it cool down, Todd. That wouldn't be good."

Todd dunked the teabag in hot water and texted Aziz Muquat, the Logic Master... 'Don't be late. Kendall is expecting you.'

Kendall Swick poked his head around the corner, recoiling from the smell in the coffee station. "Have we got a dead rat behind the partition again?"

Todd disposed of the hot, soggy, smelly teabag in the waste basket. *No*, thought Todd. *But we'll soon have a semi-comatose Logic Master in Kendall's staff meeting.*

"Why are you two always late?" the boss asked. "Come on, let's get started."

"We've brewed some tea for Aziz Mukquat. You know how much he likes an exotic cup of tea."

"Well, that's a very nice gesture, Hertle. I'm sure he'll appreciate it."

"Not as much as we will, eh, Ho Gung?"

***

Kendall sat as he usually did at the very end of his office's long rectangular conference table. Sitting on one side were Angus McCalliwag and Sun Ho Gung, and on the other side, the Logic Master Aziz Mukquat sipping his tea, Todd Hertle next to him, and Bunny Warren with Harvey.

"You're probably wondering why Darcy Gillemott isn't here," Kendall announced, bringing the meeting to order.

No, they weren't. Darcy Gillemott had discovered that his/her assistant purchasing agent, Harvey Drinkwater had made a commitment to Johann Thorsveld to deliver savings on the Peruvian Project in *two* weeks. He/she promptly called his/her gynecologist and threatened to post his/her pictures of the doctor in his suspenders and stockings on the internet if the doctor didn't reschedule Darcy's surgery. Like right now, this very minute.

"Darcy Gillemott has a medical condition."

"No kidding," whispered Todd.

"She's left on medical leave, effective today."

The Logic Master's eyes glazed over. It was starting to work. Just like Ho Gung said it would. His head began to droop. The cup slipped from his grasp. Todd rescued it and looked inside. All the tea was gone. He gave a thumbs up to Ho Gung.

The Logic Master's upper torso leaned forward. Todd guided it safely towards the top of the polished table, turning Mukquat's head so his airways were free to breathe. Mukquat's tongue slid out and saliva started to form a drool pool. Aziz Mukquat, the Logic Master, was completely, firmly and absolutely…asleep. Now, no matter how illogical Kendall Swick's decisions would be, Aziz Mukquat couldn't make them worse.

Kendall Swick, unfazed, as any good manager should be in these difficult circumstances, scanned his planner and stuck rigorously to his agenda. This was the key to success. He would not be deflected by minor distractions like the poor personal habits of Aziz Mukquat.

"With Darcy Gillemott's departure, we have an opening for a senior purchasing agent."

"No kidding," Todd whispered to Bunny. "I wonder what brain-dead moron Kendall has found to replace her?"

"Probably someone we don't know."

They were partly right. The brain-dead part.

Kendall Swick puffed up his chest, its primordial shape making him look supremely managerial: a shape that signaled he was about to make one of his typically momentous yet somewhat ordinary pronouncements. "Even though he's only been here a week," he said. "It's not gone unnoticed by management that we have a rising star in our midst."

Todd, Bunny, Angus and Ho Gung looked quizzically at each other.

Kendall continued, "I know he hasn't been with us very long. But experience isn't everything. Potential counts as well. In fact, it counts double. He's definitely proven the old maxim…that the potential inherent in possessing a Harvard MBA outstrips experience. By demonstrating his boldness to commit to a stretch target, he's made a significant impact on his future…and the future of this department."

Kendall resumed his normal chest size. One by one, his subordinates slowly turned their heads away from Kendall Swick. A perplexed Harvey Drinkwater sat motionless with his hands in his lap, admiring how Aziz Mukquat could dribble drool and then, as he snored, suck it back up into his mouth without the drool touching the table's surface.

"Oh shit," Todd said. "Oh shit! What have we done?"

Bunny threw her head into her hands. Angus leaned back, looked up at the ceiling and wheezed. Sun Ho Gung muttered something about brewing another cup of tea and seeing his ancestors.

Laying prostrate across the conference room table—sucking up his drool—was the sole person in the whole world who at that very moment could have prevented Kendall Swick from making such an immensely illogical decision. But all Aziz Mukquat the Logic Master could do was stir in his sleep as Todd Hertle's fainting body thumped onto the floor behind him.

Harvey Drinkwater had just been promoted.

CHAPTER ELEVEN

"Conglat-ulations, Drinkwater-san," Takata Hoshimei said.

Hoshimei was the first person outside the Department of Miscellaneous Commodities to extend warm wishes to Harvey. In fact, he was the first person to do so from anywhere. Harvey's colleagues were still sulking. Workplace envy. Harvey had read something about that in a magazine at the dentist's office.

After Kendall Swick's staff meeting, Sun Ho Gung had gone back to his desk and curled up asleep. Aziz Mukquat lay on the floor beside him. Todd had thrown blankets over both of them, turned the lights out and left. This morning if anyone asked, Todd would say the two had been up all night trying to find logic in Ho Gung's Baby Formula proposal.

"But we still run out of cat litta, Drinkwater-san," Hoshimei said on the phone. "My boss velly mad. He want meeting. Plonto."

Plonto? Harvey cradled the phone on his shoulder. "Bunny, do you know a buyer named Plonto?"

"No. Who's asking?"

"Takata Hoshimei."

"Give the phone to me. I'll find out what he wants."

Harvey felt like he was floating in air. He had his own office with a door on it. He had his own assistant, Bunny Warren.

And he was guaranteed to have someone in his office waiting to meet him first thing every morning. Today, his first day as senior purchasing agent, Harvey sat in silence at his new desk. Across from him was the curious old man chewing a toothpick in his mouth as if it were a saintly obligation. Occasionally, the old man adjusted the baseball cap with the logo that read *Ocean City Seed Mill*. But otherwise, the farmer did and said nothing.

Harvey decided to exercise his newly acquired effective questioning skills. "Who are you and why are you here?"

The silver-haired man wiggled in his chair, took the toothpick out of his mouth and replied, "To report my savings, sonny. Thanks for asking. Mert Hutchin's the name."

"Savings, Mr. Hutchin? You have savings to report?"

"Well," Mert drawled in Farmerese. "Yes and no, sonny."

Harvey wondered if the old man was related to Todd Hertle. Making life complicated must be a genetic disorder.

"You do? Or you don't?"

"That's right."

"What's right?"

"I do some days. And I don't others. See sonny, nobody asks me." The old man looked at the clock, picked up his brown paper lunch bag and shuffled slowly out of Harvey's office.

Oh well, Harvey thought. He'll be back tomorrow.

In the meantime, Bunny Warren had ended a long phone conversation with Takata Hoshimei. "Harvey, the Head of Z-COT wants a meeting with us right away. The cat litter situation is in a state of crisis. Darcy's dropped us in it."

Yuck! Harvey thought. Being dropped in cat litter was not how he wanted to spend the first day on his new job.

"Apparently, Darcy forgot to put in last week's purchase order. Z-COT's got a problem with honey bees as well. This sounds doubly serious. We'd better go there before Kendall finds out. You've already set the record for the fastest promotion. If we don't fix this, you may set the record for the fastest demotion as well."

"Where do we have to go?"

"Takata says his boss's office is on the Fifth Floor."

"I didn't think this building had a Fifth Floor."

"It doesn't. It's in the Globallica Tower."

"The Globallica Tower?" *Wow*, Harvey thought. *The main skyscraper? Could it get any more exciting?*

Oh, yes it could.

Someone outside his office yelled, "Pretzel Makers! Run!"

This time Harvey knew exactly what to do. Darcy Gillemott had created an escape hatch inside her office. It led into a cavity in the wall. Harvey opened it and jumped in. Bunny followed quickly, carrying a bundle of files they would need for their meeting with Z-COT. The hatch closed behind them as the jackboots of Johann Thorsveld's brigade of Presentation Expeditors clomped down the hall.

"I found one!" an enthusiastic Pretzel Maker yelled. "He's a slow old bugger."

"He'll do," Johann replied. "Bring him."

A baseball cap with the logo of the *Ocean City Seed Mill* dropped to the office floor in the Pretzel Makers' wake.

"That was a close call, Harvey," Bunny said as they emerged from hiding. "Follow me. We'll use the building's stairwell to get out without being seen. No doubt Johann was hoping to find you for a progress report."

"But I've only had my new assignment for one day. And I haven't started working on it. In fact I don't even know what the 'Peruvian Project' is."

"Tell me about it. But in Purchasing, that's no excuse."

***

The sunshine streaming through the glass felt good. This was one of those rare days in Ocean City where the sun shone without a cloud in the sky. It helped soothe the pangs of fear churning up the breakfast muesli in Harvey's stomach. Eating something for breakfast that looked pre-digested was definitely an improvement over beef jerky, something that felt like petrified wood as it was swallowed. Like the way Harvey felt about meeting the Head of Z-COT.

The old warehouse where Purchasing toiled in perpetual darkness disappeared behind them. They took the escalator at the end of the glass tunnel to the upper mezzanine of the Globallica Tower with its view overlooking the palm forest. Harvey spotted George Thaddeus the security guard on the ground floor below, sitting dutifully at his desk. His little cat Dennis sat beside him on the sleeping bag. They both looked very sad, despite the sunshine.

Harvey and Bunny walked through a bright world of energetic, nattily-dressed young executives, male and female, buzzing around them like bumblebees in flight.

"Over here, Harvey." Bunny said, directing him to a set of elevators. An elevator opened but on the directory inside there was no mention of a department called Z-COT.

"Are you sure this is the correct way to Z-COT?" Harvey asked.

"Not sure."

A pretty young lady in a white blouse and plain black skirt broke the plane of the elevator's closing door. She had a nametag that said 'Daphne'. Her eyes were like roasted almonds. They matched her soft brown hair. Bunny Warren smiled and the two women hugged.

"This is Daphne DuBois, Harvey. The person I know in Finance. We're looking for Z-COT, Daphne. Do you know where it is?"

"Yes. Fifth Floor," Daphne said in a lilting French accent, words that sent Harvey into a state of blissful adoration. If she said anything else he was sure he'd melt into a puddle at her feet. Daphne blushed and smiled at the strange young man with the silly grin.

"I'll take you," she said.

Harvey's knees felt wobbly.

The ride was short. The elevator opened into a huge room with row upon row of identical desks where row upon row of almost identically dressed young men and women clacked away at identical computers. This was Globallica Finance. Black was the haute couture color of the day. Men wore dark black suits, immaculately polished black shoes, plain white shirts with ties that had very little color in them which essentially meant they were black from a distance. The female financial analysts wore black knee-length skirts, immaculately polished black pumps and white blouses.

Harvey had seen this before. In the movies. "Do they process entry visas for space aliens here?"

Bunny looked at Harvey with her 'what-the-hell-are-you-talking-about, Harvey?' expression.

"I guess not," Harvey said. "No one is wearing sunglasses."

"Huh?"

At the far side of the open office was a corridor that sat between two black marble walls. "Follow me," Daphne said. There was a glass door at the end of the corridor. Above it, a brass plaque declared, 'The Financially Challenged Supplier Room'. But again, no mention of Z-COT.

Daphne used her pass to let them in. On the other side was a room that was the duplicate of the office outside, an open area with long rows of identically attired financial analysts, everyone busy talking on phones.

"What do they do in here?" Bunny asked.

"You know those savings checks from suppliers?" Daphne replied. "The ones Purchasing holds with such pride in the photos in your office?"

"Yes, of course."

"When the checks bounce, they come here for settlement and policing."

"Policing?"

"Finance alerts Purchasing's Supplier Relations people. That's Antonio's department."

"Antonio?" Harvey asked.

"Purchasing's Executive Director of Supplier Relations," Bunny responded. "I didn't know this place existed, Daphne. How often does one of our checks bounce?"

"Almost every time."

"Oh dear," Bunny replied. "That's not good."

"Are they made of rubber?" Harvey queried. Effective questioning, a hard skill to turn off.

Daphne smiled. "I have to go now," she said, her singsong French accent sending butterflies down Harvey's stomach. Daphne pointed to a room behind a set of glass windows in the corner of the office. "That group over there. That's Z-COT."

"Thanks," Bunny said. The two women air-kissed their goodbyes.

Harvey trundled like a lost android after Daphne.

"No, Harvey." Bunny grabbed him. "This way."

Z-COT was a small room containing two long conference tables. On top of them were crammed about as many computer monitors as the tables were structurally designed to hold. On the monitors flashed an endless list of numbers. On the wall, three plain, white-faced clocks, labeled 'Tokyo', 'London' and 'New York' told the time. A large flat screen TV was perched in the corner overlooking the twenty or so people working the computer terminals. The TV was tuned to the Ocean City Financial Cable Network.

It was a puzzling room.

There was no sign of cats or cat litter boxes anywhere.

A Japanese man broke off his phone conversation as he spotted Harvey and Bunny entering the paper strewn enclave. "Ah, Drinkwater-san!"

"Mr. Hoshimei?"

"Drinkwater-san is here!"

The Z-COT analysts looked up. They clapped. Everyone gave him a thumbs up. Harvey smiled. But he didn't move. He didn't know he was supposed to move. Soon everyone in the room realized he didn't know he was supposed to move and complete panic set in.

"For God's sake, Hoshimei! Get the Purchase Order system up before New York closes and Tokyo opens," several of them screamed in macabre harmony.

Takata Hoshimei grabbed Harvey by the shoulders and plunked him down in front of a terminal labeled, 'Restricted Access – Purchasing Only'. Harvey stared blankly at the blinking login window. Takata grabbed the employee ID card dangling on the lanyard around Harvey's neck and swiped it through a reader on the side of the terminal.

"Drinkwater-san, please enter password."

Harvey typed 'Lopez'.

The screen was suddenly filled with open purchase requisitions. Icons flashed beside each one, 'Waiting for Approval'. Takata Hoshimei leaned over Harvey, found 'Select All' with the cursor and pushed the 'Approve' icon. The list on the 'Pending' screen disappeared.

Well, that was easy, Harvey thought. Why did everyone back in the office make so much fuss? He could do this with his eyes closed.

Takata Hoshimei fell into his swivel chair, sweating profusely, his head thrown backwards, his body limp from the sudden explosive release of pent up tension.

A deep bass voice boomed from behind them, "That was too close for comfort, Hoshimei. We almost lost it. Bring this Drinkwater guy into my office! We can't have this happen again."

Harvey and Bunny were hoisted to their feet by two burly analysts and frog-marched into the office of Z-COT's manager, Lincoln Ferndale, a massive African-American man as wide as his office door and almost as tall. A square-jawed face sat on a thick neck. He resembled a medieval stone gargoyle. His shoulders looked like he was wearing football shoulder pads but he wasn't. The pictures on his office wall—ones from his playing days as a defensive lineman at Ohio State—must have been taken with a wide angle lens.

"Sit, Drinkwater. I said...sit!...now!"

Harvey mewed like a kitten, complied, and daren't look up.

"You got a problem with me, Drinkwater?"

"N-no."

"Then look me in the eyes when I'm talking to you." Lincoln Ferndale sat down. His desk chair groaned. His nostrils flared in and out like a racehorse that had just completed the Kentucky Derby seven lengths ahead of the pack. The veins in his head throbbed. "Do you realize how close we were to a meltdown out there?"

Harvey looked out of the glass window that separated Ferndale's office from the room with the monitors. The cluster of Z-COT desks didn't look anything like the control room at the nuclear reactor where his mom had worked. Either before or after the meltdown.

"But where's the cats?" was all that Harvey could think of saying.

Lincoln's mouth widened into a toothy grin. He let out a chuckle that evolved into a full-throated belly laugh.

Harvey couldn't help laughing. Neither could Bunny. But Harvey didn't know what he was laughing about.

"We don't keep them *here*...you fool."

***

"Mr. Ferndale, sir. If this is Z-COT, do you mind me asking, what is *it*?"

"It's not an *it*."

"It's not?"

"It's Zoological Commodity Trading, fool."

That really explained everything.

"I don't get it."

"You're not supposed to."

"I'm not?"

"You mean *we're* not supposed to, Harvey," Bunny chimed in. "I agree. I don't get it either."

"Okay. Look kiddies," Ferndale grumped. "If it wasn't for the persistent whining of Purchasing's Vice President Talus, we wouldn't need you. But he insists if anything needs to be bought, then Purchasing buys it. So here you both are. To annoy me with stupid questions."

"Buy what?" Harvey asked.

Lincoln Ferndale's nostrils flared again. They looked wide enough for flames to come out. It was not a good sign. "You've got a buying deck don't you, Drinkwater? And those files say Z-COT, don't they?"

Harvey had to admit they did.

"So what is *it*?" Ferndale asked in a manner which said, 'I already know the answer, fool'.

"What is *what*?" Harvey asked, in a manner which said, 'I'm still clueless, please hit me'.

"Your deck. What is… your *deck*? It's printed on your folders. Just read the labels."

Harvey read out loud:

Buying Deck – Z-COT
Cats
Cat Litter
Honey
Honey Bees
Guinea Pigs
Rhinoceros Manure
Dirt

"Dirt? Let me see that," Ferndale said.

Harvey handed over the 'Dirt' folder.

"Drinkwater, this folder's empty."

Harvey shrugged.

"We don't do no dirt here, Drinkwater. That one's not Z-COT."

"Mr. Ferndale?" Bunny's sultry, soothing voice could melt butter at a hundred yards. "Would you please be so kind as to explain why we buy what we buy for you? It would be so helpful to know."

"We don't want to cause any more trouble," she purred. "Do we, Harvey?"

Lincoln Ferndale's enormous smile and glazed eyes were a direct product of the way the beautiful Bunny Warren phrased her questions.

"Mr. Ferndale?"

He snapped out of his trance. "Well, kiddies, what you see out there—the analysts manning those desks—represents the way Globallica is growing its profits. Seventy-five percent of this quarter's profits came from here—from Z-COT, those specialists out there trading zoological commodities. But it's commodity trading with a *big* difference."

Harvey's head had slipped to his chest. Bunny poked him awake.

"What kind of difference, Mr. Ferndale, sir?" she cooed.

With that pout, Lincoln Ferndale would open up his darkest secrets to her. "We don't just trade the market, Miss Warren. We *make* it. We are the market. Take cat litter. Dogs don't use it."

Stating the obvious didn't help. The juveniles were still confused. Lincoln picked up on it quickly. "How? We find cities with a low cat population. And then we flood the market with cats. We—I mean, you Purchasing folks—buy the cats and cat litter for us. Everything. The whole enchilada. Toto mundo. My commodity traders cover your purchases with positions in the futures and options markets, and Globallica makes money both ways when we hike the price of cat litter out of sight. Boy, it's fun to be a monopoly."

Harvey, half asleep at this point, asked, "Why do you feed cats enchiladas?"

Lincoln Ferndale winced. The intricacies of the commodity market were way beyond this fool's comprehension. What Ferndale didn't know was that cats in general were way beyond Harvey's comprehension.

Ferndale continued his explanation, oblivious of the conversational risks he was taking. "This week we were short the real thing. Because 'someone in Purchasing who shall remain nameless' didn't buy any cat litter. Our butts—um, I mean, trading positions—were exposed. We almost had a market meltdown."

Harvey didn't have a clue what this goliath was talking about. He asked, "How does cat litter melt down?"

Harvey wasn't a cat person. He struck off 'get a cat' from his mental list. He didn't want to mortgage his condo to pay for cat litter. The sports pages worked great for Lopez. And they were cheap.

"And what about honey bees?" Bunny asked.

"Buy 'em all," Ferndale replied. "Then we freeze dry 'em. Honey rockets in price. We make a killing We unfreeze the bees. Sell 'em at a higher price. We make another killing. Start over. Do it again."

Honey? It always slid off his knife into his lap. Harvey would stick to peanut butter. Which frequently did. Stick to him, that is.

"And what about Guinea pigs?" Bunny asked. "There can't be much of a market for guinea pigs, can there?"

"You can make a market for anything, Miss Warren. Ever been to an Ocean City Gooney Birds AAA baseball game?" Bunny had to admit she hadn't. Ferndale flashed a pair of tickets from his drawer. "Then I guess you haven't dined on a 'Cochon Dandy', have you?"

"No, Mr. Ferndale. And I'm not sure I want to. Thank you very much."

"It's French, Miss Warren."

"That's supposed to make me feel better?"

"*Cochon d'Inde*. It's French for 'guinea pig'."

Harvey Drinkwater was intrigued. He made a mental note to add 'being intrigued' to his list of accomplishments. "What do guinea pigs have to do with baseball, Mr. Ferndale?"

One more question like that and Lincoln Ferndale would have to start therapy sessions for his superiority complex. "You must have eaten beef jerky sometime in your life, Mr. Drinkwater?"

Oh, boy. Lincoln Ferndale threw a fastball right over the plate. And Harvey obliged by belting it out of the park. Unfortunately, Harvey's treatise on the gastronomic vagaries of beef jerky was not fully appreciated.

"That's more information than I needed to know about beef jerky, Mr. Drinkwater. But thank you, anyway. A 'Cochon Dandy' is jerky made from guinea pig meat. It's a delicacy in South America, especially in Peru."

Ferndale pulled out a Gooney Birds' baseball program and showed them an advertisement for 'Pig on a Stick', explaining, "We import it, process it into jerky and sell it to catering companies. Cochon Dandies are the 'in' thing to eat in those expensive corporate boxes at baseball games. Same with basketball, football, hockey games, even the opera. Wherever high rollers want to spend big money on snacks. They don't want to buy every Joe Sixpack's ordinary beef jerky, do they? So we've cornered the market on haute cuisine guinea pig meat. With Purchasing's help, of course."

Lincoln Ferndale mentioned Peru. But when Harvey asked him, Ferndale had no clue what the 'Peruvian Project' was. So Harvey stuck to a subject he was equally clueless about, "What about rhinoceros manure?"

"An emerging market. Lots of untapped profit in that trade. We leverage it on the Zambezi Exchange. Dung options are the next big opportunity. We've invested in other varieties of dung too—elephant, giraffe, zebra. Hyena—now there's a good trade with profit potential. Lots of bone meal inside those puppies. We'll bide our time. Our day will come. There's no better monopoly than a Globallica monopoly, that's what I say."

"What do we do with rhinoceros manure?" Harvey asked.

"We don't do anything."

"We don't?"

"*We* don't. But celebrities *do*."

Harvey couldn't imagine.

"Roses, kiddies. The best thing for roses…rhino poo. Smells like shit. Sells like hotcakes. And high rollers don't care what they pay for it. These kind of people don't fertilize with just any old manure, Drinkwater. Gotta be 'designer' manure. You know, something the neighbors can't afford."

Lincoln took a giant stride and bellowed out of his office door, "Hey, Hoshimei! What's the latest quote on rhino poo?"

Takata Hoshimei switched his screen to the Zambezi Exchange and tapped his keyboard. "Closed up ten percent, boss. At two thousand dollars a pound."

"Two thousand dollars a pound!" exclaimed Bunny.

"The 'caviar' of poo, my dear Miss Warren, simply the 'caviar' of poo. So, this is your quick lesson in zoological commodity trading, kiddies. The growth revenue of the future. Run along like good little boys and girls, and make sure we don't run out of cat litter again. Okay?"

CHAPTER TWELVE

The cafeteria servicing Globallica Finance had a marvelous terrace that jutted out fifty feet from the Fifth Floor, overlooking the harbor front, high above the old piers and wharves. Sailboats and fishing boats dotted the calm ocean. Bunny Warren's friend, Daphne DuBois had obtained guest passes so she could take them there for lunch. In Purchasing, the only catered food came from a sandwich truck that backed into the ground floor loading bay to sell day-old sardine sandwiches and warm milk. Harvey usually brought his own. But at least the milk was cold.

Fate interrupted their fine dining.

Bunny's cell phone rang. It was Todd. Were they missing some files? He found some in Aziz Mukquat's briefcase when Todd was looking for Aziz's Blue Cross card. Were they missing one named the 'Peruvian Project' perhaps?

"The Peruvian Project! We've been looking all over for that, Todd. I could just kiss—no, check that, I couldn't. Thank you, Todd. Keep it safe. We'll be right back."

"He found the file?"

"He found the file, Harvey."

"Woo hoo!"

With that high-pitched exclamation, an immaculately dressed man-in-black dropped his tray. The other financial analysts on the terrace looked down their noses in scorn.

"Uh, oh, Bunny. They're not going to deport me to Regula-4, are they?"

"Huh? Why?"

Harvey was suspicious. The cell phones the financial analysts used were very silver. Extremely silver. Too silver. One touch of a button, Harvey surmised, and he would be a protein snack on the Intergalactic Express bound for the Horse's Head Nebula.

"En Finance…people aren't used to a lot of excitement," Daphne said in her sweet, musical French accent. "We haven't much to get excited about, monsieur. Someone—how you say, crashed?—an Excel spreadsheet once. The most grande excitement possib-lay here."

Daphne smiled at Harvey.

Harvey smiled back.

She blushed. "I've got to go now. Au revoir, Bunny. Au revoir, Monsieur Drinkwater. Mon play-shure to meet you. Shall I see you again?"

A massive gulp paralyzed the mouthful of head cheese sandwich searching for a way down Harvey's throat. He gagged and turned purple.

"I think that's a 'Oui', Daphne," Bunny interjected.

Daphne smiled again and left.

Harvey swallowed and gasped. He looked very pale and could barely squeak.

"Are you all right, Harvey?"

"Mm," he mewed. His face strained in every direction until it returned to its normal state of blissful ignorance. A silly grin emerged. A daydream floated into his brain cavity. Daphne DuBois and Harvey Drinkwater on a bench beside a pond in Monet's Garden near Paris.

But Fate—such a nuisance—evaporated his misty-eyed musing.

Harvey looked over the terrace's railing towards the Purchasing building below. Bunny caught the change in Harvey's expression, an appearance of stunned horror accompanied by a semi-digested polyp of head cheese that rolled slowly out of his gaping mouth. "Bunny, what are they doing to Angus!"

Harvey dropped the rest of his sandwich over the railing. A flock of seagulls chased it as it plummeted five floors.

"S-S-Soldiers…soldiers are invading Purchasing!" Harvey shouted in shock. "And they're arresting Angus!"

Below them, on the roof of the Purchasing building, the rotors of a Black Hawk helicopter whipped dust off the top of the former warehouse. The chopper bristled with machine guns and anti-tank rocket pods. Armed men in green fatigues escorted Angus McCalliwag to an opened hatchway on the side of the helicopter. Harvey and Bunny could tell it was Angus. There was no-one else who wore a kilt to work.

"Oh, *that*?" Bunny said. "Don't worry. Angus finishes work early today. He's attending a ballistic missile test."

Harvey looked at Bunny, then looked at the crowd of black-suited financial analysts who wondered what all the fuss was about. Some of them took selfies as the Black Hawk rose from the warehouse roof and flew by. Harvey wandered over to a large table of analysts, fell to his knees and pled for mercy, "I give up. I surrender. Send me to Regula-4 if you must. But please, don't turn me into a protein snack!"

Bunny grabbed Harvey by the scruff of his neck and hauled him up. "He's having a stressful day," she smiled, dragging his nearly lifeless body between the parting onlookers.

As she guided Harvey off the terrace and to the elevator, she heard someone say, "I knew those people from Purchasing were insane. This just proves it."

The elevator door closed.

"Angus should have told you, Harvey. He's such a mischievous old coot."

"Told me what?"

"His job, Harvey. What he buys for Purchasing. You remember, don't you? Ammunition and rocket fuel?"

Harvey relaxed. He hadn't been beamed to Regula-4. The 'Peruvian Project' file had been found, although Todd had the file, which was a problem. He had a dream about a beautiful girl sitting beside a pond in Paris. And Angus bought rocket fuel.

Life was returning to normal. Momentarily.

"It's okay, Bunny. I'm better now."

***

"You guys are massively, totally, utterly, beyond any shadow of a doubt…screwed."

"Thanks for your infinite wisdom, Todd."

"You're welcome, Bunny. Any time."

The conference room table was covered from one end to another with pages from the 'Peruvian Project' file, laid neatly from left to right. To Bunny Warren and Todd Hertle, experienced assistant purchasing agents, the collection of graphs, charts, internet search results, aerial photographs of the Peruvian Andes and a thick research report on the 'Nervous System of the South American Guinea Pig', didn't make much business sense. To Harvey Drinkwater, it was total, incomprehensible gibberish. Which didn't make it much different from any other file he'd read since he'd started work at Globallica. So he was fine with it and wondered what the fuss was all about.

The margins of Darcy Gillemott's draft presentation to the Savings Board were heavily annotated with red ink. Apparently she'd been working on the 'Peruvian Project' forever, at least since 'she' had been a 'he'.

"Darcy was struggling, wasn't she?" Bunny surmised. "Trying to find savings."

"No wonder she left as soon as she found out what Harvey had done," Todd said.

"What did I do?"

"It's not what you've done, it's what you committed to do, Harvey ol' boy."

Bunny looked at Todd, who looked right back. They both looked at Harvey. "Do you want to tell him, or should I?" Bunny asked.

"You're his assistant, Bunny. You tell him," was Todd's grateful reply.

"You can add 'bravery' to 'wisdom' on your resume, Todd."

"Thanks."

Bunny put down Darcy's marked-up draft presentation and took Harvey's hand. She lead him to the end of the table and sat him down. "Let's start at the beginning, shall we, Harvey?"

"That's where I like to start a story, Bunny."

"Very wise, Harvey."

Harvey loved bedtime stories. Especially when someone else told them. Outside, the sun had set. It had taken three hours to pour over the details of the massive file on the 'Peruvian Project'. Harvey had kept Todd and Bunny company, and fetched coffee. It was the least he could do. Considering he hadn't a clue what it all meant.

"Harvey." Bunny paused. "How can I approach this?"

"Keep it simple?"

Bunny sighed. "This presentation proposes that Globallica's supplier of guinea pig meat should overthrow the Government of Peru using a mercenary peasant army from Ecuador."

"Oh."

Silence.

"Why, Bunny?"

"In order to take over the guinea pig farms that our supplier doesn't already own."

"Oh."

"It gets better."

"It does?"

"Then our supplier's head of biotechnology injects every guinea pig with an experimental neurotoxin derived from seaweed which he claims will mutate the guinea pigs into the size of sheep."

"Oh."

Silence.

"Why Bunny?"

"In order, Harvey, to cut the cost of production of guinea pig meat in half. So the supplier can lower their prices."

"That's good, isn't it? Savings?"

Bunny's head fell into her hands. "Oh, Harvey, Harvey, Harvey…"

"We are so screwed," Todd moaned.

"Can it be done in two weeks?" Harvey ventured.

Bunny didn't know what was worse: Aziz Mukquat losing two days of his life in a tea-induced coma or trying to find logic in Darcy Gillemott's 'Peruvian Project'.

She muttered out loud, "Just exactly what was Mukquat going to tell Kendall Swick about Darcy's brainchild before your elixir took hold, oh brave, wise Todd?"

"If Medical can't wake Mukquat, Bunny…we may never know."

"Thanks, Todd. You're a life saver."

"All in a day's work, Bunny. All in a day's work." Todd shut down his laptop. "Well, fellow slaves. I'm going to call it a night. I'll tuck Aziz and Ho Gung into bed, and see you in the morning."

Todd's residual energy powered his legs in a blur towards the door. He was gone, leaving Bunny Warren and Harvey Drinkwater to bundle all the papers back into the enormous file box on the 'Peruvian Project' and turn the lights out.

CHAPTER THIRTEEN

Aziz Mukquat raised his head, lifting it an inch from the floor. It fell back into the drool-soaked carpet. He tried opening his eyes. That was equally as difficult. Todd Hertle looked down at the Logic Master with a pity he never thought he could feel for someone so well connected with the Savings Board. Aziz drew his knees up under his chest, raising his bum in the air. He was attempting another maneuver to emulate Homo Erectus. He failed. But he did accomplish a massive release of trapped gas. Frozen by sleep in his bum-up position, a contented grin emerged on Aziz's face. He resumed his fetal nap.

Todd wisely decided to move upwind, returning to the safety of his cube. An hour before, Sun Ho Gung's recovery had been more successful. He'd slowly crawled back to his cube. He was now sitting upright at his desk, his glazed expression staring into space. At least he looked like he was working and could control his bowels.

Harvey sat in Angus McCalliwag's office, waiting. Bunny said Angus would be in today. The Army had not kidnapped him. Harvey was relieved and sympathetic. He knew how Angus felt. Harvey had escaped a potentially similar fate in Finance and was happy not to be bound for Regula-4 as a ready-to-eat meal.

A comforting hand landed on Harvey's shoulder.

"And how's me wee laddie today then?" Angus plopped a pile of files on his desk. "Wha's tha foul smell?"

Harvey pointed to Aziz Mukquat snoring peacefully in the cube directly across from Angus McCalliwag's office.

"Let tha' be a lesson ta yee, laddie. Dunna have none o' tha piss that Ho Gung drinks. He gets it from an opium den's toilet. Just luke at wha' tha's doon to our Mukquatie friend o'er there."

Harvey watched Aziz twitching in his sleep.

Angus McCalliwag pulled two shot glasses and a silver hip flask out of his desk drawer and filled the glasses to the brim. "Na here's wha' we need. Get this doon yer cakehole." With a quick tilt of the head, a glass of amber liquid vanished down Angus' throat. "Ach, aye, laddie. Na there's a wee dram tha packs a punch!"

Harvey liked punch. But it usually smelt of fruit. This golden liquor had the aroma of Highland heather and honey—mixed with high octane, malted racing fuel.

Harvey put the drink to his lips.

"Go on, laddie. Sup up."

Harvey found the courage to swallow it. At first the sensation was warm, a soothing glow that slipped gently down his throat. But then his tongue began the Dance of the Seven Fire Maidens. The explosion that followed sent hot exhaust gases escaping through his nostrils.

Angus smiled and refilled Harvey's glass. "Bunny tells me, yee had a wee fit when me heli-bird picked me up tha' other day."

"That was *your* helicopter?"

"Ach aye, laddie." Angus McCalliwag pointed to a photograph on his office wall, his tall Scottish figure framed proudly in uniform. "I've been meaning ta tell yee. But I haven't had a wee minute. I've been busier than a one-armed wallpaper-hanger."

"You look like a general in that photograph."

"Aye, laddie. Maybe it's because…I am one."

"You're a general?"

Angus reached into his desk drawer and produced the most impressive business card that Harvey had ever seen. Gold embossed lettering. The colorful crest of the Army Reserve, Procurement Command, Western Region. 'Brigadier General A. McCalliwag, Director of Procurement and Logistics.'

"But I thought you worked for Globallica?"

"Aye, laddie. I do."

"And the Army too?"

"Aye, laddie. Here, you'll need another one o' these." Harvey's glass overflowed again. "See, laddie. Many years ago, I asked wha' these slimy gits who say they run this place had in store fer yee wee Glaswegian...me. Did they think some o' the millions o' poonds o' dosh I was saving them might someday find its way into my wee pockets? Promotion, laddie. Get my drift?"

Angus knocked back another shot glass of Scottish fire water.

"Buh tha slimy bastards said ta me...nay. Nay, Angus they said. Yee dunna have the right stuff, laddie. Yer nat 'management potential', they said."

"But you're a general? Isn't that like being a manager?"

"Ach aye, laddie. Even *yee* can see tha'. Tha's when I thought, Angus, mee lad, yee need to prove these slimy bastards wrong. So I did, laddie. If they weren't gonna promote me, maybe the U.S. Army would. And they did, laddie. They did!"

Harvey looked again at Angus's US Army business card. "And the helicopter?"

"Aye, laddie. I'm a brigadier general. I can order it whenever I want."

"And you buy the ammunition for it?"

"Nay, laddie."

Harvey looked puzzled.

"Nay, laddie. I buy ammunition for the whole Army."

Harvey's eyes widened.

"Aye, laddie. Every wee bullet I buy. Those slimy buggers here in Globallica decided they wanted a piece o' tha action. So they bought a few tarts fer the generals in Washington..."

Harvey couldn't imagine bribing someone with pastries.

"And the Pentagon brass agreed to set up the Army's buying office...right here. Using Globallica's systems, ta boot. Those lazy gits at the top of the Tower get a percentage o' every purchase I make. Just fer allowin' this wee Scottie General the privilege o' havin' an office here."

"And rocket fuel?"

"Aye, laddie. It all expanded from there. If there's a shilling to be made without a dram o' work, then Globallica's in the mix like a whore in port."

Down the hall, a muffled sound could be heard. Harvey peered out of Angus' office. Kendall Swick was in Johann Thorsveld's grasp, the Pretzel Maker's hand silencing Kendall's mouth.

Harvey bolted for his office with its trap door and hiding hole. He rushed out of Angus's office just in time to make contact with Aziz Mukquat doing a caterpillar impersonation across the aisle. Harvey tripped over the semi-paralyzed speed bump and landed face first on the carpet.

Johann Thorsveld helped Harvey to his feet, flanked by two of his burly Presentation Expeditors. "Mr. Drinkwater. It's indeed a pleasure to see you again. May I introduce you to Her Satanic Excellency, Katrina Borchevski, aka DragonForce."

Katrina G. Borchevski, Executive Director of Purchasing Process Performance, cast an impression over the office that exuded the charisma of a cobra about to strike. Her venomous karma towered over the physical presence of her dark-garbed goon squad, despite her petite five-foot-four stature. Athletically built, the stiff-collared masculine female looked like she could bend metal. Short black hair with a bright lavender streak, meticulously coiffed in place; her initials, 'KGB' elegantly embroidered on her white shirt cuffs. The Golden Dollar Sign armband on her right sleeve had extra gold braids on the top and bottom of its border, signifying her exalted executive director rank. Her armband announced, "I'm in charge, don't fuck with me." Which was also the motto on the business card she handed to Harvey.

Harvey decided wisely not to. Fuck with her, that is.

Her obedient lackey, Johann Thorsveld introduced his squirming prey, "This is Harvey Drinkwater, your Excellency. He's been hiding savings. On the 'Peruvian Project'. We caught him lying. He claims that savings are available in two weeks. We think it's sooner."

DragonForce approached the pathetic twisted figure that was her captive. "Mr. Drinkwater, we know what you've been doing. And we're not amused. Bring your presentation to the Savings Board. Immediately. If not sooner."

"But I'm not ready."

"Mr. Drinkwater…you will be."

The Presentation Expeditors escorted Harvey to his office where the bulging file box containing the 'Peruvian Project' held a prominent place on the top of his desk.

"Aha!" Thorsveld exclaimed as he plucked Darcy's marked up draft off the top of the folders in the box. "The presentation! We have it. And we have you, Mr. Drinkwater. Perfect. Now—on to the Savings Board!"

Bunny Warren poked her head around the stairwell's entrance to see if it was safe. Someone had warned her Pretzel Makers were sweeping the Department of Miscellaneous Commodities.

The limp body of Aziz Mukquat rose up, wobbling at the knees; the poor Logic Master waking from sweet dreams into a nightmare. Her Royal Darkness grinned. Johann's Expeditors grabbed him as he shook off the cobwebs of his fetal sleep. "Mukquat!" she barked. "Where have you been?"

Aziz Mukquat's brain-mouth co-ordination was lagging behind his hand-eye coordination which was currently as effective as a drunken French mime. "Marfle gab. Dee poost dorfle nag," he slurred.

"No time for a logic lesson, Mukquat. We have Savings Board this afternoon. Help Drinkwater get his presentation ready. Johann, bring both of them."

The Pretzel Makers frog-marched Harvey and Aziz out of the Department of Miscellaneous Commodities. Johann Thorsveld cradled the 'Peruvian Project' presentation folder like it was a sacrificial offering to the gods. Which it wasn't. Because Harvey Drinkwater was.

"Todd? Psst. I know you're in there," said Bunny, looking for help.

The photocopier's service door rumbled and banged. Todd Hertle's carbon-stained hand emerged as the door opened. With a careful twist of the wrist, the rest of Todd Hertle squeezed out of the compartment. The ghost of Harry Houdini was looking down on him, very proud.

"We have to help Harvey."

"No we don't, Bunny. No one can help him now."

"You're not thinking straight, Todd Hertle. Harvey will tell them *anything* they want to hear."

"Oh, I see what you mean. You mean we have to 'help' him not to 'hurt' us."

"Insightfulness, Todd. Add that to bravery and wisdom. What we need is a way to get to Harvey before he makes his presentation. And without Johann's stormtroopers finding us."

"You mean we need a miracle, Bunny."

"Yes, Todd. We need a miracle."

CHAPTER FOURTEEN

Darcy Gillemott awoke from her anesthetic, was handed a cell phone with an urgent message, and went into cardiac arrest.

The nurse picked the phone off the floor. "Could you hold, please?"

Ten minutes later, Darcy's vital signs had stabilized, the opiods had relaxed her, and she was in a fit state to resume the conversation.

"Todd, what can I do from a hospital bed?" she asked. "That presentation is a total fantasy. Okay, a horror novel. Whatever."

"You weren't seriously going to present that, were you?"

"Well, not all of it."

"What do you mean?"

"It's a teaser-deflective."

"A *what*?"

"Tease them with a savings proposal and deflect them into spin-off projects without getting them to any bottom-line."

"Oh? And how exactly does that happen, Darcy?"

"The assumptions, Todd Hertle. The trick is…building the assumptions."

"Darcy, give me the nurse back."

Darcy handed the cell phone over. The nurse listened to Todd and then returned it.

"What did you do, Todd?"

"I told her to cut back on your morphine. You're hallucinating."

"Todd Hertle. Do you want my help or not?"

"Okay."

"Then stop screwing around and listen up. You're worse than Kendall Swick. Do you know what Bjorn and Talus *really* want?"

"Tease me, Darcy. In a deflective kind of way."

"Exactly, Todd. The Savings Board wants to be teased. Every line of every savings presentation is analyzed in their demented minds as soon as you present it. They're always looking for ways to make more savings. Then they bark orders to DragonForce, who barks to Johann, who engages Pretzel Makers to search for more innocents to punish. Their theory is this—the more projects on the go at once, the more likely one of them might actually produce results. It's called a feeding frenzy. And we, Todd—*we*—are the Savings Board's all-you-can-eat buffet."

"But weren't you struggling with the savings in the 'Peruvian Project'? There seems to be a lot of red ink."

"Look, Hertle. A good teaser-deflective is like a work of art. It takes time to get the brush strokes right. That's why Aziz Mukquat was helping me."

Aziz? Oops. Dare he tell Darcy what they did to Mukquat?

No.

Discretion was the better part of valor. Todd would add valor to his resume. "He was *helping* you?"

"To find a logical way out of what you don't want to do. And then find something you *can* do—or preferably not do—by deflecting your ideas to some other dumb-ass department so they can take over the spin-offs you don't want to report back on. Get it? Aziz Mukquat's a good egg once you get to know him. If you can get him on your side, he can be a good ally at the Savings Board."

Oops.

"So you build assumptions that get the Board excited about possible spin-offs? But what if they insist on seeing the bottom-line?"

"You don't let them, Todd. That would be a big—even humongously *big*—mistake. Never get to the bottom line. Deflect it!"

"How?"

"Oh, Todd. You have so much to learn. Engage a Logic Master. Get him to validate the logic in your spin-offs but also declare your main assumption illogical. That's the one just before you reveal your 'bottom line'. That way, the presentation is stopped dead in its tracks. Regardless, you've worked the Savings Board into a lather over the potential spin-offs, so in the end they don't care. If you've done a good enough job of logically walking them to a point where the main assumption is declared illogical, by that time they've totally forgotten what the main topic was—and what its proposed 'bottom line' was—in the first place."

"So it all ends without having to sign up for impossible savings? But you wet the Saving Board's appetites with potential spin-offs that you make sure you're not responsible for?"

"Todd, someday you'll make a good senior purchasing agent. Just do me a favor."

"What?"

"Ditch the enthusiasm over Savings Reports. It's a way to win friends."

"Okay, Darcy, I'll try. But there's something we need from you urgently. Your system password."

"Why?"

"Johann took all the 'Peruvian Project' files with him, including your draft presentation. If we can access your original files, we can try to write a new presentation for Harvey. Maybe we can find a way to create that 'teaser-deflective' proposal you're suggesting. Add some new assumptions perhaps? We have to deflect everything away from that impossible promise Harvey made...a fifty percent reduction in the price of guinea pigs."

Darcy relayed her password. "One last thing, Todd. If it was that easy, why do you think I couldn't finish it? When did you say you needed it?"

"This afternoon."

"This afternoon!"

The line went dead.

"Darcy? Are you there?"

A nurse came on the phone. They would do their best once they got Darcy to Intensive Care but they couldn't promise a miracle.

"Yeah, okay," Todd replied. "I'll shop elsewhere."

***

The Savings Board was not held in Purchasing's ex-warehouse. That office's tired interior and crumbling exterior did not have the right ambience for the executives that constituted the Savings Board. They preferred surroundings a little more in keeping with the image they wished to portray as leaders of Globallica's 'secret weapon'. The Savings Board was held in the Globallica Tower in an auditorium the Purchasing 'slaves' nicknamed 'The Throne Room of the Gods'.

An Italian marble quarry had been depleted to supply the floor, columns and solid stone conference tables. Busts of Purchasing Vice Presidents, past and present, lined semi-circular alcoves carved into the solid marble walls all around the grand theater. The two-story, cathedral-style ceiling was painted with frescoes of Purchasing's greatest triumphs. Nymphs laid laurel wreaths at the feet of life-sized images of former VPs of Purchasing Diablo, Fortuna, Red Horn and Polythemus, the past Savings Board Supreme Leaders, as they strode through The Arch of Victory with satchels full of savings checks dragged behind gilded chariots. Supplier executives followed the regal procession, shackled together with chains around their necks. It was an awe-inspiring sight.

"I thought you'd better see 'The Throne Room of the Gods' ahead of time, Harvey. You can't be speechless when you do your presentation." Aziz Mukquat knew what it was like to be speechless. Speech was a faculty he'd only just recovered. The left side of his tongue was still numb.

"It's magnificent," Harvey croaked, staring at a fresco depicting Satan shoveling suppliers who hadn't given savings into the Fire Pits of Hell.

Seven steps led up to a dais made of pink marble. Here, the executive directors that made up Purchasing's Savings Board would hold court over the proceedings. In the center of the dais sat the vice president's throne, an ornate marble chair with a tufted crimson pad. It was a magnificent construct of exquisite Italian craftsmanship; the marble mosaic on its back depicting the history of Globallica Purchasing.

A lone projector and screen stood at the foot of the seven steps. On both sides, straight rows of marble-topped tables flanked the spot reserved for the presenter. Here, directors and department managers like Kendall Swick would sit in reverence. Behind these tables were less opulent tables for the senior purchasing agents. Behind those were hard metal stools for their assistant purchasing agents. Ankle chains could be used to shackle potential runaways.

Harvey approached the steps leading to the dais and started to climb them.

"What are you doing? You can't go up there, Harvey!"

"I want to see the view from up there."

"Well, you can't. It's not allowed. No one sets foot on the dais unless they're an executive director."

Harvey replied, "Well, I can dream, can't I?"

Aziz grabbed Harvey by his shirt collar and pulled him off the steps. "Come with me. To the sweat rooms."

"Oh, boy. I always wanted to try a Swedish sauna."

"It's not that kind of sweat room I'm afraid, Harvey. These are the rooms for presenters to work in while they wait for the Savings Board to start."

"Oh."

Down a narrow hallway was a row of small, plainly furnished, glass-fronted work rooms. It was one hour before the Savings Board was due to start and the rooms were beginning to fill with nervous purchasing agents and buyers working on the final touches to their presentations. Aziz spied a vacant 'sweat room' but before they could enter, a thumping cacophony of feet marched towards them.

"Let me handle this, Harvey."

"No problem, Mr. Mukquat, sir." Harvey cringed behind the Logic Master.

The group marching towards them were a vicious looking gang. They weren't wearing neat and tidy uniforms like DragonForce's Presentation Expeditors. They wore leather motorcycle jackets and jeans with chains that kept their keys and wallets attached. Some of gang had broken noses. Others had scars on their faces. All of them had slicked-back hair, bodies like professional wrestlers.

The ring leader was a squat, balding, plump man wearing a fine Italian suit with no tie, his plain white shirt opened to reveal his chest hairs. He had a thick gold chain hanging around his neck and gold chains on both wrists. His belly hung over his belt. He looked pregnant. A broad smile underscored chubby cheeks, expressive brown eyes and a furrowed brow with eyebrows nearly meeting in the middle. In one corner of his smiling mouth, he munched the end of a stubby unlit cigar.

The man peered around Aziz at the timid little fellow who was trying to dissolve into the floor tile. "My name is Antonio," he said extending his hand.

Aziz pulled Harvey in front of him, pushed him forward and whispered into Harvey's ear, "The Executive Director of Supplier Relations."

"Harvey Drinkwater," Harvey said.

"Aha! *The* Harvey Drinkwater?"

Harvey looked back at Aziz Mukquat. How should he answer that? he thought. How many Harvey Drinkwaters did Globallica have?

Aziz prodded him in the back. Harvey shook Antonio's hand. He winced under the Director of Supplier Relations' vice-like grip.

"Pleased to meet you, Drinkwater. I'm looking forward to your presentation. I'm sure you will knock 'em dead."

"We're going to wish we were dead," Aziz whispered in Harvey's ear.

"This is your first presentation to the Savings Board, isn't it?" the Italian said. "Can I give you a little advice?"

Harvey mewed, "Yes, please Mr. Antonio, sir."

"The last slide is the best one, Drinkwater. The last slide is always the best. Savings. That's what it's all about. You'll remember that, won't you?"

"Oo-kay, sir."

Antonio, Executive Director of Supplier Relations and his gang of 'Supplier Relations Consultants' left Harvey and Aziz to squirm into the last available 'Sweat Room' where they began to sweat. Aziz Mukquat wrote feverishly on a blank notepad.

"What's that, Mr. Mukquat?" Harvey asked.

"My will."

***

"I don't know about this, Bunny. I think we're farting in the wind."

"I think we're pissing in the ocean, Todd."

"Let's not split hairs."

Bunny Warren and Todd Hertle had labored for hours in the Office of Miscellaneous Commodities to muddy up the presentation on the Peruvian Project with enough assumptions it could demote Darwin's *Origin of the Species* to the ranks of a child's riddle. Proving extra-terrestrial life would have been easier than trying to inject logic into the Peruvian Project's conclusions. But they'd given it the old college try.

"Do you think we have enough spin-offs, Bunny?"

"Seaweed farming off the coast of Ecuador? Dust mops made of guinea pig fur? Hiring the Ukrainian Secret Police to train the peasant army?"

"DragonForce will like that angle."

"I don't know, Todd. How is Harvey going to walk through this maze of ideas and lead them where we want the Savings Board to go? Which is essentially nowhere."

"Harvey doesn't walk. He stumbles."

"Precisely. My point exactly."

"We just tell him to click through each slide one at a time and read *very, very* slowly. Let the spin-offs appear. If we've done the teaser-deflectives right, and the Savings Board goes off on a tangent, he'll never present the last slide—the deadly one—and it will be mission accomplished. How difficult can that be?"

"Todd, you might as well ask Harvey Drinkwater to present Einstein's Theory of Relativity."

"Great idea. Let's incorporate it. You think we can find a spin-off?"

"Todd, you know what I mean."

"Think miracle, Bunny. Channel your inner miracle-ness."

Angus McCalliwag poked his head around the partition and announced, "Yee betta get thy skates on. Tha party's aboot to start in ten minutes over in the Tower."

"Ten minutes! Why didn't you warn us sooner?"

"Do yee think it would matta, laddie? Yee are screwed anyway."

Bunny Warren glared at the Scot. "Angus, you old coot. You're enjoying this, aren't you?"

"We have to go with what we've got." Todd Hertle pressed 'print' on his laptop then emailed the revised presentation on the 'Peruvian Project' to Arkon, the Savings Board Secretary. For additional backup, he loaded a copy onto a thumb-drive.

Todd grabbed the hot sheaves of paper as soon as the printer gave birth and bolted for the exit. Anyone meeting Todd Hertle inside the glass tunnel leading from Purchasing to the Globallica Tower was about to find out what would happen if a not-so-immovable object met a definitely irresistible force.

Bunny scampered after him, buffeted in the winds of Todd's turbulence. She called ahead to Johann Thorsveld, "Johann, darling. Yes, it's Bunny. So nice to speak with you again. No, I'm not available for dinner tomorrow night. Next decade, perhaps? What am I calling about? How sweet of you to ask. I have a teensy, weensy little favor to ask, Johann darling. Would you accept a late quote from a supplier? To add to Harvey Drinkwater's presentation? It would be a nice savings for Globallica. You would? Oh, you're such a sweetie. I'll send Todd Hertle over to deliver a new presentation. He's already there? My he's efficient, isn't he? Well, blow me a kiss, Johann. Bye."

Bunny punched 'end' on her cell phone. "Creep!"

CHAPTER FIFTEEN

The Savings Board. Harvey's very first one. It was an amazing sight. The hall that earlier had been an empty cavern, echoing every footstep, was a hive of activity, buzzing with the discussions of what appeared to be a crowd of a thousand people.

In the Throne Room of The Gods, the main overhead chandelier had been dimmed. Soft lights illuminated the busts in the alcoves along the wall. Desk lamps on the long marble tables shone golden light across opened files frantically massaged by the clammy hands of the department managers. A few of them barked last minute instructions to their senior purchasing agents who in turn gave orders to their shackled assistants. A few buyers were set free to run errands; guard dogs followed carefully behind. The entire assembly was like a river of stressed-out hippopotami bellowing out their anticipation and unbridled fear.

Aziz Mukquat called Sun Ho Gung to check on the cauldron of 'Sweet Dreams on the Yangtze' he was brewing back at the office. Ho Gung replied he'd come up with a new herbal recipe he was calling 'Death by Panda Balls'. Aziz said he would give it a try.

Harvey tried to focus on something pleasant. The garden by the pond with Daphne. Happy times with Hilda and Mr. Dortmann. Sunshine.

It didn't work.

The lump in his throat was threatening to work its way forward and cause serious dental damage.

Suddenly, the hippo noise in the Throne Room ended. Uncomfortable fidgeting took its place as feet and papers shuffled. From behind enormous red velvet curtains, the members of the Savings Board entered the chamber and mounted the seven steps up to the dais.

DragonForce, Executive Director of Purchasing Process Performance. Antonio, Executive Director of Supplier Relations. Bjorn, Executive Director of All Commodities.

There was a hush as they took their seats. A final figure emerged from behind the curtain: the chancellor of the Savings Board, the vice president of Purchasing, the Head Cheese…Talus.

Arkon, Purchasing's Executive Director of Human Resources—clad in his usual drab monk robes—thumped the floor with an enormously tall, gnarled oak staff that had a carved dragon on top with red glass eyes. The Savings Board had been called to order.

Harvey heard whispering in his left ear. He turned to look at Aziz Mukquat. The Logic Master was reciting ancient Hindu script and praying to a small statue of Ganesh, the elephant-headed God. He'd converted from Islam in desperation. It was a last ditch attempt at divine intervention.

"Let the Savings begin."

Those words from Talus triggered Johann Thorsveld to extract the first victim from his shackles. The bespectacled little man had no chance. In five minutes, the Board devoured his meager savings and spit him out on the floor. Johann's Presentation Expeditors mopped up the remains.

"Who's next, Arkon?"

"Call Harvey Drinkwater!" Arkon's voice boomed across the room.

"Call Harvey Drinkwater!" resonated as Pretzel Makers scoured the tables for their prey.

Harvey clutched the script of Todd and Bunny's 'new' savings presentation close to his chest. His heartbeat began to pound out the Death March.

"Call Harvey Drinkwater!"

Harvey's shackles were unlocked and he rose from his seat behind Kendall Swick. Kendall's expression was stoic. It had to be. Success or failure, it didn't matter. Being emotionless counted above all else. As a professional manager, Kendall Swick was trained to neither yell with joy, nor cry with sorrow at any outcome. Harvey felt comforted.

"Approach, Drinkwater."

Harvey walked across the expanse of open marble floor below the dais. At that moment, the faces in the crowd sitting at the tables melted away into oblivion. Only the dais with the Savings Board mattered. He was handed a clicker by Arkon who instructed, "Push the blue button to go forward. Push the yellow button to go back. Don't push the red button."

Harvey Drinkwater's mind was a mush of thoughts. In one corner of his cerebrum was an image of a dejected little humanoid under a stairwell in the back office of Dortmann's Zipper Emporium. In the other corner, a dream of a well-dressed executive in an office with tiger maple furniture, a *Wall Street Journal* and a fruit basket on his desk. The bell rang. Round One was about to begin. Those two images would fight to the death.

"I have savings to report."

"Yes, Mr. Drinkwater. We know that."

The room twittered.

"Silence. Let Drinkwater speak."

"It's about guinea pigs, Mr. Talus, sir."

More twittering. A sound resembling knives being sharpened could be heard in the background. Harvey fingered Todd and Bunny's script then pushed the red button on the clicker. The projector shut off and the screen went blank.

More twittering.

"Um...sorry, sir."

Arkon turned the projector back on. "Blue forward. Yellow back."

"And don't touch the red one. I think I got it."

Talus was impatient. "Present, Mr. Drinkwater! Present your savings."

Bunny Warren had caught up with Todd Hertle who after delivering the script of the 'new' presentation to Harvey had been throwing up in the toilet. They entered the back of the Throne Room and sat near the exit under the watchful glare of two Pretzel Makers who stood guard.

"He was an okay kind of guy," Todd said. "I'll miss him."

Bunny dipped her head in mourning.

Harvey Drinkwater's brain could only process so many instructions at once. When too many signals came in—like blue forward, yellow back—the poor organ searched for the simplest, most profound instruction it could execute. This allowed any damage to the cerebral cortex to be kept to a bare minimum.

Harvey recalled Antonio's advice, "The last slide is the best, Mr. Drinkwater. The last slide is always the best."

That was it!

That was the answer Harvey's mind was searching for as it wandered through the maze of his confusion.

The last slide.

If the last slide was truly the best one, then that's where Harvey would start. He would present the last slide first and work his way backwards through the presentation. That way, all the savings would be explained at the very start. And he only needed to push one button, 'yellow back'. What did Harvey have to lose? Presenting from the front didn't make any sense even if Todd had insisted it did. The new presentation was full of strange contradictions Harvey didn't understand.

Harvey whispered to Arkon. The crowd hushed. The bullets on the final slide of the presentation appeared:

1) The accumulated savings from our Peruvian guinea pig supplier will be ten million dollars per year.

2) The net present value of the investment is a positive three million dollars with a six week payback.

3) With a fifty percent price reduction, lifetime savings are one hundred and twenty million dollars.

"One hundred and twenty million dollars!" Talus leapt out of his chair and pumped the air with his fists.

The rest of the Savings Board jumped to their feet. Seeing the exaltations of their leaders, the congregation of managers and their assistants rose as one and trumpeted their support in a loud boom that would strip the skin off an elephant.

Kendall Swick fainted.

"One hundred and twenty million dollars! And they said it couldn't be done!" Talus cried out at the top of his lungs as he danced a jig on the stage. "Not with guinea pigs. Time and time again, I've heard spineless cowards come in front of me and proclaim it couldn't be done. Well, today my friends—today at the Savings Board—we've seen that paradigm shattered. We've seen how a humble purchasing agent with a firm conviction in his heart, a will to succeed and a Harvard MBA can deliver the savings!"

Another roar erupted from the crowd. Harvey paused with his finger on the yellow back button. A single press of a sweaty digit would have posted the second-to-last slide onto the screen—a slide that described how the genetic engineering of guinea pigs would create an ecological disaster of Biblical proportions. But that logical destruction of the main assumption that a fifty percent price reduction was possible, would never see the light of day.

Harvey was swept up by the crowd and hoisted onto the shoulders of Thorsveld's Presentation Expeditors. He was carried in triumph through the throng, a legendary moment-in-the-making that would make a great fresco some day.

Seizing their opportunity, Todd and Bunny ran out through the exit, past two stunned and motionless guards.

"Oh, my God, Bunny. What has Harvey done this time?"

"It's our miracle, Todd. It's a miracle he still has a job."

CHAPTER SIXTEEN

Todd Hertle scrolled through the pages on his computer screen but couldn't find a match. No one wanted an energetic, brave, wise fool. Otherwise he would have jumped at the chance to apply.

"Still looking at internal job postings?"

"There's plenty available, Bunny. I'm just not sure I have the right qualifications."

Bunny looked over his shoulder. "How about this one?"

Todd clicked on the job title, 'Personal Productivity Manager – Supplier Relations' and replied, "Zip again, Bunny. Another strikeout. See, I'm not qualified."

The job posting read: 'Ideal candidate has Special Ops background in the military or in law enforcement. Qualified to train large groups in martial arts. Experience with field surgery of battle wounds desirable. Must be able to work nights. Employees in federal witness protection programs need not apply'.

"That rules me out."

Was there any hope that Todd Hertle might be pardoned from his life sentence in the Dept. of Miscellaneous Commodities?

"What about 'Savings Board Technology Analyst'? You'd be good at that."

"Bunny, I looked into it. It's not what you think it is. Read this…"

Bunny perused the job posting: 'Candidates must have electrical engineering degree with emphasis on human responses to high voltage. Mind reading skills are an advantage. The position involves some amount of routine work in support of Presentation Expeditors. Must supply own boot polish.'

"No thanks."

"I agree, Todd."

"That's it. My life is toast."

"Don't give up," Bunny encouraged him. "Check one more. I have a good feeling your new job is out there somewhere, just waiting for someone just as lame as you to apply for it. Use positive thinking, Todd."

Todd scrolled, chin firmly on his chest, disconsolate.

"There," she pointed at the screen. "How about that one? That's right up your street: 'Data Specialist – Dept. of Supply Chain Performance Metrics.'"

Todd closed his eyes and clicked. "Please, God. Let this be it."

The listing read: 'Preference is given to assistant purchasing agents in career transition.'

"See, Todd. I told you."

'Must be able to interpret complex mathematical algorithms and derive pseudo-accurate hypotheses.'

"So far so good, Todd."

'Position involves a high degree of intuitive precognition. Ideal candidates possess psychic powers and are obsessive compulsive. Will consider neurotics on an exceptional basis.'

"I told you, Todd. I told you! That's you all over."

"Bunny, I'm not sure."

"About what?"

"The psychic part."

"Buy some Tarot cards. You can teach yourself in one night, two tops. Who'll ever know if your forecasts are wrong?"

"Another psychic?"

"So what? They already know."

"Good point."

Todd completed the on-line application.

"Hey, here's an idea," Bunny said. "You could prepare for your job interview by practicing your Tarot card readings on Harvey."

"Bunny, please. I'm having a hard enough time dealing with his present. I don't know if I could stomach seeing into his future."

"Oh, don't be so hard on him. He needs our help again, Todd. Guillermo Alvarez is coming into the office at ten o'clock. I'd love to know what Harvey is going to say to him."

Todd jumped to his feet. "I'll be right back."

"Where're you going?"

"The bookstore across the street. Tarot cards. Great idea, Bunny. Good meeting prep. Thanks."

It was past 9AM. The old farmer, Mert Hutchin, shunted up the hall, lunch bag in hand, just like clockwork. He was wearing his neck collar but this was his first day without crutches.

"You're making good progress, Mr. Hutchin."

The old farmer grumbled. Bunny wondered if next time they swept the department, Johann Thorsveld's gang would take notice of the old man's visitor's pass, especially now he wore a blue 'disabled' one.

"Harvey, is there anything I can do for you before your ten o'clock meeting?" she asked.

Harvey sat in his office with his head buried in both hands.

"Harvey?"

His Friday had not started out very well at all. It was an extension of the previous four days that had not started out very well either.

On Monday, his login IDs expired when IT refreshed his computer over the weekend.

On Tuesday, he missed his appointment with Olive Olympios to get new ones. She scheduled him for the next solar eclipse.

On Wednesday, Kendall Swick had a fit when the International Video Conference was cancelled. Harvey had knocked over a glass of water inside Todd Hertle's recording studio. An hour later during a thunderstorm, a lightning bolt traveled down a metal girder, through the wet carpet and into the server room, frying Kendall's 'video feeds'.

Next week, Todd would have to outfit all the other purchasing agents in costume. Angus refused to dress up in lederhosen and speak with a German accent. Someone would have to explain to Kendall that the Frankfurt and Hamburg offices had now closed and a new one in Aberdeen had opened.

On Wednesday night when Harvey returned home, he received a letter from the State Atomic Energy Commission's inquiry into the Safe N'Sound Nuclear Reactor Company's meltdown. Radiation levels around his mother's grave were reaching dangerous levels. They needed to exhume her body. The Commission's grand jury and the Coroner's Office were now fighting over what was left of Ma Drinkwater.

On Thursday morning, Harvey woke up to find that Lopez had eaten a potted plant. On the floor was a pile of what looked like guacamole. It didn't taste like guacamole though. His week was officially turning into a disaster.

By today, Friday, last week's presentation to the Savings Board had become a distant memory. The glory had faded quickly. Johann Thorsveld had made sure Harvey was reminded of his accountability. Every day, a Pretzel Maker checked up on him. Savings couldn't be booked until a new guinea pig contract had been issued. At half the current price.

Time was ticking along mercilessly. The CEO and owner of the Alvarez Guinea Pig Meat Export Corporation of South America (AGPMEC S.A.) was scheduled to see him in a few minutes. The last time someone went to Peru to call on Guillermo Alvarez and attempt to negotiate a price reduction on his guinea pigs, the only thing that returned home was a finger in a plastic bag.

Harvey had gotten attached to his fingers.

"Mr. Alvarez is here to see you, Harvey."

The trapdoor in Harvey's office had been welded shut by Johann Thorsveld's goon squad. There was no escape.

"Let him in Bunny. And Bunny…" Harvey sighed.

"Yes?"

"Make sure Lopez goes to a good home."

"I will." Bunny wiped a tear from the corner of her eye.

A short, stocky man entered Harvey's office wearing a 1950's style, black pinstriped three-piece suit. He took off his white fedora with its black satin band and sat down. His girth filled the chair. Jet black hair. Waxed curly moustache. He resembled a booking agent for a Peruvian circus act. Or was he a fat Salvador Dali running a funeral home? Whatever.

"It is such a great pleasure to finally meet you, Señor Drinkwater," Alvarez said. "You don't look anything like I imagined you would."

"I don't?"

"No. You see, those emails I received from your office, they must have been sent by someone else. Someone with a terrible sense of humor. It couldn't have been you. You look like a very serious person to me, Señor Drinkwater."

"I do?"

"Si. You see, Señor Drinkwater, in my country we do business like we are brothers, you and I. We take our business deals very seriously. We don't joke about them."

"We don't?"

"No, Señor Drinkwater. I think there has been a terrible, terrible mistake. A mistake with terrible, terrible consequences. A mistake I'm sure you don't want to repeat."

"I don't?"

"No, Señor Drinkwater, you don't."

The chubby Peruvian's confidence mildly reassured him.

Guillermo Alvarez reached into his llama leather briefcase and produced a sheaf of printed correspondence from Globallica Purchasing. He handed the bundle to Harvey. As Alvarez smiled, the light reflected off his solid gold front teeth into Harvey's eyes. Harvey ducked under the beam to read the papers.

Johann Thorsveld had been busy. Busy accelerating Harvey's demise. Under Bjorn and DragonForce's signatures, Globallica Purchasing's price reduction demands had been emailed twice daily to Mr. Alvarez. Each one ended with the words, '…and should you wish to discuss your new contract terms and conditions, please arrange a meeting with your designated purchasing agent, Harvey Drinkwater.'

"You can't reduce your prices on guinea pigs, Mr. Alvarez?"

The Peruvian leaned forward across the desk and beckoned Harvey closer as if Harvey were about to hear a big secret no one else in the building should know. Alvarez whispered into Harvey's ear, "I can maybe give you one guinea pig at half price, Señor Drinkwater. And I'll throw a cage in for free. No charge. Since you and I are such good friends. Like brothers."

Alvarez leaned back, giving Harvey a wink. "I could have one of my men deliver it to your house? I'd *love* to know where you live. Or perhaps you would want to come to Peru yourself, to pick it up?" Alvarez grinned and twisted the thick gold ring on his finger to emphasize his point.

Harvey gulped. "Um…that won't be necessary, Mr. Alvarez. We can't accept gifts from suppliers. Besides, I get airsick."

Alvarez's smile turned into a frown. The ray of light that was causing the sweat on Harvey's face to glisten, vanished as the Peruvian's mouth closed.

Harvey looked down at the pile of correspondence sent from Globallica to Alvarez. He slowly swept it to the end of the desk. One by one, the papers fluttered gently into the waste basket. Harvey began counting his fingers.

The smile on Señor Alvarez's face re-appeared. "Then I think we have resolved this matter to our mutual satisfaction, yes, Señor Drinkwater?"

Harvey squinted as the ray of light from Alvarez's teeth returned. Alvarez got up to leave. Harvey got up to shake his hand. Alvarez noticed the large wet patch around Harvey's crotch. "Si, moy bien. It's been nice doing business with you, Señor Drinkwater."

CHAPTER SEVENTEEN

Steam rose from the mug in the middle of the desk. Harvey was not encouraged by the label on the teabag's string, 'Leper's Balm'.

"Drink it, Harvey," Ho Gung had said. "Good for you. Special Chinese recipe. Make you relax. Forget your troubles."

"Your next appointment is here," Bunny said, leaning in through the doorway.

'Cats'.

That was the label on the file folder that sat unopened in front of him. It was time to renew the contract with Paws N'Claws Animal Rescue, Inc. Another opportunity to demand savings? Or maybe not?

Unlike the last one, this meeting seemed routine. After all, how difficult could it be to negotiate with a supplier who rounded up stray cats? Harvey imagined Paws N'Claws' owner would be some gentle gray-haired old lady in a wooly cardigan, carrying an oversized tapestry handbag to bring along her knitting needles and yarn.

What Harvey got was…Freddie 'the Razor' Hogan.

Aviator sunglasses, worn indoors. Tied back California blonde ponytail under a red bandana. Black 'Harley-Davidson of Death Valley' T-shirt under a denim jacket that was frayed where the sleeves had been cut off. Dusty black snakeskin boots matching the condition of the Harley Davidson saddle bag he plopped on the floor. A longhorn cattle skull tattooed on one of his bronzed muscular arms. 'Momma's Boy' tattooed with roses on the other. Toothpick in the corner of his mouth. Pack of cigarettes wrapped under his T-shirt's sleeve.

So, no knitting needles then?

"Yo, how's it hangin', Harv?"

Harvey had second thoughts about trying Ho Gung's potion. *Would it hurt to take a tiny sip?*

He wouldn't find out. Just as Harvey was drumming up the courage, Freddie intercepted him with, "Hey, Harv. What's that great smelling brew? Whiffs like the concert I went to last night. You got more of that stuff?"

"If you want this cup, you can have it, Mr. Hogan. I'm afraid I'm not much of a tea drinker." Harvey was glad to get rid of Ho Gung's concoction. It stank of stale cigarette butts boiled in linseed oil. He would rather drink sardine juice.

"Hey man, thanks."

The cat herder took off his sunglasses, savored the aroma curling up from the surface of the mug, looked at the label and took a generous slurp. "This shit's the bomb, man. Yeah, 'Leopard's Bomb'. Cool name. Me? Call me Freddie."

"Um Freddie, is it possible, perhaps soon or perhaps sometime this year, maybe there might be some...um...savings from your company? For Globallica? Perhaps? A little?"

Freddie Hogan took a long, satisfying swig that drained the mug, nodded his approval to Harvey, then reached into the top pocket of his jeans jacket. He pulled out an ebony-handled switchblade and pointed it to the ceiling. He smiled. A gleaming alloy steel blade flashed upwards with a frightening swish.

Harvey gulped.

"Gotta keep this label, man. Gotta see if my supplier can get me some of this shit. It's good, Harv. Very good." Freddie cut the string on the teabag and popped the label into his pocket. "Is it legal?"

"Sure. You can cut a string. It's legal. I think."

"Nice one, Harv." Smiling, Freddie 'the Razor' Hogan pointed the end of the switchblade at Harvey and winked. "Who's your supplier?"

"You are?"

"No, *this*." Freddie raised the mug.

"Oh, the tea?" Harvey gulped. "His name's Sun Ho Gung. He's not a supplier. He works here."

"Here, as in *this* office? He's the boss. Gotta meet him, man. You lucky effing dog. This must be some cool shit place to work."

"No, Freddie. He's not the boss. And it's not cool. The air conditioning breaks down a lot."

Freddie 'the Razor' Hogan smiled again and closed the switchblade. "You know, I like you, Harv. You're all right. We gonna do a deal now? Or what?"

"We're not allowed to play cards at work, Mr. Hogan."

"Whoa, Harv. What's with the 'Mr. Hogan' shit? Chill out, man."

"Sorry, Freddie. I'm having a bad day. At the end of a bad week. I need some savings. Badly. You can't give me any, can you?"

"You mean cut prices, Harv? Co...yeah, no. Kinda hard to do."

"I know. It seems like that with everyone I meet," Harvey sighed. His bitter memory of Guillermo Alvarez from Peru was fresh in his mind. "Seems no one wants to lower prices."

"Can't get any lower than zero, Harvey dude."

"Zero?"

"Yeah. You know. Zip? Nada? Zero dinaros, Harv."

Harvey looked at last year's contract with Paws N'Claws. The price per stray cat, delivered, was $0.00 each. Harvey thought it was a typo when he first saw it. "They're free?"

Freddie laughed. "Well, not after I catch them, they're not."

Harvey whimpered. This was very confusing. But what else was new? A clause at the bottom of the contract—below the IRS number designating Paws N'Claws as a registered charity—read: 'Buyer will reimburse supplier for reasonable expenses incurred in fulfilling his obligations'.

"Expenses?"

"Thought you'd never ask, dude." Freddie retrieved a bundle of soiled invoices and expense receipts from his motorcycle saddle bag and plunked them in a heap on the desk. "Do you think I could get some more of the bossman's tea, Harv?"

"I'll see if Ho Gung is still here."

Sun Ho Gung was stunned when Harvey presented an empty mug and requested a second cup. He was also surprised to see that Harvey was still standing.

Bunny Warren whispered in Harvey's ear, "Processing Freddie's expense requests is routine. Just approve them. Trust me."

Harvey returned to his office, fresh mug of hot tea in hand, and found Freddie Hogan sprawled out in the chair, his hands limply overhanging the armrests, his head cocked back, looking up at the ceiling.

"That's some strong shit, Harv."

Harvey sniffed the air. "No, it's probably a dead rat."

"You're some cool dude, dude. You sure know how to treat your suppliers right. Not like that witch, Gillemott. I'll have to take a cab home and send a tow truck to fetch my bike."

"Um, Freddie? About these expenses…"

"Oh, Harv, I've cut way back from last year. That bitch Darcy laid it on pretty thick. Said he would slap me around if I didn't. How's his hormones, anyway?"

"Fine, Freddie. She's fine." Harvey thumbed through the receipts. "Um, this one, Freddie? Forty-nine massages? Signed by Trina, Candy and forty-seven others from the Rest and Welcome Ranch in Reno, Nevada?"

"Hey, Harv. Gotta treat those kitties right. Keep 'em relaxed. You know. They get pretty uptight in those little cages."

"And three weeks in the Casino Grande in Las Vegas?"

"Harv, do you know how many stray cats Vegas has? I'm doing a public service. We don't want no drunks tripping over 'em, do we?"

"Yes, but…five thousand dollars for chromed motorcycle parts?"

"Transportation costs, dude."

"Nineteen thousand dollars for beer?"

"That highway dust whips up a mean thirst, dude. But I bought wholesale, Harv at 'No Costa Lotta Warehouse'. I'm trying to save, really I am."

"But...three hundred thousand dollars worth of talcum powder?"

"Harv... Harv... this is no ordinary talcum powder. No, siree, dude. Special stuff, man. Only the best for the little kitties. Imported from Columbia."

"Columbian talcum powder?"

"Yeah, Harv," he chuckled. Freddie's head swayed around in a circle as he watched the room spin. "You know, next to Peru?"

"Peru?"

"Columbia? Peru? Whatever, man. I gotta get me a supplier of this tea shit. China? Is that far?"

Harvey's head plunked into the middle of Freddie's invoices. He sobbed. This week had been too much. He was a certified, useless purchasing agent.

"Hey, dude. Whatcha crying about? Life's a bitch, man. Tell me about it. But there's ways to chill out. Hey, you told me who your supplier was. So the least I can do is let you know mine." Freddie reached into his pocket and threw Harvey a plain white business card with no name on it, just a cell number.

"Supplier?"

"Yeah, Harv. Ask for Juan Manuel. Weed, smack, crack, crystal meth, if it's chemical, Juan has it. Whatever you want."

"Guinea pigs?"

"Guinea pigs, Harv?"

"Guinea pigs."

"They pills or what? You smoke 'em? Never heard of 'guinea pigs'."

"They're furry. Like cats."

"Man, this shit's too strong for this conversation, dude. I don't get it."

"Guinea pigs, Freddie. Little furry animals. I need someone willing to sell me guinea pigs at half the price we buy them for today. Or I'm in a whole bunch of trouble."

"Oh, yeah, Harv. Know watcha mean. Been there. Done that. Got the postcard from Leavenworth."

Freddie Hogan smiled and rubbed his fuzzy chin. He tried getting out of his chair but his legs refused to co-operate. He collapsed in a heap on the floor.

Harvey resumed his sobbing.

Eventually, Freddie hoisted his head over the edge of Harvey's desk. "Harv, I like you. You da boss, man. I wanna help you. In any way I can."

Harvey wiped the tears from his wet cheeks.

Freddie continued, although his vocal chords were now in Step Three of the process of being pickled and preserved, "I've got a good supplier. No…check that, dude. A *great* supplier. Yeah, from Columbi-ya."

Freddie's tongue lacked enough stiffness to form words. "Ish not Peru. But ish close. He can get any shit you want, man. I'm gonna ask him 'bout guinea pigs for you, Harv. Ish the least I can do. Cos' you're a cool dude, dude. An you gonna prove my spenses…yeah?"

Harvey Drinkwater sniffled and nodded. He looked at Freddie Hogan's sympathetic face. He caught a glimpse of it as Freddie slumped to the floor. "Thanks, Mr. Hogan. I guess I'll approve your expenses. Yeah, why not?"

Freddie raised his head off the floor as best he could, trying to smile. The drool washed the toothpick out of the corner of his mouth, as his cheek muscles lost all feeling. "Freddie," he slurred. "Ish Freddie. None o' tha Misser Hogan shit. C'mon, Harv. Shelebrate. Have shum tea, dude."

"No, thanks, Freddie. But you go ahead. I'm trying to cut back."

As the cat-herding biker lost consciousness, Harvey looked inside the Harley Davidson saddlebag for Freddie's Blue Cross card. He found it next to a picture of Freddie's mom. Or was it his dad? Harvey wasn't sure.

CHAPTER EIGHTEEN

A boom rattled the glasses on the conference room table. Arkon called Purchasing's HRM Committee to order. "Begin," he bellowed, as if the gong wasn't a big enough clue.

Today's Executive HRM Committee had two topics on the agenda—new hires and internal transfers, a combination known by the minions as 'the slave trade'.

"I have a deep concern over the lack of qualified people coming into our buying ranks," Talus remarked. "We've had some dreadful failures recently. Purchasing just doesn't seem to be attracting the right caliber of people."

"I have a solution, an initiative I'm particularly excited about," Bjorn said. "It's called ART...the Alternative Resources Training program. I've contracted with the Ocean City Anthropology Institute to conduct a primate computing skills trial."

"Monkeys?" Antonio snickered. A horsewhip whacked his head.

"Behave, fat boy," DragonForce sneered. "Continue, Bjorn darling."

"The Institute prefers to call them 'pre-homo sapiens'. It allows them to qualify for government training funds. The ART program has shown great promise."

"Intriguing," the VP said. "Any success stories?"

"It's still early, Talus. The chimps learn our purchase order systems quickly. But the orangutans have trouble with freight and delivery terms. The gorillas have trouble with keyboards. We need to spend a bit more money on ergonomic design. Their fingers are too fat."

"The request for supplementary funding is approved," Talus added with a yawn. "The topic of new hires is closed."

Bjorn shuffled his papers. "Internal transfers are next on the agenda. The first candidate I want as a transfer into Commodities is Louie Tartelli from Supplier Relations. He should make a good buyer. We have him targeted for surgical instruments. He's an expert in scalpels, I believe."

Antonio nodded. "Well, that's close enough. It's stilettos, really."

Talus was confused. "Antonio, how can you afford to lose someone from your group?"

"Tartelli needs to lie low for a little while, you know what I mean? Get off the streets? I'll suck up the loss."

"I want to shuffle some headcount internally within the Buying Teams," Bjorn continued. "My people are getting too knowledgeable on their commodities. Makes them cocky and mutinous."

"Your solution?"

"A fourteen person reorganization involving three promotions, nine laterals and two demotions." Bjorn handed Talus the file of his proposed people moves. "The learning curves I'll put them on should cure dissent until I move them all again. And a few demotions in the mix are good for morale."

"Approved" (*yawn*) "Anything else?"

"I'm staffing a new analytical group, 'Supplier Performance Metrics' as a result of the re-organization. Exciting stuff, Talus. Cutting edge."

"Remind me, Bjorn," the VP asked. "Which re-organization? The one, two months ago? Or the one, two weeks ago?"

"The one on Friday."

"Last week? Or the week before?"

"No, the one tomorrow."

"Have I approved it?"

"Not yet. But you will."

"Okay. That's clear now. Continue."

"Supplier Performance Metrics is a new job description within Purchasing. It's absolutely crucial to achieving the next level of savings targets. I'm developing a staff of Data Surgeons—highly skilled analysts able to dissect the minutiae of supplier metrics and determine the validity of price performance aberrations and anomalies."

"Huh?"

"The new science of predictive supplier performance engineering. Using integrated effectiveness assessments. And the analysis of discontinuities in the supply chain time-space continuum. It's the next plateau of the purchasing profession."

"Speaking of platters," Antonio chirped. "Where's the food?"

"I'm not watching you eat again. It's disgusting," DragonForce said.

"Let's stay on topic, shall we?" Talus growled.

"I plan to move someone from Miscellaneous Commodities to head up the group," Bjorn continued. "The candidate's name is Todd Hertle. Good resume. Thinks at warp speed. Has all the right eccentricities for a Data Surgeon. Off the chart energy level. Hopelessly obsessed with details."

Talus yawned again and fidgeted with his cell phone. "Fine. Approved. Next?"

"It's you, sir. Your Worshipfulness," Arkon chimed.

"Me?"

Arkon whispered in Talus's ear.

"Oh yes. Nearly forgot. EGO."

The directors groaned.

'EGO' was Talus's new baby: the 'Executive Growth Opportunities' program. It was an out-of-control freight train that Talus's executive directors desperately wanted to sabotage. Talus's idea was simple enough—identify high potential, fast-track candidates for executive development and special assignments, working of course under his personal tutelage. According to Talus, promotion to director level should not be left to chance. That's what made the whole idea so bad. Bjorn, DragonForce, and Antonio differed with Talus's approach to executive development. 'EGO' was counter to the logic of natural selection by survival of the fittest. It was dangerous free expression. 'EGO' had to be stopped. It was one of the few HR issues the three squabbling executive directors could agreed on.

"I'm going to nominate Harvey Drinkwater for EGO," Talus announced. "We need to accelerate his development. His handling of the Peruvian Project was brilliant. He cut straight to the bottom line and stood his ground under fierce questioning. He declared a confidence in achieving savings that we've yet to see from any of our current fast-trackers."

"Talus, I beg to differ on your choice of candidates. My sources—" DragonForce started to explain.

"She means her spies."

Thwack! Antonio winced as Katrina's riding crop bounced off his fat neck. "They tell me Drinkwater may not be able to deliver on his savings."

"Is this true, Bjorn?"

"I stand by my Savings Reports, Talus. Always. To the last penny," Bjorn huffed. "But if my esteemed colleague has concerns over Drinkwater's integrity, I will review his plans."

"I want everyone to agree," said Her Evilness. "If Drinkwater has lied about his savings, his fast-track status will be withdrawn immediately."

"That only seems fair," Talus said, defeated. "Let the minutes so record it. Harvey Drinkwater delivers the contract for half-price guinea pigs *before* he's put on the fast-track."

Talus rose to leave. DragonForce sent a text message to Johann Thorsveld…'Email Alvarez in Peru to withdraw our demands. Drinkwater is cooked.'

Arkon smashed the gong. The HRM meeting was over.

CHAPTER NINETEEN

Juan Manuel Jimenez kept strange business hours. He said he had an allergy to the sun. Harvey thought he must have also been allergic to people. Fortunately, Señor Jimenez didn't have an allergy to dogs. Lopez had agreed to keep Harvey company. Reluctantly.

Harvey met Señor Jimenez on Wharf Number Nine in the middle of the night in the middle of an Ocean City fog storm. The fog made it hard to tell what Señor Jimenez looked like. It didn't help that he stood with the wharf's single, lonely street light behind him.

Lopez must have had good night vision because the Chihuahua emitted a constant monotone growling, no matter which direction Señor Jimenez moved to get away from the little dog.

Señor Jimenez was an acquaintance of someone who knew Freddie Hogan's supplier of 'talcum powder'. Which was like knowing someone who had bumped into someone Harvey didn't know, and then introduced himself. At least that's how it felt. Lopez felt like sinking his teeth into the Columbian's leg.

"Are you alone?"

"No. I have a dog with me."

"Si. Moy bien. Freddie Hogan said I can trust you. Now I know why. And he told me about your little problem."

"Which one?"

"The furry one."

"Lopez doesn't have any hair."

"Que?"

"Oh…you mean…the other problem?"

"Which one?"

"The one Freddie told you about."

"Si." Jimenez sat down on a pile of oyster crates. He was getting dizzy. "I think I can help solve your problem, Señor Drinkwater."

"You can?"

"You need something cheap, si?"

"Cheaper."

"Si, cheaper. I get it cheaper for you."

"Them."

"Que?"

"There's more than one that I need cheaper. In fact, I already have one at half price. But I need more."

"Moy bien. More. And cheaper. Si. I understand. Meet me here tomorrow night."

"How will I know it's you?"

"Bring the dog."

***

Once, someone told Harvey a black cloud was always following him. Harvey could never tell. The sky was always so gray. Well, finally he'd met someone with a similar problem. It seemed wherever Juan Manuel Jimenez went, the fog followed.

Harvey's mother, bless her irradiated soul, had always told him to wear bright clothes in the dark. So that cars could see him. Juan Manuel's mother obviously didn't care about her son's safety. Which was such a shame. Because if he had worn brighter clothes, perhaps Harvey would have spotted him sooner. Before Lopez ripped off his pant leg.

"Señor Drinkwater, have you ever been to Peru?"

"No. I prefer vacations where I get to bring back souvenirs, instead of leaving them behind."

"Si, Señor. Mr. Alvarez? I understand." Juan Manuel Jimenez produced a stack of paper from inside his leather briefcase. "Well, you have no reason to go to Peru anymore, Señor Drinkwater. Here—" Jimenez flicked the pages. "Here is the solution to your problem."

"The furry one?"

"No, Señor, more than one furry one. Mucho furry ones. As many furry ones as you want. At a price you can afford." Jimenez handed the documents over to Harvey, signed, sealed and delivered, just a little damp from the fog. They were written according to Globallica's standard Purchase Order terms and conditions for the purchase of guinea pigs…at half the current price.

Harvey's eyes nearly exploded out of his head. The top page began with…'This contract binds the undersigned to supply the said goods at the said price to the said location, until someone says…forget it, we have another supplier.'

It was music to Harvey's ears.

The contract was signed by J. M. Jimenez, CEO, The Guinea Pig Meat Import Corporation of New Jersey LLC.

"Columbian guinea pigs instead of Peruvian ones?" Harvey asked.

"No, Señor. That would be too expensive. You see, where I come from the land is agricultural, used for cultivation. Plants, si? No guinea pig farms."

"Oh. But your company imports guinea pigs?"

"Si, Señor."

"From?"

"New York City."

"New York City?"

"Si, Señor. Nuevo Yorkque."

"They farm guinea pigs in New York City?"

"Not exactly 'farm', Señor. These are wild guinea pigs. But no worries, Señor. There are plenty of them."

"And they're just as good as Peruvian guinea pigs?"

Effective questioning. The key to effective purchasing.

"Si. When you eat them. No one can tell."

"Tell what?"

"You see, Señor, wild American guinea pigs look slightly different than Peruvian guinea pigs. But they are cheaper. Which is what you want, no?"

"Yes. They look different?"

"Señor, Peruvian guinea pigs have no tail, si? They are tail-less guinea pigs. American guinea pigs are a little smaller. And they have a tail. But I remove it for you. No extra charge."

"Guinea pigs with tails?"

"The finest, Señor Drinkwater…'New York Browns'."

"New York Browns?"

"Si, the finest breed. New York City brown guinea pigs. Nuevo Yorques. Just for you, Señor. An exclusive deal for Globallica."

"Do they taste the same? We have very demanding customers."

"Señor, they taste better. You see, the Peruvian guinea pigs, they exposed to a lot of sunshine. It is very hot in Peru, Señor. The light…it make the meat tough. 'Nuevo Yorques' live underground. In subway tunnels…oops, I mean burrows. No expose to light. Organically fed. Free range. It takes time to round them up. But we do it for you, our good customer. No extra charge."

Harvey looked through the papers very carefully. Just like a good purchasing agent should. There was extensive language in the voluminous contract that insisted any guinea pigs Globallica bought would be certified free from carcinogenic compounds, that they had not been raised using child labor, and that they would be recyclable to Globallica's exacting specifications. It covered guinea pig transportation and storage costs; grooming standards; warranty claims; and what to do in the case of loss or damage especially in the event of natural disasters, like tidal waves and asteroid strikes. But it didn't say anything about buying guinea pigs with tails…even if they were removed first.

Regardless, Harvey was happy. His unsolvable problem had been solved. He countersigned a copy of the Purchase Order for Señor Jimenez and stuffed the original in Lopez's mouth to carry home.

Jimenez moved out of the light, into the shadows, his voice disappearing with him into the foggy darkness. "Si, moy bien. It's been nice doing business with you, Señor Drinkwater."

Harvey had heard that one before.

So had Lopez. Even with a mouthful of paper, his growling moved up an octave.

***

"Bunny, I still can't figure out why Mr. Hutchin comes here every day."

"Isn't it obvious, Harvey? To report his savings."

"But he doesn't have any. He never does."

"Doesn't matter. Kendall wants him here until he can find some."

"What savings are we trying to get from him?"

"Well, Kendall thinks it's very important. Because Bjorn thinks it's very important. Because Talus said it's important. Savings on...dirt."

"Dirt?"

"Yes, Harvey...dirt. Remember the empty file?"

How could Harvey forget it? It was the only file that wouldn't give him carpal tunnel syndrome when he carried it.

"Well, a year ago, Talus made a big speech about it."

"About dirt?"

"Well, it contained dirt."

"Like a potted plant?"

"No...more like your potted biker."

Bunny sensed Harvey's expression cried out for her to elaborate. So she did. "Talus made a big speech about finding savings throughout the supply chain. I think his words went something like this, 'You miserable cretins, you're missing the most obvious savings of all: from the suppliers to our suppliers. They're hiding savings from us. And I want you to scour the planet to find them. I want you to drill deeper, skim smarter, burrow bigger, tunnel tougher. I want you to scrape and claw, and dig your way down through the supply chain for those savings. I want you to dig right down to…the dirt.' Then the Great Seal of the Vice President of Purchasing was imprinted on Executive Order Number 7,593 and 'Drilling Down to the Dirt' became the law."

Harvey squirmed in his seat. He still couldn't make the connection between Executive Order Number 7,593 and Mert Hutchin, the crippled farmer. Well, he wasn't crippled when the Executive Order was issued. But he is now.

"Talus," Bunny continued, "then commanded Bjorn, Executive Director of All Commodities, to be his designated champion to find savings on dirt. Bjorn commanded his legion of commodity managers—like our fashion leader and departmental poster child for incompetence in management, Kendall Swick—to drill down in every commodity group to get to the dirt. Kendall told Bjorn that since we were the Department of Miscellaneous Commodities, there couldn't be any better department to buy a commodity as miscellaneous as dirt. So he committed us to find the savings on dirt, the real kind. And that lead us to Mr. Hutchin."

"He digs tunnels?"

"No, Harvey. He's a farmer. And on his farm he has a lot of dirt. That's what farms have, generally speaking. And he sells it. Composted manure, potting soil, fill for construction sites. Kendall found out he sells dirt to the landscape company that has our gardening contract. So therefore he'd found our supplier of dirt."

"But Mr. Hutchin hasn't brought any dirt in with him. I've checked. His paper bag contains a bacon sandwich. And a Tupperware container of pickled beetroot. Every day."

"No, Harvey. It's not his dirt we want. It's the dirt on his savings."

"He has dirt on his shoes. Does that count?"

"No, Harvey. It doesn't." Bunny was about to recommend a night school course to Harvey. But she wasn't quite sure on what.

"But he says he has savings some days and not others."

"Harvey, Mr. Hutchin doesn't have any savings. If he had any, Darcy Gillemott would have found them by now."

"Then why does he show up every day?"

"Like most farmers, he gets up before sunrise, milks his cows and feeds his pigs, then delivers his dirt to the landscaping company in the early hours of the morning. When he's done, he comes in here for his mid-morning break."

"Why?"

"Because we give him a free cup of coffee. And he's a farmer. They don't like to pay for things. Especially if they're free. And because he likes company. He lives alone, you see."

Bunny's tutorial on dirt came abruptly to an end. A commotion erupted outside Harvey's office.

Cries of 'Oh my God, we're doomed!' echoed down the aisle.

Bunny popped her head into the hallway. Pretzel Makers had blocked every available exit from the Department of Miscellaneous Commodities. Others were scouring the cubicles with metal detectors and ground penetrating radar.

DragonForce and Bjorn entered Harvey's small office. Outside in the aisle way, Johann Thorsveld stood guard, stun gun at the ready. "We've come about your savings, Drinkwater," Her Depravity demanded. "Time's up, chump."

Kendall Swick was lurking in a cube across the aisle from Harvey's office, notepad in hand to record Harvey's last words for the departmental archives. Todd Hertle reluctantly videotaped the proceedings under the watchful eyes of the Pretzel Makers. They wanted it for a future training video.

"The guinea pig contract?" Harvey squeaked.

"You're a quick learner, Drinkwater," observed Bjorn. "Now cough up those savings you promised or—"

156 · CHARLES A CORNELL

The Pretzel Makers at the door parted to let someone through their ranks. Despite their faults, they respected the hierarchy of command. Purchasing Vice President Talus brushed past them. "He's a quick learner, Bjorn. That's what makes him such a fast-tracker," Talus said. "Harvey, I have great confidence in you. You're not going to let me down, are you?"

Angus McCalliwag whispered to Sun Ho Gung, "Normally, I dunna reckon yer piss is worth a pinch o' spider shit. But I think now might be an exception, Gungie Ho, laddie. Our Harvey's time has truly come. Ha' yee a way to make it a little less painful for him?"

Sun Ho Gung used the distraction of Talus's entrance to slip into the coffee station and put the kettle on. He took a teabag out of a securely locked metal tin whose label read, 'Suicide Leap Off the Great Wall'.

But Harvey wouldn't need it.

"Is this what you've come for?" Harvey replied as he opened the top drawer of his desk. He took out a piece of paper, still a little damp from foggy sea spray, and handed it to Bjorn.

Bjorn read the first sentence to the group, "This Purchase Order signifies a binding Supply Agreement between Globallica and The Guinea Pig Import Corporation of New Jersey LLC for a continuous supply of processed guinea pig meat to the enclosed specifications for the agreed price of—"

Talus peered over Bjorn's shoulder and let out a whoop. "I told you, Bjorn! I told you! I have an eye for talent. Drinkwater has delivered the savings. At exactly half the current price!"

A look of unmitigated shock crossed over Bjorn's face.

DragonForce scowled with an icy anger that even a pissed off polar bear would envy.

"He changed suppliers," the two executive directors said a cappella.

"Harvey Drinkwater has delivered on his promise," Talus crowed. "Time to deliver on yours."

Arkon emerged from the crowd with the Great Seal of Globallica Purchasing in hand. Talus produced a document for Bjorn and DragonForce to sign. Arkon applied melted wax to the paper, then pressed the Great Seal until its mark stood proud.

It was official and irrevocable.

Purchasing had a new executive development candidate.

Harvey Drinkwater had been promoted again.

Sun Ho Gung flushed his suicide tea down the sink.

CHAPTER TWENTY

The towering pile of books in Harvey's hands teetered precariously on the verge of falling as he struggled to get them through the door of his new executive office on the 129th floor of the Globallica Tower.

"My, Mr. Drinkwater, when will you ever find the time to read all these?" Nancy asked. Nancy Butterworth was Talus's executive secretary and she was laden down with his books too.

Harvey's colleagues had given him a long list of essential reading to groom his impressionable executive mind. Everyone had contributed ideas to create his library.

Aziz Mukquat said Harvey couldn't be an executive without at least touching a book on logic. The first book Aziz recommended sounded like a simple read. Aziz said that's what the author intended it to be and was perfect for today's fast-paced business environment: *Logic In The Modern Corporation: A One Page Executive Summary*. The same author had written a slightly longer one: *Confidence Games: Ponzi's Principles Adapted For Business*. Harvey liked games.

Kendall Swick had recommended, *Creating the Ultimate Supplier Negotiation: Autopsy Techniques From The LA Coroner's Office*. Kendall said this was the most influential book he'd read on his way up the ranks in Purchasing. Kendall also added, *The CEO And The Psychopath: Two Peas from the Same Pod?*.

Harvey's fellow 'slaves' wanted him to broaden his thinking, read beyond the latest fads in management, expand his universe, control his bladder.

Angus McCalliwag suggested, *Feeding Habits Of The Great White Shark* as well as *Ethics Without Borders*. Somehow the two were connected. Just like *Nero's Fiddling Tips For Managers* and *Famous Fire-Fighters Of The Roman Empire*, another of the Scot's 'must-haves' for the bookshelf.

Sun Ho Gung recommended these gems: *Chinese Secrets Of The Gastro-Intestinal Tract* and the intriguing *Alien Abductions: What The Vatican Doesn't Want You To Know*. Harvey wasn't sure about the first one. His breakfast muesli was behaving itself. But the second book sounded like it contained essential safety tips.

Bunny Warren thought Harvey should connect with his feminine side so she recommended: *Men Are From Jupiter, Women Are From Pluto: A Post-Apocalyptic View Of Inter-Personal Relationships*. Sounded like a good fit with alien abductions. Maybe it was the sequel.

"Hm, this one sounds very useful, Mr. Drinkwater. And it has such colorful photographs," commented Nancy, flipping through *A Demolition Expert's Guide To The Top Ten Mistakes in Feng Shui*.

"Sun Ho Gung recommended that one too," Harvey noted as he perused *The Art Of Public Executions: Genghis Khan's Thoughts On Failures In Marketing*.

Todd Hertle had advised Harvey to stock up on practical 'how-to' books. So Harvey added these to his list: *What You Should Know About Accents And Disguises But Were Afraid To Ask*, along with *The Idiot's Guide To Covert Videography*.

Surprisingly, even Johann Thorsveld made a contribution. He said an educated prey made the hunt more satisfying. Whatever that meant. Thorsveld's book-of-the-month selection was *Interrogation for Fun and Profit*. But with so many newly hired Pretzel Makers that one was on back order.

These books were generally thick and heavy. Serious reading could do permanent damage. Like the time Harvey dropped a book on his foot. So Harvey also picked up new releases of his favorite graphic novels, *Captain Courageous and his Sidekick, Bruce*, as well as *Space*

Druids, and *Adventures of The Lava Midgets, Super Heroes from the Center of the Earth.*

Nancy loaded the last volume into the tiger maple book case. Harvey stood back to admire his newly stocked library. And knocked the fruit basket off his tiger maple desk. If he could manage to skim through at least the first chapter of each book, Harvey thought, he would do justice to his new label of 'fast-tracker'. He'd even bought *Training Secrets of Olympic Jay Walkers* just to be sure.

"These must have cost a fortune, Mr. Drinkwater," Nancy gasped.

"Yes, Miss Butterworth, they did cost a fortune. And now I have a big problem."

"What problem?"

"If I don't get some money soon, I won't be able to pay my credit card bills. All forty-seven of them. I've been at Globallica over two months, but no-one has given me a paycheck yet."

"Really, Mr. Drinkwater? That must be some kind of mistake. But it shouldn't be too hard to fix."

"It shouldn't?"

"No, just see someone at Payroll Express."

"Payroll Express?"

"Yes, on the Bundled Services Floor. On the Fourth Level. Below Finance."

Finance? Harvey made the connection. *Oo.. Daphne!*

"I think I'll get it fixed right now, Miss Butterworth."

Harvey bounded out of his office with a renewed level of energy. He sure is a go-getter, Nancy thought. No time like the present for Globallica's newest fast-tracker.

* * *

Level Four: Bundled Services. The elevator opened into what Harvey thought was a food court but without the enticing aromas. In the center of the floor was a huge open area with bench seats like you see in airports. The room was filled with people waiting. Around the perimeter of the open space were storefront kiosks that looked like the kind of counters where you could order a submarine sandwich or rent a car.

Above the counters, a weird collection of brightly lit signs shone with a variety of jazzy logos that read 'Trish's One-Hour Consulting', 'Speedy Quik Secretarial Services', 'Accountants-to-Go' and 'Benefits by Bernie', which had a catchy slogan, 'Have You Hugged Your HMO Today?'.

Each desk had its own 'take-a-ticket-and-wait' dispenser. Harvey took the a ticket from the first dispenser he saw, not knowing the difference, and when his number was called, he ordered a crew of account temps to conduct an overnight inventory of his book collection. And then he hired a secretary, which was a very executive thing to do. Sparkles was her name. And she did. Well, the diamond in her pierced tongue did, according to the photo in her Personnel file.

He was finally led to the ticket dispenser for 'Payroll Express'. Next to the Payroll Express kiosk was a gray steel door with a small, plain black plastic sign with white lettering that said, 'Payroll Express Deluxe'. He took a ticket for Payroll Express, and after patiently waiting for half an hour found out he'd been standing in the wrong line if there was such a thing, considering he'd been sitting down. But it wasn't a problem. Quite the contrary.

"Sir," the young man behind the counter said. "Your employment status based on your security card—hmm, yes, a vice president, very nice—entitles you to use our special service, Payroll Express Deluxe."

Harvey looked at the gray door the counter attendant was pointing to. The one with the small, black plastic sign.

"You don't have to wait," the attendant said.

"I don't?"

"No, sir. Just swipe your card in the reader beside the door and go right in."

Harvey did. Inside, a red velvet carpet took him down a long corridor which opened up into what Harvey thought was a hotel lobby. It even had a Concierge desk where a smartly dressed man and woman—in bellhop-type clothing, complete with red waistcoats, bow ties and white gloves—greeted him. The man gave him a *Wall Street Journal*. The woman gave him a fruit basket, which was great because by now the fruit he'd knocked over in his office must be showing its bruises.

"This way, sir. Do you know the name of your Personal Wealth Consultant?"

"I didn't know I had one."

"Of course, you do, sir. Let me have your card and I will double check." The lady concierge took his security card and swiped it through a terminal sitting on top of an antique mahogany Louis XIV table. The gentleman concierge buffed up Harvey's shoes while he waited.

"Oh, I see the confusion, sir," the lady concierge said. "You have a new Personal Wealth Consultant assigned to you."

"I do?" Harvey never knew he had an old one. But he did know he didn't have any personal wealth. That much he was sure of.

"Yes, follow me. I'll introduce you."

Harvey followed the lady concierge through a set of tall mahogany doors into an office where there were small private meeting rooms on all sides.

"Take a seat in here, Mr. Drinkwater and your Personal Wealth Consultant will see you right away."

A few minutes later, the lady concierge returned with another young lady. As soon as he saw who it was, Harvey's knees went wobbly. And it had nothing to do with the masseuse that had been working on the tension knot in his neck while he waited.

"Daphne?" he drooled.

"Monsieur Drinkwater?"

"Oh, very good, sir. You do know her." The lady concierge brushed lint off Harvey's jacket and retreated demurely into the background to leave him in private with his Personal Wealth Consultant, Daphne DuBois.

"Such a surprise to see you here, Monsieur Drinkwater."

"I thought you worked in Finance, Daphne?"

"I did. But I was laid off last week. I have a friend who works in Payroll Express who helped me get this new job. I'm happy I left Finance. This is a much nicer place to work, Monsieur Drinkwater."

"Please, call me Harvey. I'm not quite used to being called Mr. Drinkwater yet. Maybe when you get to know me better, you can call me Mr. Drinkwater."

She giggled. "Très jolie, monsieur. That's funny. Okay. Bien, I will call you Harvé." She was so nice. And spoke like a soft, buttery croissant. "Now what can I help you with, Harvé?"

"Well, you see, it's kind of an embarrassment, really. It's about my bank account. It's empty."

"No? Pas possible, Harvé . Let me check for you." Daphne took his card and swiped it through her terminal. "But Harvé, your accounts are not empty."

"Accounts? I only have one. And I'm pretty sure it's almost empty. How many do I have?" Harvey peered over her shoulder as she scrolled through an elaborately designed personal finance website.

"Quite a few. Liechtenstein, Cayman Islands, Bahamas, Belize, Luxembourg…"

"First Third Ninth Bank of Big Buffalo Knuckles?"

"Non, Harvé. That must be a new one. Do you want me to add it?"

Harvey produced a crumpled yellow post-it note from his shirt pocket. He'd written his Big Buffalo Knuckles bank account number on it. He gave the note to Daphne. "I need my paycheck deposited in this one, please."

"All of it?"

Now this was a strange question indeed. He only had one bank account and he presumed he had only one paycheck. Well, actually he had no paycheck. Not yet. *What did she mean? All of it?*

"Um…I guess so," he replied. "Yes, please. All of it, I guess."

"You're sure, Harvé? Right now, you have your paycheck split up and deposited in many different accounts under an assumed name, Bob Gerson. Are you sure you want all of it to go into this one new account?"

So that was the problem. No wonder he didn't have any money. Globallica was depositing his paycheck to the wrong account. "Well, yes. I need money right now. To pay a few bills."

"Mais oui. Of course, Harvé. That's what I am here to do. Help you manage your personal wealth. It will only take a minute. Shall I transfer all of your balances into this one account?"

"Sure. Sounds like a good idea."

Daphne's keystrokes were as gentle and as sweet as her bonny French disposition. In an instant, she solved Harvé's problem. Au revoir unpaid VISA bills. At least for him. Someone else now had his problem. A big one. A person named Gerson.

Daphne gave him a printout confirming the transactions. He doubled checked. And triple checked. And double checked again. Yes, she'd used the right account number. And it was the First Third Ninth Bank of Big Buffalo Knuckles, not the Third First Fifth Bank of Big Billy's Pig Knuckles, which was always causing confusion with bank tellers.

Harvey gawked at the printout. Now he knew why he'd been sent to a Personal Wealth Consultant. He now had some personal wealth to consult with. All *seventy million* dollars worth of personal wealth. And an additional half million dollars to look forward to in his paycheck every month.

Harvé invited Daphne to dinner. At the Ocean City Ritz Carlton. And why not? Because today, Harvé Drinkwater officially became an executive. With a bank account to match.

CHAPTER TWENTY-ONE

Globallica's vice president of Purchasing had apparently at least one thing in common with Johann Thorsveld. They were both hunters. But there was a difference in the way Talus and Johann displayed their game trophies. Thorsveld preferred a style Todd Hertle called, 'The Dancing Bear Exhibit'. Shackled at the neck. Trained to raise its paws on command. And still breathing. Talus on the other hand, preferred a more passive display and decorated his office accordingly. Harvey called the style, 'The Museum of Dead Animal Heads'.

"Well, Harvey," Talus said. "Nancy tells me you've settled in nicely. Everything to your liking? Comfortable?"

Harvey couldn't be more comfortable. His office was exactly as he dreamt it. A *Wall Street Journal* arrived on his desk every day. So did a fresh basket of fruit. Tiger maple furniture. Corinthian leather chair. There were no cube partitions. The only problem was the view. He was several floors below Talus. Which represented the boundary between sunshine and gloom. His outlook was usually gray with overtones of smog. But everyone had to make sacrifices on the way to the top. It was Harvey's turn.

"No complaints, Mr. Talus, sir."

"Harvey, you've proven your potential. It's time to take the next step."

"Next step?"

Talus beamed with pride at the awestruck young executive. "A department of your own."

Harvey had learned so much in such a short time. Incisive cutting edge negotiation skills. Razor sharp presentation techniques. Extraordinary evasive tactics. He oozed readiness for the next challenge. He'd even learned to control his drool.

"It's not going to be an easy assignment. It will truly test your abilities. But if you win this battle—which I'm confident you will— you'll be ready to handle even greater responsibilities."

Harvey was a little intimidated. By the snarling head of a dead wild boar perched above Talus. But agreeing with Talus wasn't difficult. "Okay."

"I bet you can't wait to know what I've planned for you." Talus grinned. His eyes sparkled.

Harvey's eyes on the other hand resembled the 'deer-in-the headlights-look' of the 'deer-who-stayed-looking-in-the-headlights-too-long' that hung over Talus's desk. Next to the dead wild boar.

"Okay."

"Well, Harvey, I can tell you're a student of organizational behavior. A connoisseur of the human condition. I'm right, aren't I?"

"Okay."

"I thought so. There are misfits in every large organization. They exist. I know, why, you ask. Why?"

"Okay…why?"

"It takes all kinds of people to run a corporation the size of Globallica, Harvey. All kinds. Some you might meet on the street and dismiss as life's pathetic little losers. Well, they work right here."

"They do?"

"Yes, I know, it's amazing. Hard to believe, isn't it? But it's true. You see, Harvey, Globallica is like a large ecosystem. It's survival depends on the symbiotic relationship of a whole range of organisms, however humble and meaningless, living in harmony for the common good."

"Okay, Mr. Talus. If you say so. I think. So what will my new department buy? Aquariums?"

Talus laughed. Add quick wit to Harvey Drinkwater's résumé. Must be the Ivy League education. "No, Harvey. These poor creatures have strange habits, anti-social tendencies, poor bladder control."

"Sounds perfect…for me."

"I knew you'd be up to the challenge."

Nancy Butterworth chose an odd time to interrupt them. Harvey soon learned that oddly timing interruptions were a requirement of her job. And she was good at it.

"Talus, the travel agency says you can save two hundred dollars on your round-the-world airline ticket if you make another stop. Where would you like to stay?"

"Choices?"

"Bora Bora. Phuket. Sun City, South Africa. Casablanca."

"Sun City. I can tour a diamond mine. They give out free samples. And then I can shoot that gnu I've always wanted."

"Perfect. And that puts you in the right hemisphere for the Gaucho Carnival in Buenos Aires."

"But I must be in Amsterdam on the fifth, Nancy…I can't miss that trade show."

"Of course, Talus. Won't be a problem."

"Fine. And Nancy, has the armory finished making my samurai suit?"

"Yes. And the Japanese ambassador wants you to wear it to your bon voyage party."

"Do I have to?"

"It'll break it in."

"Good point. And my surfing lessons?"

"The company jet will pick you up tomorrow and fly you to L.A. You'll get back in time for the Savings Board."

"Sounds like you've taken care of everything as usual."

Nancy Butterworth turned to Harvey as she left, smug satisfaction written all over her face. "Sorry, for the interruption, Mr. Drinkwater."

"No problem."

Travel guides to Japan and Australia sat on Talus's desk along with the latest issue of Condé Nast and a copy of the cookbook *Kill It and Grill It.*

"You're going on vacation, Mr. Talus, sir?"

"No, Harvey, a round-the-world business trip. They're dedicating a Shinto shrine to me in Kyoto. Australian Supplier Conference in Brisbane. Guest of the Argentinean President. Then a rough week in Amsterdam."

"A trade show?"

"Relaxation Therapy Industry Convention. Checking out the latest services. Live demonstrations, promotional videos, private sales booths with dim red lighting. Tedious work. Very tiring physically. But I'll find savings for Globallica if I stay long enough. Our executive benefits contract needs a refresh. In the end, the savings should pay for the trip."

"It's a tough job, Mr. Talus, sir. But somebody's got to do it."

"Spoken like a true executive, Harvey. Don't worry, your rewards will come in due course. Especially after you've tamed the 'Unmentionables'."

"The Unmentionables?"

"Your new department, Harvey. Didn't I mention it?"

How could he? Harvey thought. They're unmentionable. "Mr. Talus, sir? I hate to contradict you but you didn't mention the 'Unmentionables' until you just mentioned them. Just now."

"Quite right, Harvey. Good observation."

"And without mentioning them again, could I ask, who the unmentionable 'Unmentionables' are?"

"Of course. We tried to keep them well fed and integrated into everyday life at Globallica. But they insisted on pursuing their unmentionable activities. So we were forced to rustle them together in one big herd and stick them down there—" Talus pointed down through the clouds to the remnants of the ramshackle harborfront clinging to the Globallica Tower like a large barnacle.

"They're Purchasing people?"

"No. Heaven forbid. Of course they're not. That's the problem. They're a barbaric tribe, Harvey. A rogue department spending money faster than we can save it. Conducting business as heathens. Brazenly flaunting the Laws of Purchasing Unbridled wild horses. Renegade lone wolves. The last frontier of bad purchasing habits for an ambitious executive like yourself to tame."

Harvey peered at the hunting trophies strewn across the office walls. A horse's head with a brass plaque that read, 'With Love, From Your Godfather' appeared to be winking at him. Was that where Talus's dead animal heads had come from? Safaris on the waterfront?

Harvey swallowed an audibly loud gulp of air.

"Courage, my young friend. As you so rightly put it, it's a tough job but somebody's got to do it."

"D-d-down there?"

"I know what you're thinking, Harvey."

"You do?"

"A man of your stature and breeding should be repulsed just by the thought of breathing the air inside those crumbling ruins."

"My new job is d-d-down there?"

"Yes, Harvey," said Talus, his comforting arm wrapped around his young protégé's shoulder. "Bringing religion to the heathens. In an abandoned warehouse. On Wharf Number Nine."

***

Harvey sat quietly in his new office. And for the first time, the gloomy rolling clouds that drifted by his window were more noticeable than his gleaming tiger maple furniture. The clouds blotted out the sun. Harvey fell back into thoughts of the times when the rising Globallica Tower blotted out the sunshine coming through the windows of Dortmann's Zipper Emporium.

He moaned, "If only things were as simple as they were when I was working for Mr. Dortmann."

Sparkles entered with his afternoon snack of warm milk and butter pecan cookies. "Oh, Mr. Drinkwater, you sound so sad. What's the matter?"

"Sparkles, have you ever wondered what it would be like to get something special you've always wanted only to find out when you finally get it, it just doesn't seem to be that special?"

"Sure, Mr. Drinkwater. That happens to me every time I have sex."

Harvey choked on his cookie and milk. He then did an impersonation of an Icelandic geyser. Droplets of milk ran down the silver framed picture of his mother.

"Oh, Mr. Drinkwater. Let me help you wipe that up."

Harvey composed himself and squeaked out a reply, hoping to change the subject. "Well, Talus gave me this assignment. And it's really scary. In fact it's so scary, it's unmentionable."

"Oh, dear. Do you need any help with it, Mr. Drinkwater? Maybe I can help?"

Harvey cringed. He couldn't begin to imagine what the 'Unmentionables' might do to poor Sparkles' closely cropped head of orangey-red hair. Not to mention her pierced tongue. Perhaps they had a trophy room like the one in Talus's office? A gallery of 'unmentionable' conquests. He imagined the Unmentionables' chief strolling up and down these stuffed exhibits, commenting on the significance of his tribe's trophies to a reporter from *The Pygmy Cannibal's Digest*. "And we bagged this one when he delivered pizza. A little chewy around the edges."

"The pizza?"

"Don't be silly."

Harvey turned pale. Transfixed by horrific images bouncing around in his head. *What was he going to do now?*

"Mr. Drinkwater? Mr. Drinkwater? Are you all right?" Sparkles asked.

Fortunately, it was a well-timed time to interrupt. And Nancy Butterworth was good at timely interruptions. "Talus thought you might like these, Harvey," she said, interrupting. "Harvey?"

"He's in some kind of trance, Miss Butterworth."

"Oh, I used to have a boss who did this all the time, Sparkles. It's easy to fix."

"How?"

"I'll show you. Just get me a glass of cold water."

Memories of Hilda and his life at the Zipper Emporium came flooding back. Well in reality, cold water down his pants came flooding back. Right down to his shoes.

"There, Sparkles. See? Everything's better now," Nancy said, the look of smug satisfaction returning.

"Neat trick, Miss Butterworth. I'll remember that."

"You'd better, kiddo. With executives, if it happens once, my guess is it'll happen again."

Harvey's eyes widened. He re-focused on his priorities as only a rising star in the executive ranks could. "Help? Yes, that's a great idea. Get help. But who?"

"Mr. Drinkwater, I used to work in Human Resources," Sparkles said. "People sent in forms all the time to ask if they could hire more help. We shredded most of them. But every now and again when my boss was in a good mood and wasn't firing somebody, we approved a few. And then we posted these job openings on Globallica's website."

Harvey remembered Bunny Warren showing him the on-line job posting system. "Do you think I could post for a Special Assistant?"

"I don't see why not," encouraged Nancy.

"But who would approve it?"

"You, Harvey. Just fill out a form and sign it."

"Really? That simple? Won't it get shredded?"

"No. You're an executive. Those rules don't apply to you."

"They don't?"

Harvey was still a neophyte when it came to wielding the tremendous power bestowed upon him by his new rank in the organization. It boggled his mind. "Can you help me prepare those forms, Sparkles?"

"Of course, Mr. Drinkwater."

Harvey's fear of the unknown was drying up. Time to deal with the spilt milk.

CHAPTER TWENTY-TWO

Harvey fidgeted. It had been two weeks since Talus had given him his new assignment and he hadn't done a thing about it. He knew he had to get started soon. But venturing down to Wharf Number Nine seemed an even more daunting task in the daylight than it had been at night. At least at night, there'd been nobody there. Apart from Juan Manuel Jimenez. And Harvey had Lopez to protect him.

But Harvey couldn't bring Lopez into work during the day. What would Lopez do in between Harvey's appointments? Deliver contracts in his teeth? That was an option. Soil expensive Persian rugs? That was a certainty. But there was no point. Harvey could do both on his own. Lopez might as well stay at home and watch TV.

Talus had left for his round-the-world business trip. When he returned, he expected results. Talus sent Harvey a postcard during an unscheduled stopover in Tibet to remind him. The stopover had bought Harvey some time, three more days. Talus had decided to go on safari in the Himalayas, hoping to bag a Yeti, thankfully. For Harvey, not the Yeti.

Time was running out. And Harvey still hadn't hired his Special Assistant. The whole process had been very disappointing. There must have been something wrong with the way he'd written the job posting. Nobody had responded to it yet. Nobody at all. As Freddie Hogan had said, 'Zip…zero…nada'.

"Sparkles, do you think I need to re-write the job posting?"

"Why, Mr. Drinkwater? I think the job description's pretty accurate, don't you?"

"I'm not sure about this bit: 'Executive seeks someone for an unimaginably difficult Special Assignment whose gruesome ending may come suddenly'."

"Well, that's accurate, isn't it?"

"Yes, but should we have mentioned: 'Responsibilities include saving the skin of your boss while sacrificing your own for the common good'?"

"But we didn't mention anything about the 'Unmentionables', did we?"

"No, Sparkles, technically, you're right. But we implied them in the required qualifications: 'The ideal candidate must possess a death wish and have no fear of heights. Especially while looking down from a wall plaque'."

"You have a point, Mr. Drinkwater. Maybe we should soften it a little."

"How about adding: 'Must have a mouth big enough to hold an apple'? What do you think, Sparkles? It gives it a more human touch, don't you think?"

Nancy interrupted them again, in her usual timely style. "I've just taken a call from Human Resources. They're sending someone up for an interview."

"For my job posting?"

"Boy, you catch on fast."

Harvey and Sparkles jumped around the room. As long as the candidate had a pulse, he or she had the job.

"I've found my Special Assistant!" Harvey squealed.

"You don't want to interview the candidate, Harvey?"

"No, Nancy. Why?"

"To see if they meet the required qualifications?"

"They have a brain function, don't they? Call Human Resources, Nancy and find out."

"No, Harvey. I'm going to call Human Resources and tell them you'll see the candidate right away."

"Oh, Nancy…"

"Hush now, Harvey. You need to be a big boy…and interview the candidate."

"Oh, all right." Harvey sat down and pouted. Being an executive was so stressful.

**

The late afternoon sun burnt through the fog. The mountains in the distance were molehills; cloudy cotton balls clung to their tops. Harvey pressed his nose against the floor-to-ceiling smoked glass. Ocean City stretched from the very edge of the harbor to the very foot of the foothills, a densely packed patch of humanity whose citizens from this height looked like tiny ants as they scurried about their work.

Here he was. Where Harvey dreamt he would be. A position he'd constructed many times in his mind, thought by thought. Irish crystal glass in one hand, half full with Scotch and ice. A pecan cookie in the other. Private secretary. Tiger maple furniture. A fruit basket. He had everything he wanted. He had everything he'd dreamt about.

He touched the tip of his finger to the glass in front of him and pushed. Its resilient surface didn't yield. He wasn't going to fall through the sky and enter Mr. Dortmann's air conditioning ducts. He sipped his Scotch and gasped at its Highland bite. He was getting used to the taste of expensive, aged Celtic drinks. He was becoming the executive his new business cards said he was. But despite the warmth of the Scotch slipping down his throat, a coldness remained. The simple person inside him didn't understand why.

"Mr. Drinkwater? Your interview candidate is here."

Harvey took one last look out of the smoked glass window in front of him and sighed. He said, without turning, "Thank you, Sparkles. I'll see him now."

Footsteps crept across his opulent office and he heard a non-descript little butt plunk down into the chair opposite Harvey's tiger maple desk. Harvey heard the person fidgeting as he waited for Executive Director Harvey Drinkwater to acknowledge the poor sod's wretched presence.

Of all the people in Globallica, only one poor schmuck had responded to Harvey's job posting. Whoever he was, whatever qualifications he had, Harvey burned with a desire to have a bit of companionship when his world came crashing down around him as he tackled the 'Unmentionable' problem. Harvey pivoted around to see who that poor little schmuck had turned out to be.

"*Todd?* Todd Hertle?"

"Hi, Harvey."

"Todd!" Harvey rushed from the window to embrace his old friend, tripped on a corner of the Persian rug, and knocked the fruit basket off his desk.

"Uh, oh."

Harvey picked himself up, brushed a pineapple slice off his Armani suit and smiled at his old friend. "Don't worry, Todd," as he gathered melon bits and orange slices and tried to re-sculpt the basket. "I'll get another one tomorrow. A new suit that is."

On his first day as an executive director, Nancy and Sparkles had gone shopping with him on the Concourse Level to pick out executive-worthy clothes. And for the first time in his miserable life, Harvey didn't care what it cost. His bank account hardly budged as the credit card was swiped, broadcasting his triple platinum credit rating to banks around the world.

"You're here about the job? The Special Assistant?"

"It sounds perfect, Harvey. I have to get out of Supplier Performance Metrics. *Fast.* Data Surgeon? It's like performing abortions on the New York telephone directory."

"Ugh."

"Oh, Harvey, it's horrible. Supplier Performance Metrics? I call it, 'The Department of Explaining Bad Data'. I just can't wait to get out of there."

"But aren't you afraid, Todd? Don't you know how dangerous this assignment's going to be?"

"Dangerous? Do you know how dangerous *I* would become if I stay there any longer? If one more moronic manager asks me to re-calculate the reliability growth curve for savings on double-sided flypaper, I'll go postal."

"So that means you're ready for a change?"

"Understatement, Harvey. Big understatement."

"Great. You've got the job."

"Which is?"

"The job I posted. That you applied for, Todd." This insightfulness differentiated the executive from the non-executive.

"Special Assistant on a Special Assignment conducting death defying, high altitude, so-scary-it-makes-your-skin-crawl *what*, exactly, Harvey?"

"We have to set up a Purchasing Department for..." Harvey drew close and whispered so quietly no lifeform beyond an inch of Todd's ear would be able to hear. "The 'Unmentionables'."

"The 'Unmentionables'?"

"That's right, Todd. The 'Unmentionables'."

"Who are the 'Unmentionables', Harvey?"

"I'm not sure. No one mentioned it. They just told me they're a gang of dangerous anti-social misfits that have set up a barbaric tribal business inside the warehouse on Wharf Number Nine."

"Wharf Number Nine? I know someone who works in the warehouse on Wharf Number Nine."

"You do?"

"Yeah. Purchasing HR wanted me to work in Wharf Number Nine. But Kendall wouldn't let me go. Said I was too valuable. Said he needed my technical skills to run the International Video Conference. That's the only thing Kendall has ever been right about."

"You know someone who works in Wharf Number Nine?"

"Yeah. Albert Duddenheim. I'll call him and set up an appointment for us."

Harvey's new Special Assistant was wasting no time. He sure knew how to hit the job running.

CHAPTER TWENTY-THREE

The location of the lair of the 'Unmentionables' was a vision of contrasts. The warehouse on Wharf Number Nine sat between the stainless steel and smoked glass tower of Globallica's headquarters and a flotilla of multi-million dollar executive yachts moored in the marina in front of it. The warehouse's flat roof had sprouted green fur. Its punky window sashes sagged with dry rot. And its brickwork, once red, had been aged by the sea to the color of elephant skin. This ancient relic of Ocean City's former Cannery Row had the appearance of a moldy hunk of meatloaf decaying on a 22-carat gold dinner plate.

All of the building's windows had either been boarded up or painted black so no natural light could enter and no innocent bystanders could peer through them. Like Harvey and Todd were trying to do.

"Harvey, why am I carrying this fire extinguisher on my back and wearing a scuba mask?"

"I saw it in the movies, Todd. If any floating green blobs pass through these walls, we can trap them in this..." Harvey had brought his Ghostbusters lunchbox with him. "We put it on the ground, open it up, and then you blast them with the goop from the fire extinguisher."

Todd Hertle's face puckered.

"Well, it's not an exact replica, Todd. But it should work."

"Oo-kay, Harvey. Now that makes much better sense."

The entrance to Wharf Number Nine—a set of weather-beaten barn-style cedar double doors—clung precipitously to the building's brickwork. A verdigris-stained brass plaque tried unsuccessfully to identify the contents of the creaky old structure. Harvey squinted. The plaque's wording was hidden under a thick layer of sea spray-produced patina. "I can't make it out, Todd. We have to go back."

"Harvey. Don't be a wuss. I didn't lug this stuff all this way for nothing. Let me try this—" Todd blasted the sign with frigid gas from the fire extinguisher. The spray frosted the plaque's surface to reveal the hidden lettering: 'New Product Development. Ring To Enter'.

"Ring to enter? Where?"

Todd pointed to the toilet chain dangling beside the plaque.

"Here?" Harvey pulled the ceramic handle down and a sound like an air raid siren drove the seagulls off the warehouse roof.

They waited.

"I don't think they heard us, Todd. Let's go."

"Harvey, with that blast, I think we just rerouted an oil tanker in mid-ocean. They heard us. Give them time."

The barn doors rattled with the unmistakable sound of a lock and chains being dismantled behind them. Harvey flung the Ghostbusters lunchbox at the foot of the door, opened its lid, scurried back behind Todd and gently pushed him towards the entrance. "As soon as the blobs appear…blast 'em, Todd!"

"Oh, Harvey. Give me a break."

"They're coming out. Quick!"

Light streamed forth from inside the warehouse, blinding the two visitors. Shapes moved in front of the light but Harvey couldn't make out their faces. The cedar doors opened wider and the silhouette of a man stood in the center of the entrance. A bank of bright spotlights shone brilliantly behind him. He stooped down and picked up the lunchbox. "Look, Marla. They brought us a present."

Harvey donned the welder's mask he'd brought for just such an eventuality and aimed his phone in warning. "Stop or I'll shoot." The phone's infrared transmitter beamed across the marina at an executive basking on board his 74-foot Lazzara super-yacht.

"Oh, Marla," the man said. "Turn off the grow lights. Our guests can't see."

"Did you hear that, Todd? Grow lights? They're incubating their young."

"Well, not exactly," said the mysterious figure, who was not so mysterious now. He was an elderly gentlemen with a Moses-like white beard, bald, thick-rimmed black glasses, wearing a long white lab coat. "We grow lettuce."

"Lettuce?" Harvey gasped.

"Albert? Is that you? Dr. Albert Duddenheim?"

"Todd? Todd Hertle?"

"I didn't recognize you with that beard."

"Yes, I know. But it kind of fits the part, doesn't it?"

"What part?" Harvey challenged. "Grand Wizard of the House of the Fried Green Tomatoes? I know your kind, mister! Now jump in this lunchbox!"

Dr. Albert Duddenheim laughed. "Todd, your friend has a strange sense of humor."

"He's not kidding, Albert."

"He's not?"

"It's a long story."

"Come in. I could use a funny story right now. Tell me what you've being doing with yourself, Todd. And bring your odd little friend with you."

"It's Harvey. Harvey Drinkwater. He's my odd little boss, Albert."

"Harvey Drinkwater? *The* Harvey Drinkwater?"

Not again, Harvey thought. He wasn't about to explain the oddity of being the only Harvey Drinkwater in Globallica. Especially to an escaped Druid.

"He's a little spooked, Albert. It's the legend of the 'Unmentionables' that did it, I think."

"Oh, that? Well, we like to perpetuate the myth, Todd. Scares off unwanted visitors. Which is just about everybody. Gives us some peace and quiet. And prevents Globallica's executives from tampering with our work."

Harvey looked up and down the walls inside the warehouse as they were ushered inside. This was not the Trophy Room he expected. There were no wall-mounted plaques anywhere. What there was instead were banks of spotlights like the ones in the ballpark at Ocean City Gooney Bird baseball games, pointing their lights down on rows upon rows of raised box planters.

In the raised beds, packed with dark, loamy soil, the strangest vegetable Harvey had ever seen grew upwards towards the light. Each plant was encased in a shoebox-like plastic envelope. The foliage was light green like lettuce. But each bunch looked like a large pack of cards standing on one end as it grew.

"Yes, it's lettuce, Harvey," Dr. Albert Duddenheim said. He plucked a bunch from inside its box and handed it to the astonished fast-tracker. "Lettuce. With a practical difference."

Harvey fondled the plant, enthralled with its square shape. He peeled off a leaf. It was flat; no bumpy, corrugated, folded curve to be found anywhere along its length. Completely flat.

"Flat?"

"Perfectly flat. And square. For sandwiches, Harvey. Organically grown. Under special lights that accelerate harvesting. With a taste to die for. We've developed the ideal lettuce. Easy to peel off. Easy to store in the fridge."

A studious looking woman had been following them around. "We're calling it the Duddenheim Lettuce in honor of its inventor." She extended her hand and introduced herself, "Marla. Dr. Marla Gorf. Head of Botanical Research."

"So this warehouse is just a big greenhouse?" asked Todd.

"No. There's much more than this," Dr. Duddenheim said. "Come and see."

Harvey munched on the bunch of lettuce like a starving rabbit. It was good. Very good. Even without mayo. And bread. And head cheese.

Duddenheim directed Harvey and Todd through a set of doors behind some enormous pallets of potting soil. Inside the next set of rooms, was another world all together. A world of whirring, buzzing, humming mini-machines dancing across work benches crammed full of discarded bits of multi-colored electrical wire, filaments of tin-snipped sheet metal and jagged shards of Plexiglas. A Noah's Ark of odds and ends. Every conceivable nut, bolt, cog, sprocket, clip, clamp, pin, rivet, screw, bracket, diode, light bulb, and circuit board were strewn about the tabletops, on the floor, in parts bins and boxes. A kaleidoscope of mechanical hodgepodge. It was Santa's Workshop meets The Terminator.

"Our Robotics Lab," announced Dr. Duddenheim.

Harvey fingered his phone nervously behind his back. Perhaps the friendly 'Saturday Morning Mr. Science' image Dr. Duddenheim was trying to project was just a clever ruse. Harvey wondered what lay behind the next set of doors. A room full of human brains floating in formaldehyde?

Harvey's fingers walked across one too many keys on his phone. A little bot the size of a small dog, with a snout to match and a mini-satellite dish on its back, snuck up behind him and grabbed the phone out of his hands. The bot raced off into the corner, yipping with a synthetically produced yap, delighted by its prize.

"Hey, my phone!"

"Oh, sorry about that, Harvey. It's programmed to respond to Wi-Fi commands. It's our Home Security Guard Bot, Dobey." The little robot chewed happily on the phone, producing a growing pile of plastic and metal slivers on the floor. "It's not totally house trained yet. We'll get you a new one."

Another little robot, looking like a mutation between a thermos and a miniature upright vacuum cleaner powered by three wheels, advanced towards Harvey's running shoe. It extended a pencil-sized probe into a crevice of the trainer's sole.

"Do you have a dog, Harvey?"

"Yes...Lopez."

"Have you recently stepped in something of his? Something he's left behind?"

"Like?"

"Like...his poo?"

Harvey blushed, embarrassed. He meant to clean it off. He pointed to the robot. "What's it doing?"

"Detecting methane. It has a sensing module that can analyze seven hundred types of organic emissions." Dr. Duddenheim checked the readouts appearing on his tablet. "Your dog's a Chihuahua?"

"What's it doing now?"

"Cleaning your shoes."

The little robot had stuck out a lever and had gently raised Harvey's foot off the ground. Another robotic arm with a whisk-like end sent out a sucking vacuum sound as it extended itself into the tread of his running shoe and removed the doggy do.

"That's amazing," Harvey exclaimed.

"The bot follows its owner and his dog around and when the mutt does a whoopsy, comes along and cleans it up. Stores the droppings in the container on its side." Duddenheim pointed. "Where genetically engineered microbes break down the poo into methane and other harmless by-products. The methane is consumed by a fuel cell which powers the robot. No batteries. Completely eco-friendly. We call him, Vinnie, the Poo-Bot."

"Sweet," admired Todd.

"Where can I buy one?" asked Harvey, his credit card burning a hole in his pocket. Or was it the fact he was getting too closed to a welding torch?

Duddenheim's smile turned into a frown. "Just another brilliant effort to advance civilization that will waste away inside Globallica's bureaucracy, I'm afraid. These bots will probably never go on sale to the general public. Most of our new products never do. Marketing's not interested in them, not sexy enough. We can't get funding from Finance. We were told they had a cung project of their own that had a higher rate of return and needed very little capital. We can't understand them. They can't understand us. It's like we speak a foreign language."

"Glaswegian?"

"What?"

"Ignore him, Dr. Duddenheim," Todd advised.

"It just doesn't seem right," opined Harvey.

"No, it doesn't," Dr. Duddenheim said as he ushered them through another set of doors. "I guess we have to be grateful they haven't shut us down completely."

In the next room, scientists, engineers and technicians—color-coded by their white, blue and orange lab coats—congregated around tables picking through the remains of a variety of foodstuffs.

"So, what goes on in this lab?" Harvey asked.

"It's our lunchroom."

"Oh."

Dr. Duddenheim gestured to Harvey and Todd. They sat at an empty table. A few moments later, Marla Gorf arrived with a tray holding several cups of coffee and a selection of sodas. "Choose your poison, gentlemen."

A good choice of beverages. An unfortunate choice of words.

Harvey stood up. "I knew it, Todd. *Run!* It's a trap. They're going to remove our brains. And play Scrabble with them."

Uh, oh, here we go again, Todd thought. "Harvey, sit down. Dr. Duddenheim is not interested in your brain. No one is. It's too small for meaningful research."

Harvey settled down. "Good point, Todd."

"Harvey, don't you see what we've just discovered?"

"A lettuce plantation? And a mechanical dog factory?"

"No, Harvey. Think bigger. Much bigger."

Harvey pondered. *Bigger?* OK, bigger. "The Garden of Eden? And a maternity ward for War of the Worlds?"

"No, no, Harvey. You don't get it, do you? It's no wonder they call them the 'Unmentionables'."

"Huh?"

"Don't you see? This place is a threat to every executive in Globallica. Everything here is something they don't understand. They *can't* understand. Their brains won't let them. And worse. They can't control it."

"Worse?" Harvey couldn't believe there was anything worse than an out-of-control brain.

"This is the only place in the whole company that's actually *producing* something. Extraordinary stuff. Stuff with real value."

CHAPTER TWENTY-FOUR

Harvey and Todd strolled along the waterfront by Wharf Number Nine, admiring the setting sun. They were carrying a much lighter load than when they had first arrived. Dr. Duddenheim's scientists had requisitioned the ragtag stuff Harvey and Todd had lugged with them. The paraphernalia was being put to better use in the name of legitimate scientific research.

Harvey and Todd's wanderings lead them past the marina, oblivious to the movement of the 74-foot Lazzara super-yacht, *Neptune's Greed* as it motored out of its executive slip. They were also oblivious to the man and woman on board relaxing in each other's arms on a cushioned settee on the yacht's polished teak deck, champagne flutes in hand.

"Katrina, have the necessary arrangements been made?"

Katrina Borchevski, aka Her Villainy, DragonForce nibbled at the ear of the VP of Human Resources, Bob Gerson until she drew blood.

"Youch, Kay-Bee!"

Katrina's eyes dazzled with deranged enthusiasm as she lapped up the redness trickling down his earlobe. "Bobby, darling. Indulge me in my little pleasures. It'll heal."

"Katrina...the arrangements?"

"How could you ever doubt me, my succulent little spare rib? Of course the necessary arrangements have been made. Haven't my plans been impeccable so far?"

Bob Gerson had to admit they had been. The last two 'Jobs' had been executed to perfection. More precisely, Vice President of

Operations, Charlie Wizzell and VP of Sales, Buzz Margoli had been executed to perfection.

"That 'diving accident' with Wizzell was a stroke of genius, Kay-Bee. Poor old Charlie."

"His contribution to the preservation of endangered Bahamian reef sharks will be duly noted in the minutes of the Sierra Club of Ocean City," Her Wickedness replied.

"And that thing with Buzz Margoli? You must admit that was a bit over the top, don't you think? Even for someone as flamboyant as our vice president of Sales."

"Margoli was such an inspirational speaker, my suckling. Now he'll have something to really trumpet about. I thought it would be a fitting tribute for the old windbag."

VP Buzz Margoli shouldn't have crossed DragonForce at last year's Chairman's Luau in Hawaii. Katrina was okay with the dancing-across-hot-coals routine. It was great fun watching the reactions of the idiots who hesitated. It gave her an adrenaline rush. And hunting the main entrée for the pig roast did fit in well with the rest of her Sports Day agenda which included force-marching overweight tourists up the Mauna Loa volcano. But enrolling Her Sadistic Majesty in a grass skirt-making class was not the right thing for the late Sales VP to do. Now he would eternally regret it.

"He looks so nice in that tutu as he whizzes by Mitchell's office, don't you think?"

"Hasn't anyone noticed that one of their gold-painted angels has gotten a little fat?"

"It'll be our special secret, Bobby," she purred into his swollen ear.

"Tell me, Katrina, what surprise do you have in store for our chairman, Byron Mitchell? And that evil lackey of his." Gerson methodically cursed each syllable of the vice chairman's name. "Bar-ry Gran-duck?"

Vice Chairman Granduck had a permanent place on the top of Bob Gerson's 'Most Hated Rivals' list ever since one of Granduck's management shuffles moved Gerson out of Finance, which he loved, into Human Resources, a position Gerson despised with a passion. This was no way to treat Globallica's star Mergers and Acquisitions wizard. Especially after Bob Gerson had helped negotiate the megamerger with ASSCO, a deal *Investment Banking Today* categorized as 'asset stripping becoming rocket science'.

Soon thereafter, Bob Gerson discovered to his delight, that his profound distaste for Globallica's ruling Politburo headed by Mitchell and Granduck was shared by a kindred spirit. His new girlfriend's career had hit a similar glass ceiling when Talus was promoted over her to become vice president of Purchasing. Katrina didn't like any of the new directions. His style was distinctly 'Roman Emperor'. Hers was instinctively 'Mortal Kombat'. It must have been a generational thing. With so much in common, Bob Gerson and Katrina Borchevski hit it off immediately. It was love at first loathing.

"Well, munchkin," Her Witch's Broom said. "I have a new recipe for Flambéed Loin of Executive Turkey Breast for Two."

"I can't wait to hear it."

"Mix one part hired Middle Eastern terrorist with one part stolen Stinger anti-aircraft missile. Put our two main dishes into a steaming helicopter. Point the launcher. Forty-five degrees to the horizon should be hot enough. Press the button and...voilà! Fireworks accompany our haute cuisine."

"Brilliant, mon petit maniac. Chef would be proud. And when do you plan this culinary surprise?"

"Next week Byron Mitchell and Barry Granduck will be taking the company helicopter for a Board Meeting on the *Floating Palace of the Seas* when the ship sails back into Ocean City from her Pacific cruise. They'll take off just fine. It's the landing that'll be a little tricky."

"Well, that puts us back on schedule, Kay-Bee. This time next week, I'll be in an ideal position to nominate the new chairman...me. And hand-pick the next Board of Directors."

"Don't forget to vote for me for vice chairman, my honey-baked honey," she cooed. "I can't wait to put the 'vice' back into the Office of Vice Chairman."

"What about Talus, dearest bloodsucker? I almost forgot about him. Has he had his hunting accident yet?"

"No. He escaped."

"Escaped?"

"We borrowed one of Bjorn's gorillas. It was not a Yeti but Bjorn's anthropologists added some makeup and prosthetics and said it would do. Besides, Yetis are so hard to find these days, you have no idea. Training it to attack a man carrying a gun was easy. Teaching it to break him apart like a wishbone was difficult. Gorillas are really more gentle than they look." Katrina slurped a sliver of liver then cracked the chopsticks in two to make her point.

"Kay-Bee, darling. You're losing me. What went wrong? How did Talus escape?"

"We didn't expect him to take a detour. He went looking for a fabled Tibetan brothel and found it. Stayed too long. The gorilla froze to death in a blizzard."

"Bummer."

"Don't worry, my saucy appetizer. Plan 'B' will work just as well."

"Plan 'B'?"

"Talus eventually made it to Amsterdam. Johann Thorsveld flew over to Holland to make sure the buffoon finds the right 'services' at the Relaxation Therapy Convention. Sweetmeat, let me tell you, with Talus's fetishes, it's like taking candy to a baby."

"You're deliciously wicked. So what's Plan 'B'?"

"'B'…as in bondage. Talus loves it. We'll just forget to untie him. Simple."

"Binding and gagging sounds like good sport. But we need a permanent fix. We don't want any residual votes on the Board voting against us."

"Don't worry, Lamb Chops. Titus won't be tied to a bed, he'll be tied to the tracks the Amsterdam to Paris Express travels on."

"Katie, how on earth do you think these things up?"

"My cultured upbringing. Daddy was Curator of the Spanish Inquisition Museum in Moscow. As a child, I had a lot of free time and a season pass. So Kidney Lips, despite a few small setbacks, everything's progressing perfectly."

Bob Gerson raised his champagne flute in triumph. "Here's to the next chairman and vice chairwoman of Globallica."

"I'll drink to that," Her Psychoticness said.

In the distance, Harvey sauntered aimlessly back into the Globallica Tower, satisfied with his day's work with the 'Unmentionables' and oblivious to the conspiracy that was brewing. It wouldn't be for long. Oblivious that is. Fate was watching over him.

On *Neptune's Greed*, Bob Gerson and Katrina Borchevski sailed insanely into the sunset, singing each other's praises. On top of the warehouse on Wharf Number Nine, seagulls added another layer of crap to the crusty moss on the roof. The universe was beginning to unfold in exactly the way Fate had ordained it would.

CHAPTER TWENTY-FIVE

When Barry Granduck was a young lad he really wanted to grow up to be a truck driver. Not a pickup truck. Or a delivery truck. A *big* truck. The bigger the better. Maybe not as big as the ones in open pit coal mines. They couldn't be driven on regular highways. But a monster tandem 18-wheeler. Hauling petrochemicals. That would do just fine, thank you very much. Ferrari red cab. Brightly polished chrome wheels and lug nuts. Twin chrome stacks. Sleeper cabin with a converted ship's foghorn on top to make sure everyone knew to get out of his way.

Psychological research says most males whose height borders on 'tall pygmy' status, like Barry Granduck's, have the same 'small-guy-drives-big-truck' fantasy. Almost all of them become accountants. Like Barry Granduck. All five-foot-one inch of him. What he lacked in height he made up for in bravado. It helped to have beady eyes, a constantly serious, frowning expression, and the valuable mentorship of Chairman Byron Mitchell.

Vice Chairman Barry Granduck had climbed the corporate ladder the old-fashioned way. He'd married the boss's daughter. But that didn't mean he wasn't skilled. No, siree. Complicated derivative trading was his forte. He could leverage a buyout with the best of them. And generating balance sheet assets while suppressing off-balance sheet liabilities was a talent worthy of an Olympic gold medal in wire fraud.

Barry had been born to do the job of vice chairman. When he was a youngster, he'd honed his skills by forcing the parents of his Monopoly opponents into legally binding liens to bankroll their bankrupt kids' game portfolios. After that, running a large publicly traded company was just a matter of mathematical extrapolation. Putting it all together, Barry Granduck was the ideal right-hand man for a chairman more interested in his collection of rare 17th and 18th century timepieces than running the largest corporation in America.

Barry Granduck had masterminded a history-making financial trading pyramid the likes of which had not been seen since the Dutch discovered tulips. "Lincoln, are we ready for the quadruple witching hour on the markets next week?"

Lincoln Ferndale tapped the keys of his laptop to confirm his trading entries for Z-COT's recent massive cross-commodity hedge. "Barry, when we squeeze the water buffalo dung market with our simultaneous call-sell, put-straddle position, my spreadsheet estimates it will bankrupt Uganda in about forty-five minutes."

"Fantastic. And you've shorted the Zambezi Exchange?"

"Every stock. At a value twenty times greater than the GDP of the countries that make it up."

"Excellent, Ferndale. Truly excellent. This trade will transcend the previous record speculative bubble in Asian currencies by at least eight billion dollars. When we're finished, Globallica won't just make the African market, we'll rule it. Did you know the King of Swaziland has twelve wives? Monarchy has its privileges, Lincoln. No question about it."

"Can I have Tanzania?"

"It's yours, my friend."

Lincoln Ferndale pumped his fists in the air. "Cha-ching!"

A call from Amsterdam interrupted Barry Granduck. "Talus, is that you? Where are you? I can hardly hear you."

Barry Granduck and Talus, the VP of Purchasing had been reluctant allies in the takeover of ASSCO several years ago. Talus had a soft spot for Vice Chairman Barry Granduck. Actually, he had a soft spot for the vice chairman's first wife, an ASSCO board member. That pillow talk had been invaluable. Ratting on the opposition's strategies proved Talus's loyalty to the takeover deal's eventual victors, Barry Granduck and Byron Mitchell. The sex-addicted purchasing executive believed his bedtime espionage had made him a lifelong confidante of Barry Granduck's. In truth, Barry was about as interested in Talus's sex life as he was in the fermentation schedule of Stilton cheese.

"It's that goofball from Purchasing," Granduck said, as he looked over Lincoln Ferndale's shoulder at the numbers on his laptop. "The nitwit is worried about missing the previews for the Board of Directors. I'll just be a minute while I figure out what he wants me for." The interruption was about as welcome as a termite at a wood carver's convention.

"You won't make it back in time? Yeah, it's okay to send a substitute, Talus," Granduck said. "I'll call your secretary. What's that noise in the background? Get some grease on that swing. Good bye."

*** ·

"Mr. Drinkwater? Mr. Drinkwater? Wake up."

"What is it, Sparkles? What time is it?"

"It's 9 o'clock in the morning."

"I had such a busy day yesterday. I must have dozed off."

"You just got here. I brought you a coffee and a donut. And a message."

Harvey looked at the scrawl on the pink message slip. "Attempt a prettier nutting?"

"Attend a preview meeting, Mr. Drinkwater. My handwriting's not that bad, is it?"

"Who's it from?"

Frustrated, Sparkles grabbed the note back and pointed to the line that said, *From.*

"Toby? I don't know a Toby. Do I?"

"Talus. It's from Talus. You know, your boss?"

"Oh. Okay. What's a preview meeting?"

"Ugh." Sparkles flung the note at Harvey and stormed out of the room. "I give up," he heard her say in the distance.

Harvey called Nancy Butterworth.

"In fifteen minutes, Nancy? I can't get a presentation ready in fifteen minutes. I don't need to? You mean I just sit there? Doing nothing? Yes, I know I'm supposed to just listen. But what if I can't? What if I fall asleep? No one will notice? So why attend? Okay, okay. Yes, I know, Nancy. I'm an executive. That's what I do."

Harvey put down the phone. He put a copy of *Space Druids* in his briefcase and wandered out of his office. He asked Sparkles for directions to the conference room where the previews of the presentations to the Board of Directors were taking place.

"Directions? Ugh! Mr. Drinkwater, you're *so* demanding."

***

A gilt-edged single page piece of paper with the meeting agenda sat neatly in front of every executive's designated place. Harvey hadn't noticed. He was reading how Regula-4 had been liberated in the Perseid Wars by Parsack, Commander of the Inter-Galactic Troop Transport, *The Margueritaville*.

"Has the representative from Purchasing arrived?" asked Vice Chairman Barry Granduck.

Harvey didn't shift from his seat, next to the tray of pecan cookies on the conference room's back credenza.

A black-suited, black-tied financial analyst took the hint and stepped out of the conference room to look for Purchasing's representative in the corridor. He re-entered the conference room and shrugged. Another black suit whispered in Granduck's ear.

"Oh, who? Harvey Drinkwater? Okay. Is there a Harvey Drinkwater here?"

Harvey perked up. "Yes?"

"Talus wants you to take the Purchasing seat."

"Take it where?"

"Here."

"But it's already here."

"But you're not in in yet, are you?"

"Where?"

"Here." Barry Granduck pointed to the chair where Purchasing should be seated. "Here. Right here is where you should be."

"You want me *there*?"

"Yes."

"But I'm okay here. Really I am."

"You, whoever you are who is 'there', please trade 'there' for 'here' and park your butt *here*. Okay, Mr. Drinkwater?"

"Okay. Okay. You don't have to yell." Harvey picked up his comic book and a handful of pecan cookies and moved to Purchasing's designated seat around the conference table.

"Ladies and gentlemen, now that Mr. Drinkwater has kindly taken his seat, we can begin. As you know, the Board of Directors will be meeting next week in the Mermaid Suite on the cruise ship, *The Floating Palace of the Seas*. Chairman Mitchell and I will be boarding her the day before to, um...check out the accommodations." Granduck slid his 'Royal High Roller' ID card for the ship's casino underneath his agenda along with the gift certificate for the ship's massage parlor.

"Today we will be screening presentations for the Board of Directors' agenda. Keep your questions crisp and on topic. We have a lot to cover. Horst, are our first presenters ready?"

Horst Gasthau, one of Granduck's black suits, strode with stoic Teutonic grace into an ante-room and summoned a waiting group of businessmen.

"The first item that will be presented to the Board," said Granduck, "will be a proposal by investment bankers, Kase, Schinken and Suppe from Frankfurt. The topic: *Leveraging the Underlying Surrealistic Value of Danish Portraiture*. Wilkommen, gentlemen. Bitte...please proceed."

Harvey understood what a Danish was. It was a fancy word for donut. Calling it a Danish made it more acceptable for refined people to eat donuts for breakfast. But when Casey, Shinky and Soup presented, they weren't making any sense. Luckily, part of what they were saying involved Purchasing. It made Harvey feel important and kept him awake.

So Harvey took notes:

Step One: Buy Danish art. But it's not from Denmark and it's not made from donuts. It's from a strange country named Bangladesh. The nice bankers from Frankfurt would loan Globallica the money to buy the 'Danish' art through something they called 'Dee Caymanlandische Island Banken'. They also did something called appraisals.

Step Two: Buy insurance on the 'Danish' art.

Step Three: Buy services from a company named 'West Coast Art Recycling Inc.'. Apparently this company took the art away for cleaning. They did their work very late at night and had a nasty habit of losing the art. They didn't seem like a very reliable supplier. That didn't seem to matter. The nice people from the insurance company would pay sixteen thousand times what Purchasing paid for the art to replace it. Based on Casey, Shinky and Soup's appraisal. See *Step One*.

Harvey checked his notes for accuracy. Yes, that's what was said. He was getting good at this executive stuff. Note-taking that is. It must have been a good deal. Granduck asked for a vote to approve it. No discussion. Just polite nods. Everyone looked at Harvey and mouthed the word, 'nod'. Harvey nodded too.

Someone asked if the Executive Benefits program would be participating in the art purchases. Granduck thought this was a great idea and authorized interest-free, non-repayable loans so the executives could buy their own Danish art. Globallica would pay the insurance premiums. What a generous company Globallica was, Harvey thought. And a patron of the arts as well.

Harvey had been so busy taking notes he hadn't noticed who was sitting next to him. And what that person was doing. The Purchasing seat was next to the Human Resources seat. Which was occupied by a familiar face...the nice VP Harvey had met on his first day...Bob Gerson. The German bankers were not the only ones talented in art. Mr. Gerson wasn't taking notes. He was drawing them, weird renditions of Vice Chairman Granduck. Was this what 'Surrealistic Danish Portraiture' was supposed to look like? It wasn't to everyone's taste, Harvey thought. But nevertheless, if you kept an open mind, it was still art.

The next few agenda topics lost Harvey's attention completely. A horrendously long discussion took place over what seemed like an eternity of charts and graphs. Never-ending columns of numbers accompanied by strange sounding topics. Incremental semi-variable cash flow. Irreconcilable differential expenses. Over-applied cyclical burden rates. Non-recurring unsustainable depreciable assets. And extraordinary, unbelievable, inconceivable paybacks.

It was awful. Harvey abandoned his note-taking. Eventually Harvey thought he heard something he understood and wrote down 'patting the budgie'. It was a mistake. Someone asked a question and it turned out the topic was something called, 'padding the budget'. The only padding Harvey knew about was the stuffing in Lopez's dog basket. Harvey was always replacing it. Lopez kept chewing through the cover and spreading it around the apartment.

Harvey had trouble keeping his mind occupied. He'd read and re-read his issue of the *Space Druids* seven times. On Harvey's right was the Public Affairs seat. According to its gilt-lettered tent card, the gentleman sitting in it was named Pierre LaFlousie. A very strange man indeed. He never looked at the speakers as they presented. He just sat staring straight across the table at two vacant chairs. One for the VP of Operations. The other for the VP of Sales. Beside Mr. LaFlousie's planner was a book. Harvey was curious and leaned over to sneak a peek at the title, *Equine Secrets for Sleeping with your Eyes Open*. Harvey didn't understand what that had to do with management. And why someone would bring it to a meeting. Harvey resumed his note-taking.

The pesky boring lists of numbers vanished from the overhead projector. *At last!* Harvey thought.

Vice Chairman Granduck, whose attention to the financial data bordered on orgasm, thanked the presenters. "Let's move on to our final topic, Executive Compensation."

Suddenly, everyone became re-energized. Heads that had been leaning to one side with eyelids that had been bouncing up and down, bobbed awake. Snoring that had progressed from a mild wheeze to a strong breeze, abruptly stopped. Granduck commented on his audience's newly acquired 'laser-like focus'.

"Please welcome Patricia Barkode from Payroll Express Deluxe…"

She received a standing ovation. She hadn't even said anything yet. Harvey was confused.

Miss Barkode, a woman whose figure was like a stork and had a beak to match, said, "Thank you. Thank you. I'm overwhelmed. Thank you so much. I'm here to present what our company believes is the best enhancement to executive compensation ever offered in the history of corporate America."

The assembly rose again in unison, ushering in another thundering round of applause. Vice Chairman Granduck was losing control of the meeting. "Please, ladies and gentlemen, this is our last agenda topic and we're running late. I've texted Chef to delay lunch. Please sit down and hold your questions and applause until Miss Barkode is finished. Thank you."

What a supremely well-executed piece of facilitation. Harvey took copious notes. And drew some pictures.

"Thank you, Vice Chairman Granduck" she continued. "As I was saying, this year's executive compensation package is ready for approval by Globallica's Board of Directors. It passed the rigorous scrutiny of the Compensation Committee. They worked on it late into last night. I have their final revisions and I must say our courier service from Bora Bora really came through for us. Just proves what a small world it is."

Harvey looked around the room. His fellow executives were transfixed and drooling. It was such a satisfying feeling to know he wasn't totally out of place among their exclusive fraternity.

"The main feature is our newest innovation in stock options: the reverse-callable, mega-leveraged Globallica stock option put. These put options place an irrevocable lien on Globallica's cash assets. If Globallica—heaven forbid (she crossed herself)—ever declares bankruptcy, the call feature of these options will liquidate all the assets the company owns and convert them to cash. *Your* cash. It's the least our executives deserve after so many years of faithful service."

Vice Chairman Barry Granduck rose from his seat. "Brilliant, Miss Barkode! Brilliant."

The crowded conference room could no longer contain its enthusiasm. Several people sustained injuries as they rushed Miss Barkode to congratulate her on her inspired presentation.

"Vice Chairman Granduck?" VP of Public Affairs Pierre LaFlousie inquired. "I move we pre-approve Miss Barkode's proposed benefit changes. After all, the Board of Directors Meeting next week is just a formality. And in these troubled times for the stock market, it would be prudent to protect our valuable compensation packages as soon as practically possible."

"Excellent suggestion, LaFlousie. I couldn't agree more. That assessment of today's market is right on the money. I move we use my emergency powers as vice chairman to institutionalize the new executive compensation package immediately. Any objections?"

A voice vote was held. The motion carried.

With the last agenda topic behind them, the meeting was dismissed. Lunch was being served in the executive dining room next door. Harvey still had a lot to learn about being an executive. The lunch buffet was a culinary masterpiece of award-winning proportions. But Harvey couldn't manage a single bite because he was full from the plate of pecan cookies he'd eaten single-handedly.

CHAPTER TWENTY-SIX

DragonForce, Katrina Borchevski loved her Saturday nights—letting her hair down, rocking to head-banging music. Unfortunately, her stuffy yacht club boyfriend, Bob Gerson, didn't like the places she frequented or the company she kept. That was fine. Women who hadn't tied the knot had a right to their independence and to making others lose their independence after tying a few knots of her own.

DragonForce had channeled her considerable Globallica bonuses and other loot into her nationwide store, 'Creative Coffins' and her chain of funeral homes, 'Chez Katrina's'. But it was her Ocean City nightclub, 'Chained Heat', that really turned her crank. Her pride and joy.

When she crossed her nightclub's threshold—dressed in a spiked dog collar and tight leather cat-suit; waterproof, so bloodstains cleaned off easily—she transformed from stiff-shirted Globallica executive to Gothic Cleopatra.

Being the owner of 'Chained Heat' had all kinds of fringe benefits. The nightspot was a magnet for the movers and shakers of the alternative economy. Stressed out from a busy work week, the in-people wanted to party heavily but couldn't stop making deals. The club percolated with the ambitious and ruthless cognoscenti of Ocean City: scammers and conmen, dodgy real estate developers, stolen exotic car dealers, corporate M&A artists wanting a little S&M, hit men, off duty executioners…and the odd terrorist.

Odd was definitely the operative word. Ahmad bin Hidin' looked a little long in the tooth for a terrorist. People questioned his clandestine credentials. There was more Long Island about him than Northern Ireland. More Chattanooga than Chechnya. Many said the only Afghan he knew was laid across the back seat of his 1995 Oldsmobile where he and his dog slept. But as old as he was, his credentials as a committed fan of punk music were never in question. When the weekend came, he didn't mind the body-pounding, ear-splitting heavy metal sound coming out of 'Chained Heat'. That's because Ahmad bin Hidin' was absolutely, positively, without question…stone deaf. He claimed his eardrums had been damaged from a lifetime of being too close to explosions. And indeed, other physical evidence supported his story. Bin Hidin' could only count to eight using both sets of fingers and both sets of toes.

Katrina wasn't about to let Mr. bin Hidin's less than impeccable references cloud her conspiratorial judgment. She needed to cut a deal with the old vagabond. He seemed genuine enough. If she could convince a bunch of Nepalese sherpas that a gorilla was a Yeti, then why not assume Ahmad bin Hidin' was who he said he was, and could do the 'Job' she planned? It was all about judging character.

The negotiation with the old warhorse at her nightclub proved to be more difficult than Katrina Borchevski originally expected. It was loud, his interpreter was his sister, and she had to use sign language to translate English into Arabic for her deaf brother to understand.

"Has Mr. bin Hidin' obtained the launcher?"

The reply came back, "No, thank you. Mr. bin Hidin' has already had lunch."

"You said Mr. bin Hidin' used one against the Soviets?"

"Mr. bin Hidin' says if he's not having lunch, he won't need a serviette."

"Ask Mr. bin Hidin', what is the price of the missile?"

"Mr. bin Hidin' says he thinks you have a nice smile, too. Do you want to dance?"

Katrina had become accustomed to awkward negotiations. She was a purchasing professional. Her extensive cross cultural training would now come in handy. She rephrased her questions with her usual high degree of sensitivity, charm and diplomacy. "Listen you dumb shit, are you going to do this job or not?"

She stuffed several one hundred dollar bills in his ears and drew four pictures on the paper tablecloth. The first picture was a stick man with a bazooka tube. The second was a stick coming out of the bazooka with a flame trail behind it. The third was a helicopter. It looked like an upside down egg beater falling from the sky in flames. The fourth was a crazy deaf old coot hauling ass with a big sack full of money.

Ahmad bin Hidin's eyes widened. His hands went up in the air. A smile stretched the wrinkles on his battle-scarred face. He garbled, "Ah. Miss Borchevski. Why didn't you say so. When do I start?"

***

Harvey had built up an impressive skills inventory. Irrelevant data entry. Reporting savings when you don't have any. Gulping without pain. Effective questioning. Presentations that worked. Negotiating win-win contracts. Being a connoisseur of fine books and fine whiskey. Finding lost warehouses. Not to forget: note-taking while sleeping with your eyes open. And of course, drooling.

But there was one skill that Harvey knew he lacked, an essential activity that every well-rounded executive was required to master at some point in his career…golf.

Once, Harvey had caddied for Mr. Dortmann. At the Oregon Retail Clothing Supply and Haberdashery Association's Annual Golf Tournament at the posh Shingle Beach Golf and Country Club. Harvey had enjoyed himself immensely. They even gave him a door prize. Something called a lifetime ban.

It all started with a little accident that almost ruined the whole outing for Mr. Dortmann. Harvey ran over Mr. Dortmann's glasses with the golf cart. What Mr. Dortmann's glasses were doing on the fairway in the first place wasn't a mystery. Why Mr. Dortmann couldn't handle Harvey's high-G turns without falling out of the golf cart certainly was.

Working fabric close to his nose, Mr. Dortmann could thread a needle through the asshole of a horsefly without the need for optical assistance. But without glasses, Mr. Dortmann couldn't see beyond the top of his knees. Which is why they use the term 'handicap' in the game of golf. Harvey quickly learned the consequences of Mr. Dortmann's loss of eyesight: the kind of pain in the crotch only a titanium-headed Big Bertha could deliver.

But this was all in the past. Harvey's life had progressed in leaps and bounds from the days of the Zipper Emporium. Harvey's omnipotent credit card could pay for just about anything. So Harvey bought himself a nice set of golf clubs with wooly hats in the shapes of his favorite Sesame Street characters. He called his driver, the Cookie Monster. The next problem was to find a golf course. One that hadn't already banned him.

That was the issue. Where to practice? Arthur P. Stottlemeyer Memorial Park was off limits for golfers. The last golfer that attempted to practice there was encased in bronze and covered in bird poop. City ordinances could be very strict.

"No, Mr. Drinkwater," Sparkles said as she grabbed the end of Harvey's golf club before it could whack the ball through his office's smoked glass window. "Not in here."

"I have to practice somewhere. How else am I going to get better?"

"Mr. Drinkwater, I probably shouldn't tell you this but when I worked in Human Resources, my boss used to go out on the cafeteria terrace and hit golf balls into the sea. That's a lot safer than this."

"But how did he get his balls back?"

"He had an assistant on a jet ski…me."

"That must have been fun."

"It was at first, Mr. Drinkwater. But a killer whale took a fancy to my jet ski and every time I got near a ball...it would nuzzle up and push me off. Most of his golf balls were swept out by the tide. So my idiot boss fired me."

"What did you do then?"

"Got a job in the Ocean City Aquarium. Training killer whales."

"So everything worked out fine in the end."

"Not exactly. Greenpeace broke into the aquarium one night and set my killer whales free."

"Oh, I know. I saw the movie."

"So this other idiot boss—the one at the Aquarium—fired me. That's when I re-applied to Globallica as a temp."

"So once again, Sparkles, everything worked out fine."

"If you say so, Mr. Drinkwater. We'll have to see, won't we?"

Harvey scratched his head. He had a profound dilemma. His executive career could not move forward without mastering the game of golf. "Sparkles, I think I'm going to do what one of your bosses did."

"I was afraid you would say that, Mr. Drinkwater," Sparkles said with a tear in her eye. "I'll pack my personal belongings. Can you give me a reference?"

"No, no, Sparkles. What do you take me for...an idiot?"

"You could have fooled me."

"No, what I meant was...that's a great idea. I'm going to hit some golf balls into the ocean."

"If you think I'm getting on a jet ski again, you're very mistaken, Mr. Drinkwater. Have you any idea what a horny killer whale can get up to when it finds you in the water?"

Harvey pondered his options. Straight below his office was the moss-encrusted flat roof of Dr. Duddenheim's laboratory on Wharf Number Nine. From this distance the roof had the appearance of fine felt. Like a manicured golf green only with bird crap all over it. But there were patches without any bird crap—areas big enough for a man, a golf ball and a tee. And in the water, directly across from the warehouse, were nets. Nets that corralled the fish in Dr. Duddenheim's fish farm. Ideal for catching golf balls.

It was settled then. Harvey would do what any self-respecting executive would do with an urgent need to solve a delicate problem. He would screw off work and play golf.

CHAPTER TWENTY-SEVEN

It was the day before Globallica's Board Meeting and Chairman Byron Mitchell fiddled with his 18th century French Revolution mantel clock. The gilded brass figures that were supposed to move when the clock struck the hour weren't working. And the guillotine wouldn't drop when the hour struck.

How am I going to cut my cigars now? he thought, exasperated.

The carefully handcrafted antique clock had survived for over two hundred years. Annoyingly, it chose to break down right at the end of a hard day's work at the very hour when Byron Mitchell usually lit up a fat Dominican stogie.

Vice Chairman Barry Granduck leered at the chairman of Globallica behind his back. Chairman Mitchell's life was an endless sequence of stress-free activities aided by an entourage of advisors, personal valets, administrative assistants, speech writers and travel consultants. He didn't even have to think. As long as he could read what was put in front of him and speak without falling asleep in mid-sentence, Mitchell could attain the aura of statesman-like leadership that his constituents inside and outside of Globallica demanded.

On the other hand, Barry Granduck's life as vice chairman was sheer drudgery. Developing excruciatingly complex financial schemes to keep this turkey of a company afloat—and its stock price soaring—was a feat of cerebral genius never truly appreciated by his boss. Fortunately Granduck's efforts had not gone totally unnoticed. Outside Globallica, the Association of Industrial Financial Statisticians had named Barry Granduck their 'Man of the Year'. They said his theories of self-actualization through financial analysis would soon make yoga obsolete as a tool in accounting. *Speculators Business Weekly* described Barry Granduck as 'the ideal person to lead a group of neurotic investment analysts through the obstacle course known as irrational exuberance'.

Vice Chairman Granduck was equally revered inside Globallica. The black-suited hordes in the Finance Department called him 'El Pitón', the python, because of his voracious appetite for swallowing astronomically large presentations of data without gagging. He was the accounting equivalent of an astronomer's black hole—an object with such immense gravitational pull that once data was sucked in, it could not escape.

Too bad Chairman Mitchell's head is too big to fit into the little guillotine, Granduck thought. *But time is on my side.*

Byron Mitchell was sixty-seven. Each year, the Board of Directors had to vote to extend his term past the mandatory retirement age of sixty-five. But this year, that was not going to happen. Granduck had solicited enough votes from board members to force his father-in-law into a much needed retirement.

"Chairman Mitchell?" Granduck asked, as Mitchell toyed with his antique clock's mechanism. "Have you forgotten? We're taking the company helicopter to the *Floating Palace of the Seas* in half an hour."

"You're right. Look at the time." The clocks in Mitchell's office ticked like a meadow full of crickets on a summer night but none of them actually told the correct time. "Who's coming with us?"

"Your secretary. Your valet. Your shoe shine boy. Your Relaxation Therapy Consultant. My secretary. Me. And Lincoln Ferndale."

"Ferndale? Isn't he that ex-football player who can't stop with that gross potty talk?"

"Dung markets, Chairman Mitchell. I've told you a thousand times. We have such a dominant market position in African animal dung that when an antelope takes a crap in the bush, a cash register rings on the Fifth Floor."

"Well, just make sure the varmint flushes the toilet, Granduck. That's all I care about. And uses some air freshener when it's done its business."

The senile old fart didn't understand modern commodity markets. He didn't understand how important Globallica's trading positions were to the company's future.

"The chopper's waiting for us." Lincoln Ferndale announced as he negotiated his way through a forest of Austro-Hungarian longcase clocks.

"Fine. Speaking of choppers," Mitchell said. "This one's working now."

A statue of Robespierre loaded a wig-wearing French Count into the guillotine and *whump*, the brass head of the aristocrat—and the end of Mitchell's cigar—fell precisely into a silver-plated basket. Mitchell lit up the stogie and his smile of satisfaction for a job well done disappeared behind a billowing cloud of blue smoke.

***

DragonForce, Katrina Borchevski focused her binoculars on the warehouse roof. Her view jumped up and down as the anchored Lazzara yacht bobbed in the water. Borchevski and Bob Gerson had taken *Neptune's Greed* a half mile offshore to witness the ultimate in high tech skeet-shooting.

"There he is," she said. "The aging cretin's unpacking it now."

She handed the binoculars to Gerson. On the warehouse roof, a camouflaged old Bedouin sat cross-legged on a little Persian mat, reading the instruction manual for a shiny new Stinger anti-aircraft missile launcher.

"Can he read English?" Gerson asked. "I thought you said he's used one before?"

Katrina grabbed the binoculars back. "Oh my goodness. This isn't the night before Christmas. And that's not a must-assemble kiddie's bike. Just pick up that thing, bin Stupid, point it and shoot."

Her hired gun attempted to load the missile. It didn't fit.

"Wrong end, dim wit! The other end!"

Head first? Tail first? Wrong end. Start over.

"How many permutations can there be?" Her Atrociousness muttered, frustrated.

"You know what they say, Kay-Bee? If you want the job done right, you've got to do it yourself."

"Oh, shut up. Just exactly how many 'Jobs' have you done on this journey, Smarty Pants? Give the old guy a chance. He's a veteran of foreign wars."

"Okay, Kay-Bee. But don't say I didn't warn you."

Katrina panned from the roof to the dockside. Standing at the end of the marina's quay were a group of men in suits holding briefcases along with someone who looked like the Executive Secretary for the local chapter of Satan's Choice. "Hey, mutton cheeks, who are those stuffy types over there?"

"Oh…them. Just a few bankers I know."

"Bankers? I recognize one of them from my nightclub. It's Freddie 'the Razor' Hogan, a part time repo man. He's pretty good. I use him when customers fall behind on their coffin payments. He dug up one dearly deceased and deposited him in a muslin sack on his wife's doorstep. So what does he want with you, my little bacon rind?"

"The boat."

"Which boat?"

"This boat."

"As in…the one we're sailing on?"

"As in the only one we're sailing on that I no longer own."

"You missed a payment?"

"A few."

"As in…how many?"

"As in…most of them."

"Why?"

"It's complicated, Kay-Bee. A banking mix-up. Seems the wire transfers from my accounts in Luxembourg to Belize via Panama have somehow…um, fallen through a cyber crack. Apparently a big one. Payroll Express Deluxe says I charged the account where the deposits from my Globallica paycheck are directed. But I don't remember doing that."

Katrina Borchevski was not impressed. She could forgive a few minor faults with personal hygiene. She actually preferred her men with a slightly natural, musky smell. It brought out the animal in her. But poor personal financial management was a character flaw she abhorred in a boyfriend. There was a saying in the nightclub, 'the thinner the wallet, the smaller the…'. She usually didn't keep a relationship of that kind going long enough to find out. Financially challenged suitors were sushi with her, figuratively speaking.

Katrina panned back to the rooftop of Wharf Number Nine. Ahmad bin Hidin' had finally figured out how to load the rocket launcher. She panned over to Globallica's helipad, jutting out from the side of the skyscraper. The chairman's JetCopter fired up its rotors. Eight figures emerged from the building into its downdraft, their suits and dresses whipped up by the wind.

Katrina returned her sights to the warehouse's roof to confirm that Ahmad was pointing the Stinger in the right direction. He was. But he was no longer alone.

***

In the past week, Harvey had made a lot of new friends in Dr. Duddenheim's laboratories on Wharf Number Nine. When he visited, they seemed to go out of their way to make him feel at home. Although they were very busy, they still found time to answer Harvey's many questions.

Harvey had read in one of his management books that asking a lot of dumb questions was a really good thing for executives to do. Harvey was extremely skilled at this. Funnily enough, the scientists of Wharf Number Nine liked him asking a lot of dumb questions. It made them feel important. Harvey input 'asking dumb questions' into the skills inventory in his planner, underneath 'drooling'.

"What's in that bottle?"

"Don't touch that, Harvey. It's dangerous."

"What's in that box?"

"Nothing. It's empty, Harvey. It's just an empty box."

"If the bottle is dangerous, and the box is empty, why is the knife sharp?"

"Huh?"

"If those numbers on that dial go up, will the box become full? Is a full box dangerous?"

"Huh?"

"If you put the dangerous bottle and the sharp knife in the empty box, would the numbers on that dial go down?"

"*What*?"

"If the numbers on that dial never changed, would that mean the box could never be sharp?"

"Excuse me?"

"If the knife was inside the bottle…and the bottle was inside the box…would the fish swim upside down?"

"Um, *what*?"

"How dangerous is a fish in a box? If a fish swallowed a bottle, could it cut its way out of the box without a knife?"

"Harvey, would you like a job working here? You're not just a possibility thinker, you're an *impossibility* thinker."

"I am? Gee, that's sounds great. But no thanks. I already have a job. I'm an executive."

"Oh…that explains everything."

Harvey couldn't linger in the labs very long today. There was a vital skill in urgent need of fine tuning. If this managerial skill was not mastered soon, it would provide the answer to another very important question: is a golf club a weapon of mass destruction?

The way up to Wharf Number Nine's roof, which was about to double as Harvey's driving range, was not a straightforward process. To Harvey it was a test of his shrewdness and dexterity. It began by going through a door marked, 'Do Not Enter'. Harvey was used to seeing signs that lied. Like the one over Dortmann's Zipper Emporium. Passing through, he became drenched in a shower of quick-grow nutrient. It created enough lubrication for Harvey to squeeze up the air-conditioning duct on the inside wall of the building. Climbing an air-conditioning duct in real life was definitely harder than falling into one in your dreams. Especially with a Big Bertha in one hand and a bucket of golf balls in the other.

Once the rooftop was reached, the rest of the journey involved dexterity. The next step involved walking across a clothesline suspended between two radio antenna towers to get over a skylight. Balancing the bucket of golf balls as a counterweight was not the real knack. Stopping the seagulls from pecking at your nutrient rich clothing was. Without hurting yourself. With the golf club. As you flailed at them.

Firmly on the other side, Harvey negotiated his way through large patches of bird droppings which had various levels of viscosity. He found an unmolested patch of moss to tee off. After several practice strokes, most of the mossy greenery was propelled off the roof along with the golf ball. The smart fish in the fish farm below swam for cover. The dumb ones thought they were being fed. That gave Harvey something to aim at.

Finally, Harvey emptied his bucket of golf balls. The next test of shrewdness was finding a way to get down. Reversing the process would be a logical choice. But Harvey liked a new challenge. He found it. They were called stairs.

On his way to the stairwell, Harvey discovered he was not alone. An old man sat cross-legged on a carpet, taking a little time at the end of the day to enjoy his hobby. Harvey thought it was unusual to look through a telescope when the sun was still up. What would you see? The stars were not out yet.

Harvey put down his empty bucket and crept up quietly behind the man, Big Bertha in hand. The oddly dressed gentleman seemed to be fiddling with a focusing knob as he looked through the eyepiece of the telescope. The telescope's instruction manual was opened up on the carpet. Harvey thought the section said, 'Troubleshooting'. It actually said, 'Turning-and-Shooting'.

It sure takes extreme patience to master amateur astronomy, Harvey thought. The old man, in a state of intense concentration, didn't move a muscle as Harvey approached, golf club in hand. What Harvey didn't understand was that Ahmad bin Hidin' could sleep like a baby next to a railway yard during rush hour. Harvey tapped the deaf terrorist on the shoulder to get his attention. With the Big Bertha. Which made the old man jump with surprise. For a brief instant in time, Surprise was muscled out of the way by Fate. Because Fate had decided it was also an opportune time for a hungry seagull to nibble at Harvey's tasty nutrient-rich shirt collar.

By the time Fate was done, it was hard to tell which of the three of them was the most surprised. Harvey seeing a seagull on his shoulder? The seagull seeing a golf club swung in his direction for perhaps the first time in its life? Or a grizzled old mujahedeen seeing stars when the sun was still shining?

Harvey chased the seagull away and turned back towards his new found friend. This was puzzling. Why was the man taking a nap? Silly Harvey. So he could stay up late to star gaze. Harvey picked up the telescope and looked through the eyepiece. It seemed to be working just fine. As Harvey moved it around, things came sharply into focus. Like people. Below him on the marina's quay, Harvey made out an old friend, Freddie Hogan.

"Yoo-hoo, Freddie!" he shouted.

Harvey waved back and forth to try and catch Freddie's attention. It didn't seem to work. Harvey jumped up and down. The safety catch became unlatched. The priming pin was dislodged. The 'Automatic Aim' button was pressed. And finally, the 'Target Locked' indicator light came on.

Down on the quay, Freddie spotted a funny little man on the rooftop of Wharf Number Nine. Anyone imitating a kangaroo—especially one that was desperate to go to the bathroom— deserved a second look.

On board *Neptune's Greed*, Katrina Borchevski and Bob Gerson watched as Globallica's executive helicopter, with the chairman and vice chairman and their entourage onboard, rose gracefully from its pad as it began its ascent out over the sea. This was the moment they'd so patiently been waiting for.

Harvey's wild animal-like gyrations were getting results. Not entirely the results that Harvey had hoped for. It was amazing how little finger pressure was required to depress the trigger of a Stinger rocket launcher.

One of the perks of being an executive at Globallica was the expensive fitness club membership the company paid for. Because of it, Katrina Borchevski and Bob Gerson's reflexes approached the caliber of Olympic gymnasts. However, the synchronization of their diving routine needed some work. Give them some credit. After all, their leaps in the pike position with a double twist were executed under a particularly high degree of difficulty: diving off *Neptune's Greed* when a streaking Stinger anti-aircraft missile hurtled towards them at subsonic speed.

However imperfect their jumps were, their entry into the water was well synchronized—synchronized with the Stinger missile as it entered the yacht's galley. The pair were safely submerged when Harvey's airborne mixture of high velocity and high explosives reacted nicely with the assortment of canapés and fine cheeses that Chef had packed for their afternoon hamper.

Harvey looked down the telescope tube and discovered that stars did indeed come out in the daytime. He was amazed at the telescope's impressive magnifying ability. He'd never seen an exploding supernova up close before. It was truly a spectacular sight.

Harvey made a mental note to take up astronomy. And give up golf. After all, he had to admit, he was useless at it.

CHAPTER TWENTY-EIGHT

What would a day be like, Harvey thought without Mr. Fortinelli saying, "Itza a great-a day in Ocean City?"

Harvey couldn't imagine it.

He preferred his *Daily Oregonite* over *The Wall Street Journal*. It didn't come with a fruit basket but came with Mr. Fortinelli's words of wisdom instead.

"Itza bigga. Itza really, really bigga. Isn't it?"

"What?"

"Mama Mia, you dodo. The boat. The picture. Inna front of you. Inna your hands."

"Oh?" Harvey looked at the front page of *The Daily Oregonite*. Taking up most of the page below the headline, 'All Aboard for the Board', was a photo of the cruise ship the *Floating Palace of the Seas*.

"I'm going on that."

"You gonna what?"

"I'm going on that boat, Mr. Fortinelli."

"You?"

"Yes, *me*. Today. For Globallica's Board Meeting."

Harvey could hardly remember a time when Mr. Fortinelli was speechless. But today was that day. Talus had called Nancy Butterworth who'd called Sparkles who'd called Harvey at home to tell Harvey that Talus couldn't make it to the Board of Directors Meeting. Not this year. Not next year. Not ever. Talus was retiring from Globallica to move permanently to Amsterdam to become the president of the International Relaxation Therapy Association. Talus appointed Harvey to be the acting Executive Vice President of Purchasing. Which now meant Harvey Drinkwater was a member of the Board of Directors of Globallica.

On the front page of *The Daily Oregonite* below the picture of the cruise ship was a smaller article titled, 'Globallica Executive Charged With Insurance Fraud'. The article stated, 'Yesterday, Globallica VP of Human Resources, Bob Gerson was arrested after Ocean City Fraud Squad officers uncovered his scheme to defraud Swiss insurance company, Glockenspit after a fire that destroyed Gerson's luxury yacht, the *Neptune's Greed*.'

'Mr. Gerson made the highly absurd claim,' the article continued. 'That a terrorist's anti-aircraft rocket had sunk his boat. The Chief Prosecutor of Big Buffalo Knuckles County said Mr. Gerson was swimming upstream without a paddle. Mr. Gerson was charged with arson and fraud. Apparently he could no longer afford the re-payments on his boat loan. An eye-witness has come forward to testify for the prosecution. Miss Katrina Borchevski, another Globallica executive, said she was dining on board Mr. Gerson's yacht when she saw Mr. Gerson deliberately tip a flambéed brandy drink into an engine compartment that had been leaking gasoline fumes.'

Harvey was shocked and stunned. How could a respected executive such as Bob Gerson—a true paragon of virtue—get mixed up in such skullduggery? Fortunately, someone with greater integrity had stepped forward to stand up to his villainy. Harvey made a mental note to congratulate Katrina Borchevski. It was comforting to know that in her determined quest for justice, Executive Director DragonForce was making sure the reputation of Globallica's executive class would not be tarnished by the unwholesome acts of one bad apple.

Today's *Daily Oregonite* was chock full of Globallica news. There was a photo of Angus McCalliwag, dressed up in his Army general's uniform, handing a check over to someone Harvey thought looked somewhat familiar. The caption read, 'Ocean City Citizen Given

Reward for Finding Stolen Army Hardware'. The article said that 'an unspecified weapon' had been stolen from an Army test firing range and had been returned by a Mr. Ahmad bin Hidin' who claimed the ten thousand dollar reward. However, Mr. bin Hidin' was only given half of the reward. Apparently there was a piece missing. Harvey didn't think this was very fair. It wasn't Mr. bin Hidin's fault the Army had been so careless.

The photo of Mr. bin Hidin' reminded him of someone. He looked a little like the amateur astronomer Harvey had met on top of Wharf Number Nine. It was only the vaguest resemblance. The man standing with Angus in the newspaper photo had some kind of unfortunate facial deformity like he'd been hit by a caveman's club. Harvey concluded it wasn't the same man.

"Good gracious, Mr. Fortinelli. Look at the time," Harvey said. "I can't stand and chat with you all day. I'll be late for Globallica's Board Meeting."

Harvey bundled the newspaper under his arm and strode confidently down Sardine Way. He heard a foghorn blast coming from Wharf Number Thirteen, the berth of the gigantic cruise ship, *The Floating Palace of the Seas*.

Fate was beckoning him to the most important meeting of his life.

***

When Harvey arrived in the Mermaid Suite for the Board of Directors Meeting, Vice Chairman Barry Granduck went out of his way to give him a tutorial on the nuances of life at the very top of the corporate ladder. It began with Harvey signing some kind of attendance sheet that read like a pledge of allegiance to the vice chairman. Granduck called it a 'proxy vote' and said it was a formality. Assigning his 'proxy' to Granduck he assured Harvey, was simply a way for his new mentor to give Harvey a little advice. Especially when it came to voting. That seemed more like a necessity than a formality.

Harvey also learned that every progressive modern corporation had outside directors sitting on their boards. Like the solid corporate citizen it was, Globallica was no exception. Vice Chairman Granduck introduced Harvey to them. They were all stalwarts of the business world. Captains of industry. Society potentates. Mr. Granduck said they'd been carefully chosen to contribute their profound wisdom to Globallica.

Representing the old guard of Ocean City's establishment were the Stottlemeyer brothers, Roger P. Stottlemeyer and Arthur P. Stottlemeyer IV, descendants of the city's founding father. Together, the Stottlemeyer twins had a wealth of business acumen. Their keen perspective on the laws of supply and demand had been forged from a tough, lifelong struggle to dominate the US head cheese market. They had succeeded. The brand name 'Stottlemeyer' had become a household word.

"It's a privilege to meet you," Harvey said.

Next, there was Senator Jimmy Crawdad, Oregon's senior Senator in Washington. It was rumored that in his youth, Crawdad had been a personal friend of Henry Ford and Thomas Edison. Which would make him one hundred and thirty-eight years old. Many doubted that claim. Few doubted his age. It was certainly the age of the wheelchair he sat in. It said so on the label on the back. Senator Crawdad was a battle-hardened veteran of political wars. His white-coated medical staff were battle-hardened veterans of the senator's legendary grumpiness. When he was awake.

"Senator," Harvey acknowledged, as the politician snored.

Harvey discovered he was not the only board member brought in at the last minute as a replacement. The outside board seat belonging to the head of the Ocean City Anthropology Institute, Dr. Tristin Postlewhite, also required an alternate. Dr. Postlewhite had contracted a rare tropical virus, simian succulent fever, on his last trip to Africa. His good friend, Purchasing's Executive Director Bjorn, had arranged for a suitable academically-inclined substitute to replace him and cast the professor's vote on the Board. A chimp named Boris.

Representing the humanities was Ocean City's most flamboyant personality, Yoodah Earth. Mr. Earth had worked his way up the social ladder from humble beginnings as a musician. His rising fame in the music business had produced a sizable fortune. He had his own recording studio, 'Zoundz of Da Hood'. Yoodah Earth's artistic nature nurtured a deeply spiritual side, a side the rap artist was only too willing to share with Harvey. Yoodah told Harvey he owned a casino, 'The Shrine of Babylon', which he said was "designed to purge the pennies of perdition from the pockets of the populace". Yoodah's entourage chanted, "Amen, Brother Earth."

So there it was. Great care had been taken to populate Globallica's Board with the finest minds Ocean City could offer in the fields of business, politics, the sciences and the arts. The formal introductions were over. The stuffy chitchat subsided. The luncheon ended. Senator Crawdad's plasma was topped up. The serious business of Globallica's Board of Directors was ready to begin.

Harvey grabbed a plateful of pecan cookies from the luncheon buffet and sat next to Boris the chimp. Unlike the other board members, Boris warmed up to Harvey right away. Perhaps it was because they were both newcomers to the executive suite. There was a certain chemistry between them. There was also a bunch of bananas between them. Harvey made a mental note. Add 'networking' to his skills inventory.

***

While the Board of Globallica toiled away tirelessly in the Mermaid Suite on board the cruise ship, Lincoln Ferndale sat alone with his laptop and cell phone in his office in the Globallica Tower, a shot glass of tequila ever present by his side, traumatized by what was unfolding with his commodity trades. The market appeared to have a mind of its own. Which for a trader accustomed to controlling the market, was tantamount to unfair manipulation by the hands of Fate.

Ferndale felt like a thundering herd of gnus was about to trample him. Why wasn't his short position in African bat guano counterbalancing his in-the-money call options on hippo poop? Why would an unexpected Rwandan monsoon drive the price of hyena shit through the roof? What macroeconomic theory supported an almost disastrous drop in the value of rhino dung? The market was becoming a zoo. For some strange reason, cash seemed the safest place to be. Which is not where he was. He couldn't escape fast enough from the zany Zambezi into the fireproof funds of the Fed. Right now life was a bitch...as bitchy as an African spiral-horned bongo in heat.

Lincoln Ferndale was not the only one ready to have a tantrum. Back at the Board Meeting, Senator Crawdad had been building up to it all afternoon. Even Chairman Mitchell commented that the cantankerous near-cadaver was threatening to spoil the tranquility of the Board's proceedings. It didn't help that Boris the chimp was trying to drink from the Senator's saline drip.

A break in the Board's deliberations was in order. Vice Chairman Granduck was relieved. He needed to take a walk. Wipe off the sweat and tension. The crucial vote on Mitchell's tenure as chairman was about to be taken. And Granduck was afraid he didn't have enough votes in the bag to depose him.

The Stottlemeyer twins could always be counted on to vote for Chairman Mitchell. They had to. They had married the chairman's other two daughters. To cancel their votes, Granduck was counting on Yoodah Earth's support. The vice chairman had made sure Yoodah's application to expand his casino was stuck in Ocean City's Planning Committee. Which Granduck controlled. Granduck had Yoodah—and his vote—by the short and curlies.

His Purchasing friend, Bjorn had made sure that Boris the chimp's vote was a shoe-in for Granduck. An electroshock sensor implanted in the primate's skull would guarantee that. So Granduck knew he could neutralize the Stottlemeyer twins' votes. Using a chump and a chimp.

Cancelling out the chairman's own vote was easy. Senator Crawdad hated Chairman Byron Mitchell's guts. Mitchell had political ambitions. He'd tried in the past to oust Crawdad from the party ticket. Despite his age, the wily old Senator had always been too clever for his would-be political rival. And that's how Crawdad became indebted to Vice Chairman Granduck. If it wasn't for Barry Granduck, Senator Crawdad would have been ousted from Globallica's board a long time ago.

So there it was. If the outside directors voted as they should, it would not decide the contest. It was a stalemate. It would then be up to the company's executives on the Board to settle the fate of the chairman. In the past, Globallica's executives had been equally divided between Mitchell's camp and Granduck's. Mitchell's loyal old-timers versus Granduck's young bucks; both sets of votes equally weighed around the table, again canceling each other out.

The VP of Human Resources Bob Gerson never voted for Granduck. Luckily, he'd been arrested for insurance fraud. That might tip the scales. Barry Granduck was now counting on Talus's vote to swing the balance in his favor. But Talus was swinging somewhere else. In his place, an up-and-coming Globallica executive had been put in a position to cast the deciding vote for the next chairman.

Before the Board Meeting started, Granduck had tried his best to rig the election. But Boris the chimp had eaten the papers authorizing Granduck to cast Talus's proxy vote for him. The key vote was now free to decide the fate of Globallica.

Fate was now in the hands of one man.

A wild card, the joker in the pack.

Harvey Drinkwater.

CHAPTER TWENTY-NINE

Martha Biggelsdorf was the glue that bound the Board of Directors together, Chairman Byron Mitchell's loyal secretary of thirty-seven years. Ever since Byron Mitchell had taken control of Consolidated Remanufacturing's board, and then Globallica's board, Martha Biggelsdorf had meticulously recorded every second of every proceeding, all in immaculate but painstakingly tedious handwritten notes. Martha refused to use modern technology. In any part of her life. She walked everywhere. Hand knit her own sweaters. Made her own bread. Pickled her own onions. At the office, Martha thought computers and word processing software were the work of the Devil.

Vice Chairman Barry Granduck called Martha Biggelsdorf 'The Mother of All Techno-Peasants'. As far as Martha was concerned even multi-part forms and carbon paper—if you could still find some, outside of a museum—were the writing instruments of a witch's coven. Call her old-fashioned if you want to, but Martha Biggelsdorf insisted upon handwriting the agendas, handwriting the minutes, handwriting everything. It was a blessing and a curse.

So when Barry Granduck announced it was time for the Board to take a break, Martha was relieved. Not to rest, but to catch up. To translate the minutes from shorthand to longhand. To distribute revised agendas. And of course, to make ballots…handwritten ballots. The ones that would be used by the directors to vote. Like the vote on the last motion of the day…electing the next Chairman of the Board.

Martha Biggelsdorf followed very formal protocols in everything she did. Preparing these ballots had become an annual ritual practiced over decades of faithful service. She took great pride in constructing each ballot by hand in expressive calligraphic script. The election ballots for chairman listed two nominees, 'Byron Mitchell' and 'Barry Granduck'. But as tradition dictated, Martha always included a line for a write-in candidate. According to the strict rules of corporate governance, it was the right and proper thing for the Secretary of the Board to do. And proper, Martha Biggelsdorf certainly was.

The Mermaid Suite had emptied. The lounge bar next door had filled up with thirsty board members. During the break, Martha labored alone at her tasks, watched by a clever chimp named Boris. Martha wrote eloquently on the ballots. Boris munched happily on a bowl of bananas.

In the bar next door to the Mermaid Suite, the Board's most senior member was setting a good example. Senator Crawdad piped a bottle of Courvoisier into his intravenous drip. It went downhill from there. The Board of Directors of Globallica were rapidly becoming wasted. Barry Granduck was nervous. Very nervous. Were the directors capable of voting according to the deals he'd struck?

Martha completed her work. Boris finished his bananas. Martha went to the bathroom. Boris went to the bathroom. Behind a potted plant.

Granduck returned to the Mermaid Suite to check on Biggelsdorf's preparations for the important vote. She wasn't there. But he saw her stack of handwritten ballots. Her neatness was not up to her usual immaculate standards. Somehow a banana peel had slipped into the middle of the pile. No matter. He took a ballot to cast his vote. He put the ballot in an envelope, sealed it, put the envelope in the ballot box and left.

Boris the chimp had been watching Martha carefully. At the Institute, he'd been trained to imitate everything humans did. As a star pupil in Purchasing Executive Director Bjorn's Alternative Resources

Training Program, Boris had been trained to write. Apparently this was a prerequisite for being a purchasing agent. After Martha Biggelsdorf left for a tinkle, Boris looked at what she'd been writing. Names. Seemed simple enough. Then the Boss arrived. He'd watched him too.

Everything was simple. Simple enough for a chimp to imitate. Boris picked up Martha's pen and the rest of the ballots and returned with them to his seat. He looked at the tent card beside him and copied what he saw. 'Harvey Drinkwater', it said. So 'Harvey Drinkwater' he wrote—in the line marked, 'write-in' candidate. It was the only blank space to copy anything on to. This chimp wasn't dumb.

Boris the chimp had several aptitudes distinctly better than others. Imitating handwriting was one. Convulsing when electrical shocks were applied to his head, was the other. Although he was good at both, he preferred the former to the latter. Which was very wise for a chimp. It made decision-making easy.

He'd seen Barry Granduck with the ballot. He remembered the little 'test' Granduck had conducted on him before the Board Meeting to check out the electrodes wired into his head. Boris was a quick learner. He knew if he copied what humans did, it would prevent electrical sparks from shooting out of his nipples.

Boris was indeed a very smart chimp. No one had to show Boris what to do more than once. When the Boss jumped, he jumped. When the Boss picked his nose, he picked his nose. When the Boss stuffed a ballot in an envelope, he would stuff a ballot in an envelope. So that is what Boris did. Just like Barry Granduck, the Boss. Just like a good trained chimp with wires in his head was supposed to do. He'd written on every ballot. Now he put each ballot in an envelope. And then he stuffed the stack of envelopes in the ballot box. Just like he saw the Boss doing.

Harvey returned from the bar. "Oh, you poor thing," he cooed, just like everyone cooed when they saw a cute monkey. "Did somebody leave you here all alone? With nothing to do?"

Boris chirped, "Oo-oo, ee-ee." *Stupid human.*

"Come on, lil' buddy, I'll treat you to a banana milkshake."

Boris happily followed Harvey, satisfied that good behavior would now have its just desserts.

Martha Biggelsdorf returned from the ladies room. Her carefully prepared ballots were gone. Had they been stolen? No. She saw an envelope peeking out of the top of a well-stuffed ballot box.

Had the board members already voted for chairman?

Apparently, they had.

**

Lincoln Ferndale knew defeat when he saw it. His 'Grand Gamble in Uganda' had become his 'Swan Song on the Serengeti'. The Zambezi Exchange had seen a trading session like nothing in its history. Lincoln Ferndale had seen his life flash before his eyes. The dung market had collapsed in a smelly heap. And so had Globallica's fortunes.

He called the vice chairman, "I can hardly hear you. Where are you?"

"The bar. What's up?"

"Mr. Granduck, it's not good."

"How 'not good', Ferndale?"

"Extremely 'not good'. As in, so 'not good' as to be as 'not good' as 'not good' can be."

"That good, eh?"

Lincoln Ferndale explained.

"Ferndale," Granduck said, white as a ghost. "Trigger the 'Escape Plan'."

"Are you sure?"

"Are you some kind of idiot?"

Ferndale took the hint. Self preservation was a powerful force of nature. More powerful than animal dung. Lincoln Ferndale put Granduck on hold and dialed the number of a seedy law office he never thought he'd be asked to call. The voice at the other end of the line mumbled in response to his instructions. Once Ferndale was done, no-one could stop the ball from being set in motion. Globallica was filing for Chapter 11 bankruptcy.

And Barry Granduck's plan? Leave the sinking ship before the other rats were given their wakeup calls.

"Cash flow?" he asked Ferndale.

Ferndale tapped into Globallica's accounting systems.

"Exiting now…"

Cash began to flow out of Globallica like water over Niagara Falls. Granduck's amendment to the Executive Benefits Plan had been programmed into the accounting system. Money equivalent to the Gross Domestic Product of four small Caribbean nations gushed into the executives' offshore bank accounts.

"What about the lease documents?"

Ferndale's laptop thumped along to the tune of the War of 1812 Overture. "I'll put a records trace on it right away, boss."

Apparently, the Globallica Tower was not actually owned by Globallica. It was owned by a Trust in Bermuda who leased it to Globallica. The Trust had been set up under the names of three former ASSCO executives, a condition of their agreement to support the company's merger with Consolidated Remanufacturing to form Globallica. Two of the ASSCO executives had died. The third could not be located. In the event the last ex-ASSCO executive died, the trust's partnership would be dissolved and ownership of the Globallica Tower would revert to another trust controlled by Vice Chairman Barry Granduck.

Needless to say, Barry Granduck wanted those documents badly. "Ferndale, get those papers out of Globallica. Now!"

Lincoln Ferndale's fingers attacked his keyboard. "Boss? Wouldn't cash flow be improved if we fired all our contract employees?"

"Your point?"

"Should I?"

"This is no time to be conservative, Ferndale."

Several keystrokes later and every contract employee in Globallica was sent an electronic pink slip in their email. The cash flowing out of Globallica was now accelerating faster than a Formula One Ferrari. But despite Ferndale's frantic electronic search, the Records Department had no trace of the lease documents.

"Hey boss," Ferndale said. "Looks like the lease docs were never scanned. A paper copy must be in the Globallica Tower somewhere."

Vice Chairman Barry Granduck's dream of being chairman of Globallica had evaporated along with seven billion dollars worth of dung options. The shareholders would be left holding the bag. But Granduck—along with the rest of Globallica's executives—would depart with their bags full of Globallica's cash.

"What do we do now, boss?"

"You're definitely an idiot, aren't you, Ferndale? Choices?"

"Leave?"

"Bingo."

"What about the Board?"

A tiny kernel of fiduciary responsibility still existed inside Barry Granduck's cold heart. Lincoln Ferndale was right. The last duty the vice chairman had before resigning was to inform the Board of Directors that the largest corporation in America was now a bankrupt shell.

"Ladies and Gentlemen," he screamed over the noise in the bar. "I have an important announcement to make."

He told them the news about Globallica's Chapter 11 filing.

Vice Chairman Granduck's announcement was met with mixed feelings. For the outside directors on the Board, it meant their quarterly boondoggle had ended with a piss-up never to be repeated. For Globallica's executives it meant celebrate like never before! Because the value of their put options on Globallica's now worthless stock, combined with exit bonuses that milked Globallica's cash reserves, meant each executive could own the Third World country of their choice with change to spare.

A fight broke out. The executives jostled over who would buy Aruba. It was a frenzy of exuberant irrationalism fueled by intoxicated irreverence.

"It's B-Day! B-Day!" VP Pierre LaFlousie screamed into Harvey's ears.

"B-Day?"

"Chapter 11, Harvey. Woo hoo!"

B-Day? Chapter 11? Oh, no. Harvey hadn't read Chapter Eleven. Chapter One was as far as he'd gotten. On all of his books. With the exception of *Alien Abductions: What the Vatican Doesn't Want You to Know*. He'd read the whole book twice.

"Here's to B-Day, Harvey old chum," LaFlousie said, dancing a jig.

"B-Day? Is this somebody's birthday?"

"No, Harvey. B-Day…Bankruptcy Day. Globallica's bankrupt. And we're rich!"

Harvey was puzzled. Not for the first time. Bankruptcy? That was good? He sure had a lot to learn.

***

Martha Biggelsdorf collected the ballot box. Her last job of the day was to count the ballots and duly note in the official minutes the august decision of the Board of Directors of Globallica pursuant to the motion to elect a new chairman. With the exception of only one vote—Barry Granduck's—every director had voted for the same candidate. Even the incumbent chairman, Byron Mitchell, hadn't voted for himself. The new Chairman of the Board of Globallica was someone new. Someone she was unfamiliar with.

Martha Biggelsdorf wrote his name in her record of the Board's meeting in penmanship so precise it made monastic manuscripts in the British Museum look like Neolithic cave drawings.

The new Chairman of the Board of the largest—and most recently bankrupt—corporation in America was…Harvey Drinkwater.

CHAPTER THIRTY

Today was not like every other day. Harvey didn't get up at the same time he always did. In fact, if it weren't for Lopez, Harvey might have stayed in bed until sunset. He managed to open one eye. A wet tongue applied canine moisturizer to his nose and cheeks.

"Oh, my head. What time is it?" Harvey glanced at his bedside clock. "11:30. Oh, boy. Am I ever late!"

Harvey pushed the little dog aside and sat bolt upright in bed. Bad move. He thought his temples were going to explode. Whatever he drank yesterday, it had the after effects of a rodeo ride on a Brahma bull.

What happened after the Board Meeting? It was still a fuzzy blur, facilitated by more than a few lingering Fuzzy Navels. Harvey vaguely remembered some kind of odd celebration. Several brain cells clubbed together and brought a tiny recollection of it to the surface. It seemed like a strange daytime dream. Something bad had happened. But some kind of tidal wave of euphoric optimism had flushed the angst away.

Harvey remembered flushing some of his lunch down the toilet. His stomach was queasy. His head still pounded. And his pajamas felt uncomfortable. They felt like they were tied in a knot around his neck. Harvey discovered he'd slept in his suit and tie. That was good. It wouldn't take him long to get ready.

"Lopez, no time for a body wash. I'm late for work."

Which also meant no time for muesli. No time for two slices of toast with strawberry jam. One slice for Lopez. The poor little dog whimpered pathetically. Okay. Time for one slice. And one slice only.

Harvey grabbed a jarful of pink antacid tablets to munch on, put on his coat and rushed out the door. Well, into the door... head first. Then he went out of it.

A comforting certainty could always be found in Ocean City's metropolitan transportation system. It was as reliable as ever. The train was late as it always was. The station was packed as it always was. And the people were as rude as they always were. But outside the station, Mr. Fortinelli's newspaper stand was closed. It had a 'Gone to Lunch' sign hanging from it. There would be no 'Itza a great-a day in Ocean City' today, and no *Daily Oregonite* with Mr. Fortinelli's built in entertainment and wisdom.

If that wasn't punishment enough, Harvey had another ordeal to endure. A crowd. Not the usual lunchtime-line-outside-Stottlemeyer's-Deli kind of crowd when it was 'Buy One, Get One Free, Head Cheese Sandwich Day'. No. This crowd was bigger. Much bigger. It stretched from the train station to the plaza in front of the Globallica Tower. It stretched up the granite steps under the 'People are Our Greatest Asset' bronze façade and then inside the building's glass-doored entry. It stretched throughout the glossy marble-and-palm foyer right up to the revolving security doors.

In the middle of the crowd, reporters and cameramen buzzed like wiretapped bees. Correspondents from LA, DC, NYC. ABC, NBC, QVC. MTV, the BBC, the SEC, Sex in the City. USA Today, the Today Show, Entertainment Tonight, Saturday Night Live, the Tonight Show, the New York Dog Show. Vogue, Monday Night Football, Masterpiece Theater. They were all in the crowd somewhere.

Why here? Harvey thought.

Some commentators were commentating on the number of commentators commenting about something. But what was it?

Harvey ignored them. It was the best strategy. He weaved and squeezed his way through the crowd, tripping over cables and light stands. Rival camera crews fought for turf like 'Battle Bots' overdosing on electricity. Harvey pushed his way towards the revolving doors that lead up to the Executive Suites. At first he wasn't noticed as he moved through the throng. Until he swiped himself across to the 'Other Side'.

Wow, what a strange feeling, Harvey thought.

He was on one side of a gigantic glass wall, alone.

The reincarnation of Attila the Hun's Mongol hordes were on the other side. They surged forward to get a camera shot of the first person to enter Globallica's inner sanctum since the day began. But Harvey didn't know that. How would he know? He'd slept through the morning news. And missed his morning paper. All he could see were the frothing, near savage faces of the paparazzi, their cameras pressed against the glass.

With their mikes thrust forward in the crush, anchormen and anchorwomen desperately blared out questions Harvey had absolutely no chance of understanding. The din was so terrific, seismographs were being tripped all the way up and down the Pacific Northwest. The reporters all seemed to want answers to something.

Answers from Harvey.

But what?

Flashbulbs flashed until Harvey's movements looked like he was under strobe lights. It was cool. He started to air guitar. He always wanted to do that. Who didn't? Then he noticed someone on the other side of the glass, in the crowd, hiding her head in her hands, embarrassed. It was Bunny Warren.

"Bunny? Bunny!" She couldn't hear him. He pounded on the glass until he got her attention. They could just about tell what each other was saying by reading lips.

"Harvey. What are you going to say?"

"Say about what?"

"About this?"

"This?"

"*This*. This frigging unbelievable, screwy murfle garb…"

"I can't hear what you're saying, Bunny. Come here and tell me."

"In *there*? With you?"

"You prefer your side?"

"Let me in."

Harvey pushed the button on his side of the revolving glass door. It would let someone—and only *one* someone—through at one time. Bunny emerged through the door, a little tussled and creased up, but fine. On the other side of the glass, a phalanx of reporters flashed their wallets at them. Cash fluttered in the air, as the reporters exercised their constitutional rights. "Name your price for an interview!" It was called freedom of the press.

"Harvey, we have to get out of here. *Soon*. I don't know if that glass will hold up much longer." Cracks like spider webs appeared at random locations along the window wall which was starting to groan in the crush.

"Let's go up to my office, Bunny. Maybe Sparkles or Nancy Butterworth knows what's going on here."

"No one can get past the Fifth Floor into the Executive Suites, Harvey. Everyone's access has been denied."

"Well, let's go see the VP of Public Affairs. Pierre LaFlousie must have some idea how to handle the press. That's his job."

"Harvey, nobody—as in no *body*, no *one*, nada *soul*—has come through these doors today until you just did. As far as we know, the Executive Suites are empty. The executives have all disappeared."

Harvey was afraid of something like this. He'd told Talus on the very first day as an executive that Globallica shouldn't have a floor full of black suits processing aliens. But Talus didn't believe him. "What if the aliens turned on us?" Harvey had said. It had happened before. In the comics. Why not in Ocean City? Maybe the Vatican was right about abductions. Globallica's executives were probably locked up right now on a prison starship somewhere out in the deep cosmos. Waiting to be deloused at Regula-4.

Harvey and Bunny entered the elevator to the Executive Suites. As the elevator door closed, they left the chaotic din behind. The fear of what he might find around the next corner caused the antacid tablets in Harvey's stomach to churn. Harvey was defenseless against aliens. His Ghostbusters lunchbox was in Dr. Duddenheim's lab.

A pleasant lady's familiar voice provided a calming influence. She said, "Which floor?"

"My office," said Harvey.

"Taking you to…the office of the vice president of Purchasing."

"Well, that's a relief," Harvey said. "At least someone's here today to run the elevators."

***

Someone else was in hiding in the Executive Suites. The news media hadn't noticed him come in because he'd been there all night. Lincoln Ferndale's mission was two-fold, summed up simply: damage control and theft.

In the crowded lobby, the commotion over Harvey Drinkwater's appearance and disappearance was just the distraction Barry Granduck needed to keep hidden so he could orchestrate Ferndale's exit from the building. Lincoln Ferndale's work was almost done. The last and most important task was locating several documents that were as valuable as treasure from a sunken Spanish galleon: the lease papers and title for the Globallica Tower.

"Ferndale, you've got company," Granduck said over the phone from behind a palm in the foyer.

"I know, Boss. I'm in 'Executive Security'. Two people have entered Talus's office. I can see them on the surveillance cameras. One looks like Harvey Drinkwater. Yeah, it's him alright. He's just knocked over a fruit basket."

"Did you find the lease documents?"

"And more. I've got all the files, Boss."

Barry Granduck pumped the air. *Yes!* This time tomorrow he would be cruising the Bahamas in a catamaran and shopping the darknet to place a 'contract' on ex-ASSCO executive Number Three, the last barrier between himself and ownership of the Globallica Tower.

"Ferndale, we've got a problem," Granduck said. "The SEC has agents everywhere. The poor bastards have some delusion they'll find someone to question. So far, I've counted only three possibilities: you, me and Drinkwater."

"So how do we slip their net, Boss? With all this stuff I've scoffed?"

"I'm beside the mail tube, Ferndale. Send the documents down. I'll collect them and when you're done, get the hell out of there. Fake your way through the lobby."

That was actually pretty easy. Late last night, Lincoln Ferndale had pretended to be a cleaner from West Coast Art Recycling. An innocent, 'I know nothing' as the uniformed nobody exited and he should escape the news gauntlet relatively unscathed.

Barry Granduck flashed a one hundred bill in the face of the sleepy security guard sitting at the foyer's reception desk. He told the poor slob to hand over any mail when it came down the chute. George Thaddeus thought it was odd a man was wearing sunglasses inside the building. Perhaps he was from the CIA and was trying to look inconspicuous.

Thud. Plonk.

The first mail tube arrived. The records of Globallica's decisions on executive compensation, the Danish art purchase scam, stock options.

Thud. Plonk.

The honey bee monopoly swindle. Option trading records. Honey cartel pricing agreements. The secret honey bee warehouse locations.

Thud. Plonk.

Confidential minutes about the merger deal with ASSCO. Offshore bank account statements showing funds still held in 'trust' for ASSCO executives. Invoices for grave sites and funeral expenses.

George Thaddeus wasn't the only one watching Barry Granduck extract a mittfull of papers from the mail tubes. To an undercover agent from the Securities and Exchange Commission, every *Thud, Plonk* downstairs meant someone upstairs in the Executive Suite was sending stuff down. Even the SEC could add two plus two. Well almost.

Thud. Plonk.

More papers. Falsified statements to the FDA. About a surgical instrument sterilization treatment that didn't work. Something to do with the toxicity of armadillo spit.

That was it. The SEC had enough evidence to choke a gnu. The agent barked a code word into his concealed mike, 'Tora. Tora. Tora.' A black-helmeted, black-garbed SEC SWAT Team rappelled down the granite wall. Other agents sprung from camouflaged hides in the palm forest. They descended on Barry Granduck. They jammed their automatic weapons into the back of his head.

"We have the suspect. Repeat. The suspect is down."

The SEC agent read him his rights, "You have the right to remain silent…etc, etc…Barry Granduck, you are charged with assault with a deadly financial weapon…derivatives."

Lincoln Ferndale viewed the fracas in the main lobby on the security cameras. Ferndale had arranged his own plan 'B'. He proceeded to the terrace of the Finance cafeteria. He was going to parachute down to a waiting speedboat. But someone else was waiting. The U.S. Coast Guard.

Thud. Plonk. Again.

This time, the arrival of the mail tube was ignored. The SEC SWAT Team was being interviewed by CNN. A gaggle of literary agents were waiting to sign them to a book deal. MTV was setting up to make the music video. Vogue e-mailed New York…black was 'in' again.

244 · CHARLES A CORNELL

George Thaddeus unloaded the last mail tube and read the papers inside. He paused to let it all sink in. The gray skies in George Thaddeus's world lifted. And the sun shone brightly in. After so many poverty-stricken years, it all finally made sense.

CHAPTER THIRTY-ONE

"Angus? I need your help."

Angus McCalliwag hadn't heard from Harvey Drinkwater in weeks. But somehow he knew he would eventually get this call. "Wha' do yee need, laddie?"

"Everything, Angus. I need everything," Harvey sobbed.

"Yee got it, laddie. Hang in there."

Bunny Warren had not stopped making phone calls. To Angus, Todd, Darcy, Sun Ho Gung. As the new chairman of Globallica, the press was baying for Harvey's blood. Harvey needed help from someone.

A recorded message on the line for the VP of Public Affairs said, "This is Pierre LaFlousie. If you want to leave a message and know where Martinique is, place it in a bottle and pray the trade winds get it here. Otherwise tough luck, sucker." Not the best PR Globallica had ever done.

Harvey had turned on the TV and heard the news. Fortunately even a snail's brain could understand what it meant. It was truly, frigging, unbelievable. Somehow Harvey's dream of rising to the top of the largest corporation in America had been put into a food processor and pureed into a Reader's Digest version of 'Nightmare on Elm Street', with Harvey entering the creepy old house alone and the rest of the world waiting for him inside with a chain saw.

"Todd? It's Bunny. How soon can you get here? Angus's helicopter is picking you up now? Good. I'll meet you on the terrace of the

Finance cafeteria. Bring Sun Ho Gung. And his tea. We're gonna need it."

This was Harvey's plan: he would do what anyone else would do in his situation. If he was about to die, he would surround himself with friends. He made a list. It was amazing how many people he'd met since he joined Globallica. Maybe some of them would be willing to help. Dr. Albert Duddenheim and Dr. Marla Gorf. Daphne DuBois and Takata Hoshimei. Aziz Mukquat. Freddie Hogan. Nancy Butterworth and Sparkles. Mert the farmer. Boris the chimp.

But there was someone he really, really, really wanted help from. Someone he admired tremendously. Someone who'd started him in his business career. Someone who'd given an idiot a chance. Someone who really knew how to run a successful company and someone who Harvey had regretted not saying goodbye to. Mr. Dortmann. Oh, what Harvey wouldn't give now for some of Mr. Dortmann's precious advice. He would even put up with hearing him say, 'Oi vey' as only the old shopkeeper could say it.

"Bunny? Can you ask Angus to pick someone else up?"

"Sure, Harvey. Who?"

Harvey handed her his long list.

"Harvey. This is a lot of people. I don't think Angus' chopper can fit them all in."

"Order another one?"

"Harvey…"

Harvey put on his best hound dog look. He might be the saddest excuse for a Chairman of the Board that anyone could ever expect to find, but somehow he always managed to pull it together.

Bunny Warren took the list. "I'll see what I can do."

✂* *

They convened on the 147th Floor in the office of the Chairman of the Board of Globallica. Ocean City lay hidden below them underneath a velvety cotton blanket of clouds. One hundred and forty-seven floors down, at the base of the Globallica Tower, news crews from over one hundred countries had set up a permanent media city. The bright yellow glow produced from the media's lighting equipment illuminated the cloud blanket from underneath.

The sun began to set.

"Oi vey. So many clocks. Why are all these clocks here?" Mr. Dortmann pushed his bifocals to the end of his nose and admired the fine craftsmanship and ornate decoration. The legacy of expert tradesmen from three centuries ago filled display cases and shelves throughout the opulent chairman's office.

"Harvey?" Todd Hertle said. "There's someone at ground level that insists we meet with them."

"Todd, I'm not up to doing any more interviews. That call I took from the *Bass Fisherman's Gazette* was frightening. They said the Governor of Missouri was extremely upset I wasn't going to open the fishing season tomorrow like the previous chairman of Globallica had promised. Todd, I don't know anything about fishing. Or Missouri."

"No, Harvey. You don't understand. It's more serious than that." Todd was wearing his it's-more-serious-than-that expression.

"It is? How serious?"

"Bankers."

"Bankers?"

"As in…they want to know how we're going to pay our bills."

"VISA?"

"No, Harvey. We can't pay our bills with VISA. We pay our bills with something called revenues. Which apparently we no longer have."

"Oh? Well, let's get some then."

"Oo-kay, Harvey. I'll order some right away. What do you want on them? Pepperoni and mushrooms?"

"Ham and pineapple, Todd. Pepperoni repeats on me."

"Harvey, we're not ordering pizzas."

"We're not? I'm hungry. Here, use my credit card. I've got money. Really, I do."

"*Ugh.* Angus, I give up."

"Todd, take it easy on the wee laddie. He's doon everything he can."

"Which is… nothing, Angus."

"Tha's wha I said, Todd. He's doon everything he can."

Mr. Dortmann turned away from ex-Chairman Mitchell's clock collection and surveyed the worried, despondent faces of Harvey's colleagues. They knew what trouble the company was in, even if Harvey didn't. It was time for Harvey Drinkwater to get a dose of bitter reality, delivered in a way only Mr. Dortmann could deliver. "Harvey. Come here. I want to talk to you."

This reminded Harvey of the time he microwaved Mr. Dortmann's car keys. He'd dropped them in a puddle and thought it would be a good way to dry them off. It didn't work. The fireman's hoses got them wet again. Mr. Dortmann had said, "Harvey. Come here. I want to talk to you."

"Yes, Mr. Dortmann, sir."

"For some extremely bizarre reason, the shareholders of Globallica have decided in their infinite wisdom to entrust you with the running of this company."

"Yes, Mr. Dortmann. I know that. I'm not stupid."

"Well, that's a debate for another time, Harvey. Trust me on that one."

"Okay."

"So what do you plan to do about it?"

"About what, Mr. Dortmann, sir?"

"Running the company, Harvey."

"Oh, that. Well, I thought maybe I would just let it run itself. And then hide."

"You can't do that, Harvey."

"Oh, yes I can."

Mr. Dortmann was smarter than Hilda. He never needed to wear red lipstick. "Harvey, who do you work for now?"

Harvey opened his mouth to answer. He'd always had a boss to look up to and to work for. Mr. Dortmann was trying to trick him. This was a riddle. The answer was easy when he worked in the Department of Miscellaneous Commodities. He'd worked for Darcy, then Kendall. Then he worked for Talus. But now? There was no one. No one obvious.

Harvey struggled for a solution to this mystery. In the background, the clocks began to chime. First one, then another, until the bings and bongs filled the room with sound.

"It's time, Harvey."

"Time, Mr. Dortmann? Time for what?"

"It's time *you* ran this company, Harvey. That's your job now, isn't it?"

"But where do I start?" Harvey answered, his voice croaking with desperation.

"First, you, the chairman, have to decide what kind of company you want to run."

"I decide that?"

"Yes, Harvey. You do."

"Which means?"

"You decide what products the company makes."

"I do? How do I decide that?"

"Customers tell you."

"I'm confused. I thought it was *me* who decided that."

"You do. But only after you first ask what your customers *want*."

"Like the 'Idea'?"

"Yes, Harvey. Exactly like the 'Idea'. That's exactly what you need to find out."

"How?"

"Look at the people around you, Harvey. Why did you ask them to come here?"

Mr. Dortmann pointed to the people crowded around ex-Chairman Byron Mitchell's French-polished mahogany conference table. Dr. Duddenheim doodled on the chairman's handmade parchment paper. General Angus McCalliwag had the Pentagon on one cell phone and the Army's Procurement Corps on another. Todd Hertle nervously paced up and down. His high energy level demanded constant activity. Fortunately, the chairman's carpeting had the highest level of wear resistance Globallica's money could afford.

"Friends?"

"Not just friends, Harvey. They're now your staff. Like you and Hilda were to me at the Zipper Emporium. Ask your staff for *their* 'Ideas'. Ask them what they think Globallica's customers want. Ask them how to get it. Try it. You'll like it. Believe me, you'll be surprised what you might find out."

"So I find out. Then what do I do?"

"Have a plan. Have a business plan. Deliver it. And hope your customers like the results."

"What about the bankers?"

"Oh...*them*. Well, if the bankers want their money back, they'll have to co-operate, won't they?"

"Co-operate? Co-operate with what?"

"The 'Plan', Harvey. Your plan. You're the Chairman of the Board, am I right?"

"I guess so."

"Then start acting like one."

"Yes sir, Mr. Dortmann."

*＊＊

Globallica already had a business plan. Harvey asked Nancy and Sparkles to fetch a copy from Talus's office. An hour later and the conference table was filled with piles and piles of binders so high you couldn't see who was sitting on the other side. Every volume had been carefully filled with what an army of business planners had thought was essential, distilled from the collective wisdom of an army of executives who extracted it with great pain from their armies of analysts, strategists, subject matter experts, specialists, certified accounting professionals and consultants.

But it didn't make any sense.

Not just because it didn't make any sense when you read it. Which is what happened when you tried. But because it didn't make any sense that anyone with half a brain—or even Harvey Drinkwater, with arguably a quarter of a brain—would even attempt to try to read it, let alone implement it.

"Laddie, this is the biggest load o' stinkin' tripe I've e'er clapped me eyes on. No wonda our troosers are hangin' doon by our wee ankles."

Harvey conjured up that image. He checked his own pants. They were fine. "Okay, Angus. Now what?"

"This isn't a plan, Harvey," Todd said. "This is a recipe for disaster."

"Thank you, Todd. For stating the obvious."

Angus and Todd looked at each other. Was that Harvey Drinkwater who'd uttered those words? Or perhaps Dr. Duddenheim had learned ventriloquism?

No, it was Harvey.

Mr. Dortmann's tutorial on customers had been followed up by one on revenue generation. The company needed cash and didn't have any. Selling stuff was how you got cash to pay your bills when you couldn't get cash any other way. VISA was OK to buy pizza. It was not OK to fund the cash flow of the largest corporation in America. Even Harvey Drinkwater finally understood that.

Harvey brought the bankers up to the office. They explained Globallica's cash flow problems in terms that were quite simple to understand: pay up or else.

For Harvey Drinkwater, the 'or else' would probably mean a lifetime of toil underneath the stairwell at the Zipper Emporium. Harvey was determined to avoid that. He liked the view from the 147th Floor better. So he rolled up his sleeves and got to work. Harvey Drinkwater, the new chairman of Globallica, made his first real decision on his own. Well, it was more like a decision disguised as a riddle. But it would have to do for now.

"What do you do if you need some money to pay for something but you don't have any money in the bank to pay for it?" he asked his staff.

A PhD in Biomechanical Engineering, a registered commodity trader, a General in the Army Reserve, an expert on Chinese herbal remedies, and an assistant purchasing agent with the hyperactivity of four hundred gerbils, and everyone else, hadn't a clue what Harvey was talking about.

"We give up," Todd said bravely.

"Hold a garage sale."

"A garage sale?"

"Well, look at these clocks. We don't need all these clocks to tell the time up here, do we? We only need one. We'll keep one and sell the rest. There's stuff on every floor we don't need any more. When I don't need something, I sell it. Then I have money to buy something I do need."

"Aye, laddie. I see wa' ya mean," Angus said. "Toddie, our Harvey's got a really greet idea. Who'll help do an inventory of tha' buildin' wi' me?"

Daphne DuBois and Aziz Mukquat volunteered right away.

"Todd, dunna be a wee wimp. If any legs can whip aroond tha' buildin', it's yours laddie."

"OK, Angus. Count me in." Todd leaned over and whispered into the ears of Bunny Warren, Nancy Butterworth and Sparkles. "Ladies, contact Sotheby's. Tell them Globallica's going to unload enough rare one-of-a-kind antiques to cause their commissions to be listed separately on the New York Stock Exchange. Then contact the Smithsonian, the Guggenheim, the Louvre. Whip up a frenzy amongst the bidders."

"Gotcha, Todd."

It was Freddie Hogan's turn to get a shot of Todd's focused energy launched up his wazoo. "Freddie, check the ownership records in the marina and in the executive garage. Contact the Yacht Brokers Association. The Porsche Owner's Club. Get ads placed in the Robb Report. If it hangs on a wall, it shines, it floats, hits sixty miles per hour in under five seconds, we'll sell it. I'll bet my calculator, there isn't a bauble or a toy within two miles of this building that isn't owned by Globallica."

"I'm with you, dude."

Chairman Harvey Drinkwater's new business plan was being set in motion. As his staff sprung into action with a renewed sense of purpose, Harvey sat back in the chairman's overstuffed Corinthian leather chair, a slight smile of smug satisfaction on his face. He looked at the piles of binders stacked up on the conference table.

"Aziz?"

"Yes, Boss."

"Put this old business plan up for sale. We don't need it anymore."

Harvey took an apple out of the fruit basket and opened up today's edition of *The Wall Street Journal*. To his surprise, an ink-sketched portrait of the new chairman of Globallica was front and center on the first page. Somehow that person looked very familiar.

CHAPTER THIRTY-TWO

"Harvey? You have a call on line four ..."

"Thanks, Sparkles. Who is it?"

"George."

"George? George? Do I know a George, Sparkles? Is he from *Fortune*?"

"No."

"*Forbes*?"

"No."

"*GQ? Rolling Stone?*"

"No, Harvey. He's from the lobby."

"Which lobby? The Surgical Instrument Political Action Committee? The Ocean City Port Re-Development Task Force? The Sardine Processing Trade Association?"

"No, our lobby. As in 'the lobby downstairs'."

"Huh?"

Sparkles asked the person calling for more clarification. Who was he? And why did he want to bother an important, busy person like the chairman of Globallica? Especially while Harvey was playing with the French Revolution mantel clock. Harvey didn't want to be disturbed while he was slicing salami for his sandwich.

"He says he's the George with the cat named Dennis who likes marshmallows. Apparently that's important information for some reason."

"Of course it is, Sparkles! George!"

"That's what he says his name is, Mr. Drinkwater…George. From the lobby."

"Why didn't you say so?"

"I thought I did. Do you want to speak to him or not?"

Harvey was on a break from the all day planning session for Globallica's garage sale, the sale his new executive team was calling, 'The Most Humongous Garage Sale in the History of the World'. It was easy to get embroiled in details and forget simple things. Like George and his cat Dennis. "Sparkles, tell George to come up. I can find time to talk to an old friend. Tell him he can bring Dennis. Lord knows we have plenty of cat litter around here somewhere."

"Yes, Mr. Drinkwater."

As Sparkles left, Nancy Butterworth came in with a completed executive summary from the morning planning session for 'The Humongous Garage Sale'. Bunny, Angus, Sun Ho Gung and Freddie Hogan stood behind her to gauge Harvey's reaction to their first set of plans.

"Impressive results," Harvey said, in his best 'I'm-the-chairman-and-I-bestow-upon-you-my-heartfelt-congratulations' voice.

The sale catalogue was going to the printer's today. 'The Most Humongous Garage Sale in the History of the World' would be scheduled over two weeks. That's how big it was. It was so big that *The Antiques Roadshow* had applied for trademark protection for a new definition of 'cleaning out the attic' that had to be invented to describe it.

Bunny Warren had finalized negotiations for the TV and movie rights. Todd Hertle had cut a deal with a toy distributor in Taiwan to sell souvenir bobble-head dolls of Harvey. Sun Ho Gung had worked with Freddie Hogan and the Red Cross to set up a tea tasting tent. Ho Gung's tea was already a big hit with the TV cameramen although viewers were now complaining about the out of focus news coverage.

Angus had bartered with the Pentagon to provide event security in exchange for Globallica's old business plan. Apparently, someone in the military could see some value in the massive document. Strategic Air Command wanted it as a battle plan for a war game simulation with North Korea.

Todd Hertle buzzed past Sparkles as he rushed excitedly into Harvey's office. "Harvey, we've found a mother lode on the 146th Floor." Todd handed him an addendum to the sale inventory.

"*Whoa*! That's big, Todd."

The others looked over Harvey's shoulder as he fingered through the wad of paper describing the new finds.

"We had some trouble decoding the security systems but we finally got into Barry Granduck's office," Todd explained. "And when we did, it was *so* worth it." Todd showed them the digital photos he'd taken for the auction catalogue. "I think we have time to include everything. Daphne and 'Accountants-to-Go' have been working double-time to help Sotheby's with the appraisals."

Bunny agreed. "Accountants-to-Go are very efficient, aren't they?"

"Aye, lassie," Angus replied. "Have yee no noticed? There's more tha' a few wee Scots amongst them. We were coonting our pennies before the English knew how ta make fire."

"Sh, Angus, you old Scottish coot. Can't you see Harvey's concentrating?"

Harvey looked again at Todd's list and photographs. It was an odd collection indeed. "Todd, do you think this stuff will actually sell? Who will want to buy old used cigars for example?"

"They've got great provenance, Harvey. They're Winston Churchill's. We've got the DNA tests of his saliva to prove it."

"These books look in really bad shape. If they were mine, I'd just throw them in the garbage."

"The Gutenberg Bible? Leonardo da Vinci's sketchbook?"

"Who'd buy these old ratty papers?"

"General Custer's handwritten last will and testament, penned at the Little Big Horn. Adolf Hitler's love letters to Eva Braun."

"What's a 'Magna Carta'?

"Kind of like an antique business plan, Harvey."

Harvey kept looking through the list. "Ah, now these are useful. We can make money selling sandwiches and pasta at the auction."

"What? Where do you see that?"

"From Salvador's Deli. Reubens sandwiches. An Italian dish called Modigliani. I haven't eaten a Toulouse Lautrec before. Sounds like it has a lot of garlic in it. What is it?"

"No, Harvey. Salvador *Dali*, not 'deli'. It's art."

Todd showed Harvey photos of the Renaissance, Impressionist and Surrealist masterpieces he'd found hanging in the ex-vice chairman's office.

"*Yuck*! I don't like this Picasso thing. I think I'd rather look at a dead fish in an aquarium."

"Oh, we have that too, Harvey. See page 178. The Tate Gallery in London will love it."

Harvey thought Todd was kidding. He turned to page 178. "Double *yuck*!"

***

The system Harvey had set up to get around the media—so that visitors to his office could meet him without being hijacked—was somewhat bizarre. But then, for the post-apocalyptic survivors of Globallica's Chapter 11 filing, reality was about as far removed from normalcy as a computer tablet was from the Dead Sea Scrolls.

It started by taking a cab to Dortmann's Zipper Emporium. Then a visitor had to use a secret password to get by Hilda. The password was changed every day. Today's was 'Wildebeest Dunghill'. It was Takata Hoshimei's turn to make it up.

Once that test had been passed, Hilda made a 1-800 call to a number which was a front for Angus's friends in US Military Intelligence. They were posing as telemarketers for a hosiery outlet in case the Russians eavesdropped on Hilda. Apparently, this process was modeled on the most effective way to monitor enemy troop movements. Who knew? After a while, Hilda negotiated a bulk discount on queen-sized support stockings. Every job has its perks.

That's how the helicopter came to collect George Thaddeus from the rooftop of the Zipper Emporium. The rest was easy. A short five minute ride to the terrace of Finance's cafeteria and the media was stymied. This rigmarole bypassed the cordon of wolves who pounced on anyone trying to enter the Executive Suites the conventional way. One good thing about this new procedure was the bankers had given up and went home.

George Thaddeus thought it was strange that he worked only fifty feet away from the revolving glass doors but couldn't use them. But his world had now turned upside down just like Harvey's. As he was let into Harvey's office by Sparkles, the quietness was a welcome relief from the constant day-and-night chatter in the Globallica Tower's foyer. Sleeping had been a problem. Most of the SEC's SWAT Team was still in hiding in the greenery, hoping to make more arrests. And they snored like old pigs.

"Tea?"

"Oh, no thanks, Harvey. If it's anything like the tea they're brewing downstairs, I'd have to go into rehab."

"This is just regular tea, George. Really, it is."

"It's okay, Harvey. But maybe I could give Dennis some of that milk." George placed a saucer on the floor. The poor cat, completely frazzled by the helicopter ride, quickly made himself at home.

"Harvey, you remember I told you that I used to work for ASSCO?"

"Yes. You told me the first night I met you. Around the campfire. With the marshmallows."

"Well, look at this…"

George Thaddeus passed him a sheaf of legal-sized papers. Harvey pushed the intercom button, "Nancy, could you come in here, please? I need someone to prepare an executive summary."

"Harvey, you don't need to bother her."

"I don't?"

"No. I can summarize it for you. It's pretty simple. I own the building."

Harvey looked again at the papers. Buried in a plethora of heretos, whereases, who-so-evers and where-for-art-thous was a smattering of real English which said that George Thaddeus was a partner in a trust in Bermuda and that trust owned the Globallica Tower.

"I'm the sole surviving member of this trust, Harvey. My former colleagues and I exchanged our entire lifetime's worth of hard earned wealth, represented by our holdings of ASSCO stock, for this pile of papers. Then the scumbags from Globallica hid them from us."

"Why?"

"So that when we died, it would all come flooding back into their bank accounts."

"What would?"

"Ownership of the Globallica Tower. The lease payments on it. Your rent. You see, Harvey, I'm your landlord. And all the time that I slept in that lobby, with my cat and my sleeping bag, with barely enough money to buy a bag of marshmallows, look what was being sent into a trust account in my name in Bermuda. A trust account I didn't know how to access. A trust account that would have passed on to Barry Granduck if I died."

George took out a crumpled envelope from inside his old tweed sports jacket and handed it to Harvey. It was a freshly printed statement from The Bermuda Triangle Trust.

"Jumping Je-hosophat, George!"

"That's exactly what I said when I saw this statement for the first time. And you know what else, Harvey?"

"No."

"I've been listening to a lot of conversations down in that lobby. There's really not much else to do. And that tea you sell down there has a funny way of loosening the tongues of the people that drink it."

"Before it paralyzes them, you mean?"

"Exactly. Well, a few Swiss bankers spilled the beans so to speak."

"Yodel."

"Huh?"

"Yodel, George. Swiss people are very neat. They don't spill anything. But they yodel a lot."

"Oh? Right. Well, as I was saying, these Swiss bankers told a lot of stories. And one of them is quite interesting. I don't presume you know exactly how much money Globallica owes these bankers, do you Harvey?"

"Well, no. Not really. You see I'm too afraid to ask."

"That's too bad. Because if you did, you would find out that Globallica doesn't really owe them that much."

"We don't?"

"No. You see the company's cash flow problems are basically down to one thing."

"Which is?"

"The rent, Harvey. You pay an ungodly amount of rent on this building."

"To you?"

"Yes, Harvey. To me. That's what's so great about it, don't you see?"

"Not exactly."

"Well, I now have this ungodly amount of money in the bank. More money than any one person would ever wish to have. In fact, the interest on it every year is probably more than I can spend for the rest of my life."

"So you're here to raise our rents?"

George laughed. "No, Harvey. No, no. I just want a job."

"You have a job."

"No, a real job, Harvey. Like the one those bastards took away from me."

Harvey looked puzzled. "A job with us?"

"Yes."

"But we can't afford to pay anybody, George. We're probably not paying you right now. To be our security guard."

"Oh, Harvey, have I got a deal for you."

Uh, oh, Harvey thought. The last time he heard that, he ended up with enough steak knives to fill the armory at the Tower of London.

"I can see you don't know where I'm going with this, do you, Harvey?"

"Not exactly, George." The only thing Harvey could see was Dennis going pee-pee in a potted plant.

"Harvey, I now have enough money to pay off all of Globallica's debts. And I can hold off collecting my rent until the company gets back on its feet again."

"You would do all that for *us*?"

"I would do all that for a new job title. And an office with a polished mahogany desk. Yes, Harvey, I would."

"A new job title?"

"Vice chairman, Harvey. Your new vice chairman."

"Does that mean Globallica will no longer be bankrupt?"

"Yes, Harvey Drinkwater. It does."

CHAPTER THIRTY-THREE

The 'Most Humongous Garage Sale in the History of the World' had started. Outside the Globallica Tower, the arrival of the celebrity glitterati coming to bid on Globallica's baubles resembled an invasion by the 101st Airborne. To let the little people get a peek, scalpers rented binoculars for two hundred dollars a pop. Which was also the price of pop inside the auction. In souvenir crystal decanters. Thirsty hip hop divas and parched mega-movie moguls lapped up the limited edition crystal on sale, with relish.

And you could buy relish too. In kiln-fired commemorative ceramic pots, both the jar and its pickled ingredients lovingly made by hand by Martha Biggelsdorf. Martha was having the time of her sheltered corporate life. Just like all the other Globallica employees who were making products to sell at the marathon auction.

Initially, the spin-offs and concessions—souvenirs, refreshments, boutique cuisine, aphrodisiacs—had been a sideshow to the main event. They were just a collection of last minute money-making ideas cobbled together by the auction's Planning Committee. But that's not how entrepreneurs from all over the world saw it. They came to buy Globallica's surplus high end art and antiques. But sitting through the bidding soon bored the brash, high-energy buccaneers of the New Economy. Sitting still for longer than two minutes was not in their DNA.

Once a canny venture capitalist saw an opportunity and made a move, others pounced. They all wanted in on the action. If there was a way to manufacture, franchise, cross market, or license the new products and services Globallica was putting in the auction's sideshow, they tripped over each other to find it. No one was fooling them. This wasn't a garage sale. This was 'The Ocean City Marketing Expo'.

Sandwiches? Come on. These New Economy sharks knew better. What a clever way to launch a new product. Disguised as simple sandwiches. Dr. Duddenheim's square, flat lettuce was a big hit. Every fast food chain and supermarket wanted to be the first to market the most amazing vegetable since Native Americans showed the settlers how to boil corn.

And while the celebs emptied their bank accounts to buy the trinkets and trash left in the wake of excessive executive spending, the star attraction was not to be found in the auction catalogue. No siree. It was cruising in and out between the aisles and underneath the seats, cleaning up after the beautiful people's prissy poodles and pugnacious pit bulls. The pungent piles on Globallica's pristine polished floors were sucked up, sanitized and incinerated by Vinnie, the Poo-Bot.

Tremors could be felt all the way back to Tokyo and Shanghai as the contest to cut a deal with Globallica on this new technology took on the appearance of a martial arts tournament. To the victor, the spoils. Dr. Duddenheim and his New Product Development Team were wined, dined and signed. The Chinese, Japanese and Koreans were shrewd businessmen. Why spend five million dollars for a crusty portrait of a long dead Italian Renaissance dignitary when you could use the same amount of money to kick off the design of a factory to make the invention of the year: robotic dog-poop-sweepers?

After the first three days, an extravaganza of high-rollers had fought over old cigar stubs. But the entrepreneurial elite had buzzed over new product deals. This cocktail mix of diamond tiaras and dynamic energy created a firestorm of curiosity amongst the general population.

Whipping up this frenzy was as easy for the news media to do as squirting cream on top of a cappuccino. Everyone in the country, everywhere, wanted to know one thing. Where was the mastermind behind the scenes? Because Harvey Drinkwater, chairman of Globallica, had yet to make an appearance.

"This is Bonnie Chow reporting for the StarStruck TV Network from Ocean City, Oregon. It's the 'Media Event of the Century'. We're now witnessing a gathering of celebrities at the headquarters of Globallica, the likes of which have never been seen before and may never be seen again. For the past three days, Ocean City has been the place to be and the place to be seen. London, Paris, New York. Cannes, Nice, Rio. Oscar night in Hollywood, the Grammies. They're all taking a backseat to Ocean City, Oregon."

"You can feel the electrifying excitement in the air," she continued. "Stretch limousines are arriving every ten minutes to deliver this blockbuster country diva, that A-list movie star, a Rock n' Roll Hall-of-Fame living legend, a world champion mud wrestler. From the entertainment world, the sports world, TV, politics, the music business, they're all to reserve their seats at 'The Most Humongous Garage Sale in the History of the World'."

"But the big question my viewers have been asking," she said. "Where is the leader of this orchestra? 'The Maestro'? The marketing and financial genius that has taken the world's worst bankruptcy and transformed it into the 'coming-out' party for a rejuvenated New Globallica? A company many had written off as 'so much stale rigor mortis'. A company that has taken innovative new products and emerged as 'The Mother of All Phoenixes', rising from ashes that Wall Street thought were stone, cold dead. This is Bonnie Chow reporting, from Ocean City, Oregon for the StarStruck TV Network."

As the 'Sale of the Century' continued, this was the question every network anchor was asking. Where was the chairman of Globallica? Where was Harvey Drinkwater? All of the media pundits had pretty much the same story to peddle. Globallica had been front and center in the business press for weeks. First as 'The Poster Child for Gross Incompetence on a Mass Scale' or so the headlines in *The Wall Street*

Journal said, then for the 'Renaissance of Business Strategy on a Pork n'Beans Budget' according to *The Harvard Business Review*.

All of the talking heads on the cable networks had parroted the same tune on financial chat show after financial chat show. There was a New Globallica. The Old Globallica was gone, vanished, banished and forgotten. This dramatic turnaround was being attributed to the brilliance of one man: Globallica's chairman, Harvey Drinkwater.

As he watched his TV on the 147th floor, Harvey was terrified.

It was amazing what a relatively few, common sense decisions could do in such a short time. Especially when it wasn't you who made the decisions. Of all the management skills Harvey had carefully inventoried in his planner, the last one he'd thought of using was 'common sense'.

"This is Bonnie Chow again with an 'Eye-Witness Newsflash' from the lobby of the Globallica Tower. Beside me I have Hilda Ausfahrt, someone who worked with Harvey Drinkwater before he became the most famous executive on the planet. Hilda, tell our viewers what it was like to work with someone who's now the world's brightest star in the business sky."

Hilda adjusted her hosiery to make sure her fifteen minutes of fame, or less, would be just perfect. "Well, Harvey was a simple man. He didn't have expensive tastes."

"So you would conclude, Hilda Ausfahrt that he did not approve of the excessively lavish lifestyles of the previous administration at Globallica?"

"No. I don't think he did."

"So how did Harvey Drinkwater change Globallica's corporate culture so suddenly?"

"Well, um…"

"Our viewers are waiting."

"Well…well…"

Without a nail file in her hand and a hands-free headset in her ear, Hilda was lost for words. "Well, he…he…he murkle crabbed…"

"Excuse me? What did you say?"

"He murkle crabbed his barfle murg."

"There you have it, viewers of StarStruck TV. An eyewitness account has conclusively concluded that Harvey Drinkwater, chairman of New Globallica, um...murkle crabbed his barfle murg. Exclusive coverage. As only StarStruck TV could deliver it."

***

The sale was in its final hours. The pressure on Harvey to make an appearance on the 'Stage of All Stages' was building. *Saturday Night Live* had petitioned the Supreme Court of the United States to rule Harvey Drinkwater was a national treasure that deserved special status as an 'Icon of the People' and therefore should be granted an all-network broadcast time slot. After much deliberation, it was unanimously agreed, the first such Supreme Court decision since the invention of television.

It still hadn't forced Harvey's hand. That task fell to Daphne DuBois. In her gentle French way, she convinced Harvey that a public speech was not only unavoidable but desirable, an essential requirement to build upon the mountain of goodwill New Globallica was generating. So it was decided. Harvey Drinkwater had to emerge from his self-imposed exile to make a public appearance. That is what the chairman was paid to do.

As the time for the broadcast of his first speech as chairman drew closer, to say Harvey wasn't nervous about it was to say that global warming was caused by a single cow fart. To help him relax, he decided to bring Lopez along for company. He needed someone to share the misery of being in the spotlight. The little mutt's mutterings would hopefully take his mind off his own mutterings.

The speech was scheduled to be delivered on the auction's final night, at the Evening Gala. The Evening Gala was another serendipitous piece of brilliant marketing. The idea started out as a 'thank you' evening for Globallica's hard working employees. But after media attention reached hurricane force, the Planning Committee decided to orchestrate it like a Hollywood premier. Searchlights in the sky. Red carpets everywhere. Champagne. Guys in their tuxedos. Gals in their haute couture. When the photographers' flashes went off, the reflections from the celebrity crowd's multi-million dollar jewelry looked like someone had thrown the switch for indoor fireworks.

To support the power needs of the Evening Gala, Angus McCalliwag had requisitioned portable generators from the Army. It was just as well. When Harvey descended from the 147th Floor and passed through the glass revolving doors, the media's lights came on all at once, causing the rest of Ocean City to be plunged into darkness by the brownout. Only the Globallica Tower stayed lit up.

Harvey Drinkwater, chairman of New Globallica, strode along the plush red carpet like a conquering Roman emperor, his radiantly beautiful and very cutely French girlfriend Daphne DuBois on his arm. Which fit nicely with his destination, the Great Hall, Purchasing's Savings Board, formerly known as 'The Throne Room of the Gods'.

From the dais where Talus, Bjorn, DragonForce, Antonio and Arkon had held court, Harvey Drinkwater would make his inaugural public speech as Chairman of the Board. Afterwards, Harvey would announce that the 'Great Hall of Savings' would be given to the employees of Globallica to become their new recreation center. Harvey couldn't wait. He'd already signed up for bingo night and the badminton tournament.

The procession moved along rhythmically. Soon, the moment Harvey's adoring public had waited for had arrived. Harvey Drinkwater approached the bottom of the seven steps that lead up to the pink marble dais and its throne, the chair with ornate Italian marble mosaics depicting the history of Globallica Purchasing. From this throne, Harvey would read his speech. But afterwards, the lavishly decorated objet d'art would be auctioned off for charity. It served no useful purpose in his new organization. Besides it looked uncomfortable.

The word had leaked out that the chair would be sold—the chair where the new chairman of Globallica had given his first public speech. Bidders hovered like vultures. The Smithsonian vowed it would be theirs. No one could outbid them. Once they snagged it, they promised limited edition replicas would be made available to collectors.

Harvey was happy to get the chance to sit in it just once. For someone unaccustomed to pomp and ceremony, once was not only all he needed, it was probably all his nervous system could take. He mounted the first step and paused. Lopez walked beside him, his tongue lapping in the air. The room fell into a hush. TV cameras filmed the moment from every conceivable angle. Harvey hesitated. It was such an overwhelming feeling. The last time he put his foot on that first step, he remembered Aziz Mukquat admonishing him, "What are you doing? You can't go up there, Harvey. No one goes up there unless they're an executive director."

To which Harvey had replied, "Well, I can dream, can't I?"

Was it a dream? He pinched himself to check.

Lopez had seen Harvey's transfixion fits many times before. They were always an opportunity for the pooch to get into mischief. At least until whatever spell had entered Harvey's head had worn off. So as Harvey paused, the little dog ran up the steps ahead of his master and jumped into the throne's plush seat.

That broke the spell.

Harvey bounded up the last steps, "Lopez, get out of there! That's *my* seat, you dumb dog!"

The room burst into applause. The chairman of Globallica had finally spoken his first words.

Lopez settled down on the marble floor beside him. Harvey took out a single scrunched-up piece of paper where he'd written a few words. No one—not Daphne, not Bunny, not Sparkles or Nancy—

knew what Harvey's speech contained. Secrecy was the chairman's prerogative. They just prayed it would make sense.

Harvey fumbled with the paper. At first, it didn't look as if he could make out his own writing. Then he turned the paper right side up. And began, "Ladies and gentlemen. Distinguished guests. Filthy rich bidders. Welcome to the New Globallica. Today is a special day in the history of our company. It's a day when a humble man has the great honor to present the new faces that will restore Globallica's reputation."

Harvey waved his new executive team onto the platform. George Thaddeus, Vice-Chairman; Bunny Warren, VP Sales & Marketing; Todd Hertle, Chief Information Officer; Angus McCalliwag, VP of Purchasing; Sun Ho Gung , VP of Health and Safety; Dr. Duddenheim, VP of Product Development; Sparkles; Nancy Butterworth…and more. The employees of New Globallica erupted into thunderous applause.

Harvey looked again at the crumpled paper in his hand. There wasn't much more he'd planned to say. But, although he didn't know it at the time, Harvey Drinkwater would say what no leader of Globallica—Old or New—had ever said before.

"I pledge, with everyone's help, to bring real value to our products, to our services…and to our lives. Only then, can Globallica call itself a truly 'new' company. That is my solemn promise, so long as I am chairman."

Not a bad speech for someone who'd never given one before.

Fate was pleased. Its work was done.

Fate would finally leave Harvey Drinkwater alone.

At least for a little while.

ABOUT CHARLES A CORNELL

When Charles isn't trying to survive the chaos of everyday life, he's dreaming up all kinds of bat-shit crazy fiction. He specializes in science fiction, science fantasy, dieselpunk & steampunk. He's known to write award-winning mystery thrillers too!

A survivor of thirty-nine years of BigCorp dysfunction, Charles has a BSc. degree in Metallurgy & an MBA. He worked in materials engineering, quality management, logistics & purchasing for a big name Fortune 500 company. That's why he knows so much about BigCorps, their dysfunctional cultures & how to survive them!

Charles A Cornell was born in England, raised in Canada and now lives in Florida.

His first published novel, *Tiger Paw*, won the 2012 Royal Palm Literary Award for Best Thriller from the Florida Writers Association.

His dieselpunk work, *DragonFly* was a 2014 Royal Palm Literary Award Finalist in Science Fiction. *DragonFly* is a retro-futuristic collision of science fiction and fantasy with a generous dash of alternative history.

Charles's short stories and novellas have appeared in the anthologies, *The Prometheus Saga*, *Return To Earth* and *In Shadows Written*. His Prometheus Saga science fiction story *Crystal Night* won the Royal Palm Literary Award for Best Novella in 2016.

Works By Charles A Cornell

Satirical Non-Fiction & Fiction

A Survivor's Guide To Working At A Big Corporation
Harvey Drinkwater & The Cult Of Savings

Science Fantasy/Dieselpunk:

Missions Of The DragonFly Squadron

DragonFly (Book One - Illustrated)
Spies in Manhattan (Book Two - Coming Soon)
Die Fabrik / The Factory (Novella)

Science Fiction Novellas:

Crystal Night
Children Of The Stars

Scott Forrester FBI Thrillers

Tiger Paw

Anthologies

The Prometheus Saga
Return To Earth
In Shadows Written

www.CharlesACornell.com
www.BigCorpSurvivor.com
www.DragonFly-Novels.com

More About DragonFly

DragonFly explores the incredibly turbulent times during the 1940s and the 'what ifs' that might have been. *DragonFly* follows the journey of Veronica Somerset as she battles the odds to become Britain's first female fighter pilot. Packed with full color illustrations and black and white 'retrographs', *DragonFly* conjures up a whole new world of fantastic technology, dangerous fighting machines and wizards battling across the boundary between good and evil in a World War re-imagined like never before.

"The thrilling climax... outdoes any big action flick for sheer sweep and menace. Cornell hits a home run!"
> - Ken Pelham, award winning author of the mysteries,
> 'Brigand's Key' and 'Place of Fear'.

"There is a lot to like about Dragonfly... surprises... intrigue... in a world that doesn't particularly follow the history that we know."
> - Bard Constantine, author of 'The Troubleshooter' series and
> 'Silent Empire', dieselpunk novels.

"It was fantastic ... Charles has done a wonderful job blending alternate history with the mystical. His characters are well developed. I was disappointed when it ended."
> - John Charles Miller, award winning short story writer and
> author of the alternative history novel, 'Citrus White Gold'.

www.DragonFly-Novels.com

www.ingramcontent.com/pod-product-compliance
Lightning Source LLC
Chambersburg PA
CBHW060009050426
42448CB00012B/2679